The Short Oxford History of the British Isle

General Editor: Paul Langford

The Nineteenth Century

Edited by Colin Matthew

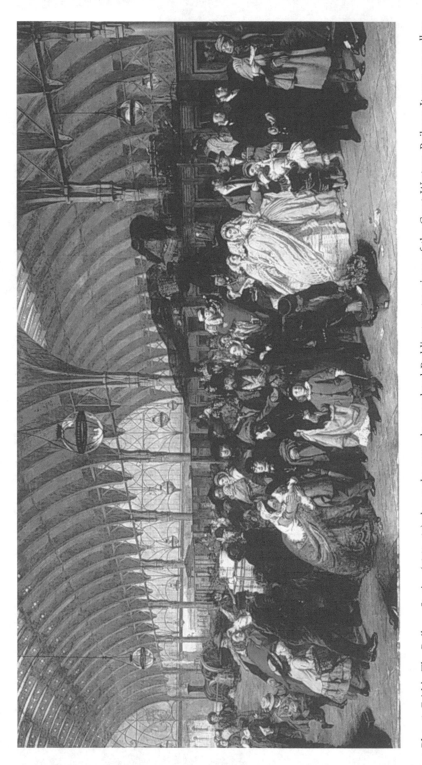

Plate 1 Frith's *The Railway Station* (1860–62) shows the recently completed Paddington, terminus of the Great Western Railway. It uses, as well as celebrates, the latest in Victorian technology. The family group in the centre is Frith's own.

The Short Oxford History
of the British Isles

General Editor: Paul Langford

The Nineteenth Century

The British Isles: 1815–1901

Edited by Colin Matthew

OXFORD
UNIVERSITY PRESS

OXFORD

UNIVERSITY PRESS

Great Clarendon Street, Oxford OX2 6DP

Oxford University Press is a department of the University of Oxford.
It furthers the University's objective of excellence in research, scholarship,
and education by publishing worldwide in

Oxford New York

Auckland Cape Town Dar es Salaam Hong Kong Karachi
Kuala Lumpur Madrid Melbourne Mexico City Nairobi
New Delhi Shanghai Taipei Toronto

With offices in

Argentina Austria Brazil Chile Czech Republic France Greece
Guatemala Hungary Italy Japan South Korea Poland Portugal
Singapore Switzerland Thailand Turkey Ukraine Vietnam

Published in the United States
by Oxford University Press Inc., New York

British Library Cataloguing in Publication Data

Data available

Library of Congress Cataloging in Publication Data

Data available

ISBN 0–19–873144–2 (hbk)
ISBN 0–19–873143–4 (pbk)

5 7 9 10 8 6 4

Typeset in Minion
by RefineCatch Limited, Bungay, Suffolk
Printed in Great Britain by
Biddles Ltd., King's Lynn, Norfolk

General Editor's Preface

It is a truism that historical writing is itself culturally determined, reflecting intellectual fashions, political preoccupations, and moral values at the time it is written. In the case of British history this has resulted in a great diversity of perspectives both on the content of what is narrated and the geopolitical framework in which it is placed. In the late twentieth century the process of redefinition has positively accelerated under the pressure of contemporary change. Some of it has come from within Britain during a period of recurrent racial tension in England and reviving nationalism in Scotland, Wales, and Northern Ireland. But much of it also comes from beyond. There has been a powerful surge of interest in the politics of national identity in response to the break-up of some of the world's great empires, both colonial and continental. The search for new sovereignties, not least in Europe itself, has contributed to a questioning of long-standing political boundaries. Such shifting of the tectonic plates of history is to be expected but for Britain especially, with what is perceived (not very accurately) to be a long period of relative stability lasting from the late seventeenth century to the mid-twentieth century, it has had a particular resonance.

Much controversy and still more confusion arise from the lack of clarity about the subject matter that figures in insular historiography. Historians of England are often accused of ignoring the history of Britain as a whole, while using the terms as if they are synonymous. Historians of Britain are similarly charged with taking Ireland's inclusion for granted without engaging directly with it. And for those who believe they are writing more specifically the history of Ireland, of Wales, or of Scotland, there is the unending tension between so-called metropolis and periphery, and the dilemmas offered by wider contexts, not only British and Irish but European and indeed extra-European. Some of these difficulties arise from the fluctuating fortunes and changing boundaries of the British state as organized from London. But even if the rulers of what is now called England had never taken an interest in dominion beyond its borders, the economic and cultural relationships between the various parts of the British Isles would still have generated many historiographical problems.

This series is based on the premise that whatever the complexities and ambiguities created by this state of affairs, it makes sense to offer an overview, conducted by leading scholars whose research is on the leading edge of their discipline. That overview extends to the whole of the British Isles. The expression is not uncontroversial, especially to many in Ireland, for whom the very word 'British' implies an unacceptable politics of dominion. Yet there is no other formulation that can encapsulate the shared experience of 'these islands', to use another term much employed in Ireland and increasingly heard in Britain, but rather unhelpful to other inhabitants of the planet.

In short we use the words 'British Isles' solely and simply as a geographical expression. No set agenda is implied. It would indeed be difficult to identify one that could stand scrutiny. What constitutes a concept such as 'British history' or 'four nations history', remains the subject of acute disagreement, and varies much depending on the period under discussion. The editors and contributors of this series have been asked only to convey the findings of the most authoritative scholarship, and to flavour them with their own interpretative original- ity and distinctiveness. In the process we hope to provide not only a stimulating digest of more than two thousand years of history, but also a sense of the intense vitality that continues to mark historical research into the past of all parts of Britain and Ireland.

Lincoln College   PAUL LANGFORD
Oxford

Contents

List of plates

Maps

List of contributors

MARTIN DAUNTON is Professor of Economic History and Fellow of Churchill College, Cambridge. He has published widely on economic history since c.1700 and has written a history of the Post Office. He recently published *Progress and Poverty: An Economic and Social History of Britain 1700–1850* (to be continued in a companion volume) and has completed a study of the politics of taxation since the 1790s.

KATE FLINT is Reader in Victorian and Modern English Literature at the University of Oxford. Her books include *The Woman Reader, 1837–1914* and *The Victorians and the Visual Imagination*. She is currently working on the place of the Americas in the Victorian cultural imagination.

JANE GARNETT is Fellow and Tutor in Modern History at Wadham College, Oxford. She has published on Victorian religious, intellectual, and cultural history and is currently working on the cultural history of religious images in Italy.

JANET HOWARTH is Fellow and Tutor in Modern History at St Hilda's College, Oxford. She has published on women and the history of higher education (editing Emily Davies's *The Higher Education of Women*) and on late-Victorian county politics.

COLIN MATTHEW was Professor of Modern History and Fellow of St Hugh's College, Oxford. With M. R. D Foot, he edited *The Gladstone Diaries*. His two-volume biography of Gladstone won the Wolfson History Prize in 1995; it is now available in a one-volume paperback as *Gladstone 1809–1898*. He was Editor of *The New Dictionary of National Biography*.

ANDREW PORTER is Rhodes Professor of Imperial History in the University of London, at King's College. His many books include *The Origins of the South African War* and *European Imperialism 1860–1914*. Most recently he edited and contributed to *The Oxford History of the British Empire: Volume 3 The Nineteenth Century*.

ANDREW SAINT is Professor of Architecture at the University of Cambridge. His many publications include a biography of Richard

Norman Shaw and *The Image of the Architect I* and *Towards a Social Architecture*. He has been Architectural Editor of the Survey of London and an historian for English Heritage.

Colin Matthew, the editor of this volume, died in October 1999 after the typescript had been completed but before it had proceeded through the press. His colleagues have overseen the final stages of its publication, and deeply lament his passing.

Plate 2 The Forth Rail Bridge under construction, 1888. Designed by John Fowler and Benjamin Baker, its cantilevered construction boasted spans of 1700 feet, a world record at the time. It was officially opened on 4 March 1890 by the Prince of Wales.

Introduction: the United Kingdom and the Victorian century, 1815–1901

Colin Matthew

The times have changed in nothing more than in the rapid conveyance of intelligence and communication betwixt one part of Scotland and another.

Thus wrote Sir Walter Scott in the opening sentence of his most characteristic novel, *The Heart of Midlothian* (1818). He referred to the brief period of rapid stage coach travel—soon ended by the railways—but he indicated what was to be the decisive characteristic of nineteenth-century Britain: the rapidly increasing velocity of ideas, of people, of goods, and of money. With speed went profit, and with profit went power. Power and success oozed from Victorian Britain: a dominant economy, a worldwide empire and banking system, an unassailed fleet and most of the world's merchant shipping, a 'race' transplanted across the globe, a political and social system whose stability astonished Europeans, especially the Germans—and all from small islands whose population, though rapidly increasing through the first two-thirds of the century, barely exceeded 40 000 000 in 1900 (England and Wales, 32 249 000; Scotland, 4 437 000; Ireland, 4 469 000).

Britain's moment in world history: progress and caution

The nineteenth century was Britain's moment in world history. She seized it with an odd mixture of self-confidence and self-doubt. It would not be unreasonable to see Victorian Britain as one of the most successful states in the history of the world. Yet her success was unintentional, unplanned, and unanticipated, seen as a curious and only half-deserved bonus from providence; and right through it ran a sense of caution, even of alarm. The British had a strong sense of hubris and little sense of 'manifest destiny' (the American phrase of 1845). Her ruling class must have been the most cautious imperialists in history. The scale of Bismarck's boldness as he forced unification on Germany was outside the thinking of nineteenth-century British cabinets. Their equivalent was a carefully crafted moderation, a refusal to panic, a willingness to listen and to compromise, a readiness to reform within the existing constitution and to let the institutions of the country play their part. Attempts at the end of the century to provide an ethos of imperial rule suitable for so extensive an empire were regarded with suspicion. The 'khaki election' of 1900 (fought after the supposed defeat of the Boers in South Africa) rang hollow even to the jingos who won it. The sense of change from progress qualified by caution to alarm qualified by the possibilities of scientific advance can be seen dramatically and in an exaggerated form in the poetry of Alfred Tennyson, who succeeded William Wordsworth as Poet Laureate on the latter's death in 1850. Tennyson's poem, *Locksley Hall* (1842), faced the future boldly in many famous lines:

> Not in vain the distance beacons. Forward, forward let us range
> Let the great world spin forever down the ringing groves of change.
> Thro' the shadow of the globe we sweep into the younger day:
> Better fifty years of Europe than a cycle of Cathay.

But his poem, *Locksley Hall. Sixty Years After*, published in 1886 as the Liberal Party split over Irish Home Rule, struck a very different tone:

> Gone the cry of 'Forward, Forward,' lost within a growing gloom;
> Lost, or only heard in silence from the silence of a tomb . . .

'Forward' rang the voices then, and of the many mine was one.
Let us hush this cry of 'Forward' till ten thousand years have gone.

Though the United Kingdom had triumphed in the wars against France, and though her national security was for the time being unthreatened, the victory of 1815 left a sense of unease. The doctrines of the French Revolution were not defeated, and the British propertied classes took a considerable time to come to take the Tennysonian view of progress in the first quotation above. 'Liberalism'—by the mid-century a term which almost equated to the opinion of the political and intellectual majority—was initially seen by many after 1815 as a foreign idea, and was often equated with the strict secular liberalism of the Continent by which British Radical and Liberals were taken to have been captured. It was in this context that J. H. Newman doubted that Thomas Arnold, one of the great liberal Anglicans of the century, could be a Christian. Contemporaries visiting France and Italy in the 1820s did not know which was the more shocking: the popery of the revived Roman Catholic Church or the secularism of the remnants of the revolution. It was to be a generation before there was again confidence in a progressive government.

The *first* industrial nation: work and discipline

An important part of British uncertainty, both in the aftermath of the war and in the century generally, sprang from the absence of precedent for the extraordinary transformation the country found itself experiencing. No precedent in any country existed for the economic dominance of industries such as iron, steel, and manufacturing, or for the extent of urbanization which accompanied them. British society and its economy was an unprecedented experiment in industrial and financial capitalism, as Karl Marx spotted from his desk in the British Museum. Marx strove, better than most, to give shape to the astonishing development he saw around him. He brilliantly described the commodity, that central object of Victorian life, round which revolved labour and profit in the factory, 'getting and spending' (in Wordsworth's phrase), comfort and variety in the home, the office, the pub, the club, and the pavilion. And he analysed the spasms of the capitalist economy which generated the surges of expansion followed by crisis which created a sense of instability running right through society. Limited liability legislation (1855–62) prevented the extreme forms of bankruptcy for investors, but, short of that, life was precarious, whether at the labouring or the middle-class level (except for the clergy). Even the aristocracy, accustomed to be so assured and self-confident, saw the repeal of the Corn Laws[1] in 1846 as symbolizing a loss of power and found themselves seriously affected by agricultural depression from the 1870s to the 1890s.

Life in the nineteenth century was hard, raw, and unreliable, as the United Kingdom laid the foundations of a mature capitalist economy and stood on the cusp of the national comfort which came to it in the second half of the next century. There was accordingly a complex mixture of wealth, show, and power amidst uncertainty, squalor, and deprivation. Those whose calling did not take them into industrial areas rarely visited them. When they did, they were usually appalled: Queen Victoria's reaction to a visit in 1852 to the Black Country to the west of Birmingham—one of the most prosperous of the industrial areas—is similar to Dickens' sense of alienation described in *Hard Times* (1854), a novel conditioned by a visit to Preston. The queen wrote in her journal:

It is like another world. In the midst of so much wealth, there seems to be nothing but ruin. As far as the eye can reach, one sees nothing but chimneys, flaming furnesses, many deserted but not pulled down, with wretched cottages around them . . . Add to this a thick & black atmosphere . . . and you have but a faint impression of the life . . . which a 3rd of a million of my poor subjects are forced to lead. (Cited in Elizabeth Longford, *Victoria R. I.*, 1964, p. 305.)

For an age which saw itself as moral, work was the justification for living with such conditions—and the change from frivolity and

---

[1] The Corn Laws, which are discussed in several chapters of this book, were a tariff set up in 1815 to protect domestically grown cereals from being undercut by foreign imports and to maintain high domestic production in the British Isles at steady prices. Details of the scheme were varied from time to time, but its effect was to favour the rural producer against the urban consumer. The Corn Laws quickly gained a symbolic as well as a practical significance, and the Anti Corn-Law League was founded in 1838; when the Corn Laws were 'repealed' in 1846, a shilling duty was in fact maintained, until final repeal in 1869.

corruption to work and probity was the change on which the nineteenth century especially prided itself over the eighteenth. This change was most obviously exemplified by the evangelicals. But it was to be found in most areas of nineteenth-century society and opinion, including the utilitarians—apparently the antithesis of the evangelicals. The utilitarians, despite their claim to use happiness as their criterion, were as dour and determined as any religious sect. Work and the discipline of work, whether in employment, for a charity or a church, for the family and the home, became its own justification: men worked, women worked, children worked, and if they could not work, they went to the workhouse. 'You saw nothing in Coketown [Preston]', Dickens wrote in *Hard Times*, 'but what was severely workful.'

The cult of work led to Sunday (the Sabbath Day) being, at least in principle, exclusively dedicated to praising the works of the Lord. Even the opening of high-minded places of self-improvement such as galleries, museums, and libraries on Sundays was a controversial matter. The labouring classes came to regard 'St Monday' as much as Sunday as their day off. Nothing appalled Protestant visitors to the Continent more than to see Sunday treated as a day of recreation. In fact, the Sabbath was not as closely observed as some would have liked and from the 1840s societies for the proper observance of the Sabbath were active. Legislation to prevent the opening of public houses on Sundays was often proposed, and was passed for Scotland in 1853 (with provision for 'bona fide' travellers to refresh themselves), Ireland in 1878, and for Wales in 1881; but a bill for England failed, though quite often introduced. Lord Robert Grosvenor's bill in 1855 to stop Sunday trading in London was abandoned following vast popular demonstrations against it. By 1880, a number of galleries were opening on Sundays, and in 1886 a bill was passed permitting their opening on Sundays in London. Even so, Sunday in most parts of Britain, and especially in Scotland and Wales, was a joyless, frustrating day for those not inclined to frequent worship.

With this intensity of work came rules and codification of behaviour. Influenced by evangelicalism, which encouraged living by rules as well as by faith, and by the very different demands of the processes of factory and commercial life, and by the complexities of the division of labour within social living, rules and codes were drawn up for most aspects of public and private life. Categories of living were established, whether by the classifications of occupations in the census, of the Indian castes, or of the aristocracy (Burke's *Peerage* codified earlier rules of precedence so that all peers and baronets and their relations had a rank number in one of 57 classes, so that they knew the order of entering and leaving rooms; for example the wife of the younger son of a knight was 57 838). And with the railways, the telegraph, and the post—which together made possible the rapid velocity of goods and money—came timetables, local, national, and international, and consequently national time. *Bradshaw's Railway Guide* became the bible of commerce and Greenwich was agreed as the international meridian in 1883–84—an important victory over Paris—and hence Greenwich Mean Time became the basis for world time and timetables.

Rules governed work and made it profitable. To be a 'workjng man' was a source of pride as well as a mark of insecurity and Rudyard Kipling was, as always, not uncharacteristic of his period when he described heaven as pure work:

> And no one shall work for money, and no one shall work for fame,
> But each for the joy of the working . . .
>
> ('When Earth's Last Picture is Painted', 1896)

When the American artist James McNeill Whistler sold a picture for 200 guineas which, in the impressionist style, suggested rapid inspiration rather than sustained application, John Ruskin, the art critic and social reformer, accused Whistler of 'flinging a pot of paint in the public's face', thus provoking a famous libel action. Ruskin prized dedicated individual craft-work above all other social activities. His view that mass production of the sort developed in Victorian factories was the antithesis of a good economy was in some respects similar to Marx's view in that it identified an alienation of the worker from the product. Popular criticism of the queen in the 1860s and early 1870s was based not on widespread republicanism—though there were some republicans—but on the fact that she was clearly not working.

Yet within this culture of work developed, as we shall see, a culture of leisure, of 'time off', more complex than anything since the Roman Empire. This counter-culture of leisure was for the most part organized, and initially sparse and dour: sport was hard and earnest, and relaxation was to be bracing and improving. The middle-class culture of walking and mountain-climbing related to an emphasizing of masculinity and 'proving one's self'. Sportsmen logged their sport with the enthusiasm of office foremen meeting their production targets. A somewhat different ethos was epitomized by Albert Edward, Prince of Wales, and his aristocratic circle; but his appetite for excess was so gargantuan—with his five meals a day and up to twelve courses at dinner—that to match it was, in fact, hard work, as several of his courtiers complained. To kill 30 000 head of game in a season at Sandringham, even with help, required application of a kind. Fox-hunting, as the novels of Anthony Trollope and Robert Surtees record, was a very popular rural activity, especially in England. Midway between a participatory and a spectator 'sport', it was as important as a forum for social advancement as a means of killing foxes.

Commodities and ownership

For a society which praised work as highly as did the Victorians, the ownership of its products, in the form of commodities, took on an especial fascination. As Marx remarked, commodities are 'merely congealed quantities of labour', ownable by anyone with the money to buy them. A mass market in commodities of remarkable complexity developed, with advertisments stressing in detail the variety of choice available to the individual in a cheap form, whether of clothes, furniture, books, pictures, or any other of a myriad of products. Houses became showplaces of numerous objects, the walls cluttered with pictures and decorations, the furniture elaborately carved, the atmosphere made claustrophobic with the abundance of detail. Museums became packed with collections of anthropological and imperial commodities, including the ultimate form of labour ownership: the display of the skulls of a variety of 'primitive' peoples. On the other hand, while the British might collect examples of the dead from their colonies, they ceased directly to own the living, for by abolishing slavery in the empire they replaced the sovereignty of slave labour with the individualism of wage labour. The British navy played a major part in the worldwide elimination of the slave trade, especially by blockading the coast of West Africa.

The commodities produced by British work represented the wealth and complexity of the society which produced them. The extent of the 'division of labour' (the political economists' term to describe the specialization in the workplace and the home which made possible complex production) was reflected in the 1851 census, which listed 17 classes and 91 subclasses of different categories of occupation, the basic classification still used in British censuses. (By 1911, a dictionary of occupations maintained from 1861 by the census office contained upwards of 30 000 different terms.) It was no accident that it was in 1851 that the basic classification was made, for by the time of that census, in the same year as the Great Exhibition in Hyde Park, the extent and character of the switchback of change on which the Victorians were riding was becoming much clearer, and therefore measurable. The 1851 census also confirmed a remarkable growth of population without the accompanying starvation (save in Ireland) which Thomas Malthus had anticipated. It also confirmed an extent of urbanization not equalled in other large European countries until early in the twentieth century, and the extent to which the Church of England was threatened by other churches, and religion in general, by non-attendance at church.

1851: the achievement of balance

1851 marked a taking of stock, and the start of a period of relief on the part of the propertied classes that the fears of the earlier part of the century were passed: the economy had not failed, the huge debts left by the wars against the French had not proved crippling, the working classes had not revolted, the Chartist movement of the 1830s and 1840s had collapsed, the modest modernization of the political system made by the Whig governments through the Reform Act of 1832 and other legislation in the 1830s had been adequate for the time being. Public health crises, notably the cholera epidemics of 1831–32 and 1848–49, were becoming avoidable through improvements in public health. The very strong reserve powers of the state, used energetically to suppress radicalism in the 1816–20 period, were rarely used subsequently in the century, except in Ireland and parts of the empire. The repeal of the Corn Laws in 1846, which gave a primacy to those who consumed food rather than to those who produced it, showed that the country could move peacefully from agricultural to urban priorities, matching the trends which the census so clearly indicated; and the accompanying ethos of free trade created a sharp division between 'government' and 'the economy' which received very widespread support. The intense debate about class privilege which the Corn Laws provoked between 1815 and 1845 ended almost overnight. No political party after 1848 until after the end of the century supported protective tariffs or departed significantly in practice from a free-trade approach. The land campaign in England which, armed with David Ricardo's *Principles of Political Economy and Taxation* (1817), had underpinned the Anti-Corn Law League, could not sustain sufficient passion to make a serious political impact, despite Richard Cobden's efforts to maintain momentum. Land ownership remained central to the politics of Ireland, and to the politics of parts of Scotland and Wales, but in England reformers despaired of support. Joseph Chamberlain's Radical Programme of 1885 reflected a revival of attack on the role of the large landowner, but its force was quickly blunted when Chamberlain threw in his lot with the landowning party over Ireland.

Free trade, civilization, and cooperation

'Classes' there might be, but free trade would prevent, as William Gladstone, the leading free-trade chancellor of the exchequer, observed, any assertion 'of the most selfish instincts of class against the just demands of the public welfare'. Parliament, consequently, would be above economics and would be perceived as 'fair' by all sections of the community. 'Fair dealing' was a much-prized Victorian value, and it had a worldwide significance. 'In reforming your own fiscal and commercial system', Gladstone told the Commons in his first great budget speech in 1853, 'you have laid the foundations of similar reforms—through every country of the civilized world.' Such was Britain's mission, but Gladstone's confidence of worldwide success proved over-optimistic. In the last quarter of the century, Victorians' self-doubt deepened while their empire expanded and diversified. Every country in 'the civilized world', including Britain's own settled dominions and India, introduced protection, leaving Britain the only wholly free-trading economy.

Free trade was not seen by Victorians as simply an open world market, for they believed market economics should be balanced at every level by voluntary associations. Thus there should be an international order through the cooperation of states in the Concert of Europe, a solution to the question of world order supported by many, but not all, free-traders, for some, especially those in the peace movement and associated with Richard Cobden, saw any form of diplomacy as likely to deteriorate into aristocratic corruption. Cobdenites saw world peace as best assisted by vigilant peace associations promoting arbitration and non-intervention in a free-trade context. At home, membership of a host of associations was looked to as a way of balancing the lonely life of the individual in the marketplace ethos of a capitalist economy, whose regulation was at best minimal. Many saw the established churches as providing this sort of associationalism at a national level. At the local and quasi-national level, cooperative, building, and friendly societies, trades unions, professional associations, civic clubs, local parliaments, and debating societies, and a myriad of other voluntary bodies, including the Nonconformist and Roman Catholic Churches, provided a financial and psychological shelter. Perhaps the most famous of these was the Rochdale Society of Equitable Pioneers, one of the first cooperative societies. 'Self-help'—the title of Samuel Smiles's famous bestseller (1859)—meant self-improvement within a context of penny banks and friendly societies. Government looked to such bodies to provide welfare services, and to an extent they did, especially the established churches. Intellectual life, also, developed associations, the two great meeting places for the development of ideas and exchange of information and opinion being the British Association for the Advancement of Science (from 1831) and the National Association for the Promotion of Social Science (from 1857 until 1884), each annually holding large meetings in a major city and each seeing itself as a guardian of the civic and intellectual welfare of the nation.

Established churches, the parish, and welfare

Whether an established church was to be seen as a voluntary body or an agent of the state was a much-contested question. Its status and its responsibilities were mostly given to it by law, but its ability to finance them became increasingly a voluntary matter, as church tithes and compulsory rates were abolished. In practice, an established church stood astride the line between state and voluntary. In ending taxes earmarked for the established churches, the United Kingdom went the opposite route from most Protestant countries on the Continent. In the early years of the century the established churches provided, through their parishes, a wide range of services largely controlled and prioritized by the members of those churches. The nineteenth was the last century in which the parish was the natural unit through which most people's lives were lived. Charles Dickens described a family man falling on hard times:

What can he do? To whom is he to apply for relief? To private charity? To benevolent individuals? Certainly not—there is his parish. There are the parish vestry, the parish infirmary, the parish surgeon, the parish officers, the parish beadle. Excellent institutions, and gentle, kind-hearted men. The woman dies—she is buried by the parish. The children have no protector— they are taken care of by the parish. The man first neglects, and afterwards cannot obtain work—he is relieved by the parish; and when distress and drunkenness have done their work upon him, he is maintained, harmless, babbling idiot, in the parish asylum. (*Sketches by Boz* (1835–36), 'Our Parish', Chapter 1.)

By the end of the century most of these responsibilities had passed to secular authorities, and the parish had become chiefly a unit of religious worship. The Poor Law was secularized in 1834 and the Elementary Education Acts for England and Wales in 1870 and for Scotland in 1872 recognized that even bodies as large and well-endowed as established churches were unable by themselves to supply a national educational system. By the end of the century the inability of voluntary associations to meet the rising expectations of the population caused many to revise their view of where the boundary between state and voluntary responsibilities should fall.

Even so, most of the new cities tried to maintain the parish spirit on a larger scale, and to preserve the idea of the parish as, in the words of Dickens, 'a little world of its own' or, as put by the great Scottish theoretician of parish life, Thomas Chalmers, in his remarkable book, *The Christian and Civic Economy of Large Towns* (1821):

We think that the same moral regimen, which, under the parochial and ecclesiastical system of Scotland, has been set up, and with much effect, in her country parishes, be introduced into the most crowded of her cities, and with as signal and conspicuous an effect on the whole habit and character of their population . . . the simple relationship which obtains between a minister and his people in the former situation, may be kept up with all the purity and entireness of its influence in the latter situation . . . there is no dissimilarity between town and country.

Intense local pride was manifested in fine civic centres, the endowment of museums, galleries, and libraries by those who had made their money out of the area, and it is a point of importance that though London was the chief financial centre, the ownership of industrial wealth was largely held and banked in the locality where the production was carried out: civic pride related to local money. Some named their buildings after the dominant liberal ethos of the period (the Free Trade Hall in Manchester), others after their benefactors (the Usher Hall in Edinburgh). It was only gradually that Peel's Bank Charter Act (1844), with a roughly similar act for Ireland (1845), phased out local banknotes, and it was only after our period that 'clearing banks' became national institutions based in London, rather than local or regional institutions; in Scotland and Ireland separate national banking and note-issuing systems continued, Sir Walter Scott having written a powerful defence of the Scottish notes in his *Malachi Malagrowther* letters (1826).

London: an imperial city?

With voluntaryism and self-improvement went self-respect, a code of honesty and a sense of respectability. The preservation of personal dignity in conditions of deprivation was a striking and much-noticed feature of society at all levels, what Dickens called 'shabby-genteel'. London—William Cobbett's 'great wen . . . the metropolis of the empire'—was often seen as the antithesis of the city-parish spirit of the rest of the country: 'It is strange', Dickens observed, 'with how little notice, good, bad, or indifferent, a man may live and die in London ... he cannot be said to be forgotten when he dies, for no one remembered him when he was alive' (*Sketches by Boz*, 'Characters', Chapter I). Yet as it expanded London, too, retained its villages and its parishes: for a city which housed a government with ultimate responsibility for almost a quarter of the world's population London was remarkably informal and unimperial in its planning, or absence of planning. Indeed, its haphazard development mirrored the haphazard expansion of the empire which was ruled from it. The Mall, Buckingham Palace (built 1825–37), the new Palace of Westminster (built 1840–52, and at that time the largest building in the world), and the museums to the west of the city at Kensington were grand by any standard and showed what the British could do if they chose, but they were exceptional. For the most part, a much more humdrum approach was preferred with considerable eclecticism of style—there was to be no Baron Haussman in London and the development of Paris was caricatured as the monotonous consequence of an unhealthy alliance of autocracy and money. The sort of imperial capital which might have been built to the north or west of London was never seriously contemplated. The British prime minister lived in an ordinary if commodious house with an ordinary address—10, Downing Street. New Delhi was planned from 1906 as an imperial capital, but the use of taxation for national institutions in London such as the National Gallery, the National Portrait Gallery, and the British Museum, or for their equivalents in Edinburgh and Dublin, was seen as something profligate.

The most dramatic innovation in London took place beneath the streets, as a huge underground city of tunnels was built, for sewage, postage, water, communication-tubes propelled by air or water pressure, and for transport. Cesspools were made illegal in 1847, the sewers initially depositing the sewage in the Thames. Its pollution required a system of main-street sewers and pumping stations. These were completed by 1875, Frank Forster and Joseph William Bazalgette supervising the construction of 1300 miles of sewers, integrated with the development of the Thames Embankment. By the 1880s new houses were connected as a matter of course to sewers. The expanding city posed considerable problems of transportation, especially in the central area. Cabs were introduced in London in 1823 and omnibuses in 1829. The relaxation of licensing control on horse-drawn cabs in 1831 led to a great and necessary increase, J. A. Hansom inventing his famous cab in 1834. But it also led to constant traffic jams in the centre (by 1893 there were 10 806 cabs, plus personal carriages, and 2366 omnibuses). Attempts to regulate numbers and fares led to a series of cab strikes. The first (partly) underground railway in the world was the Metropolitan Line, expanded into the Metropolitan and District Line, linking the new railway stations to the north of the city and running just under street level. It was inaugurated in May 1862 by a steam train containing Gladstone (a major shareholder) and other dignitaries, the railway opening officially in 1863 (its stations today are largely unchanged). But the narrow, winding streets in much of London prevented easy develop-ment of a sub-street underground (as was relatively straightforward in Paris). Though innovative, the underground was only marginally effective as an alternative to surface travel until electric engines in the 1890s permitted deep-level underground transport. By 1900 London (north of the Thames) had a somewhat haphazard and embryonic underground transport system poised for the extensive developments of the Edwardian years.

A United Kingdom: unity and pluralism

London was the capital of the United Kingdom of Great Britain and Ireland (the state's name declared by the union with Ireland on 1 January 1801) and of the empire. Dublin and Edinburgh (Wales had then no capital) had their administrations but the nineteenth century was the century of the Union, the point towards which, at least according to English Whiggery, state-formation in the British Isles had been developing since the Saxons. William Stubbs remarked in his great *Constitutional History of England* (1873) that 'England, although less homogeneous in blood and character [than Germany], is more so in uniform and progressive growth. The very diversity of the elements which are united within the isle of Britain serves to illustrate the strength and vitality of that one which for thirteen hundred years has maintained its position either unrivalled or in victorious supremacy.' Stubbs, writing soon after the publication of

Charles Darwin's *On the Origin of Species* (1859), saw this process in Darwinian as well as Whiggish terms: the union of the English kingdoms under Wessex showed that the 'process of natural selection was in constant working'. But the Union, as Stubbs also noted, was never homogeneous and, as with its franchise and voting system, set out to avoid the French model of systematized centralization.

The centripetal force of a much more integrated economy was to an extent offset by a revival of national traditions and identities. With its parallel administrations, its separate series of law for each of the three kingdoms, its religious pluralism, with the monarch an Anglican in one part of her realm and a Presbyterian in another, the Union was self-evidently partial, except in one vital respect: the Crown in Parliament at Westminster had an absolute sovereignty in legislation. The Union's various parts were semi-separate but unequal. Scotland, Ireland, and Wales were always subject to an English majority in both Houses of Parliament which was usually willing to assert itself. Yet the politics of these proportionally minor parts of the Union, and particularly Ireland, took up a great deal of English time and at the 'heart of the empire' there was in almost every decade of the century a debate about the constitution—a debate greatly intensified when Gladstone and the majority of the Liberal Party proposed Home Rule for Ireland in 1886.

Differing views of the Union: politics and history

The Union was of different advantage to different national ruling groups, some of which felt themselves protected by its wider framework from more general pressures. Some of such groups were social: the landed class in Scotland and Ireland was shielded by Westminster from the sort of socio-legal reform it might otherwise have expected in the face of the clearances it so energetically promoted in both those countries (and thus in Ireland when such reform did come it was accompanied by lavish cash inducements in the form of land purchase, and in Scotland in the modest Crofters Act (1886)). Enforced rural depopulation is given special importance in Irish history, but its effect was perhaps the more profound and long-lasting in Scotland, where, unlike Ireland, it was accompanied by the imposition of new forms of rural economy: sheep farming or the sporting estate, the latter of especial significance to the Union as it opened the Highlands for English recreation, exemplified by the queen's development of the Balmoral estate on Deeside in the 1850s. The landed class in England used the land crisis in Ireland to argue against any reform of land tenure in England, partly by allowing Parliament to exhaust itself by periodic bouts of modest Irish land reform, partly by successfully alleging that the property of small landowners and even householders would be endangered by any change in the holdings of large landowners (and some nineteenth-century landowners were very large: 80% of the land in the United Kingdom in 1873 was owned by fewer than 7000 people).

The professional class varied in its view of the Union. In England, the desirability of the Union was taken for granted. In Scotland, the professional class was generally strongly Unionist after 1886, though with some support also for Home Rule; and the revival in 1886 of the Scottish Secretaryship of State—administrative rather than parliamentary devolution—exactly suited their priorities. In Ireland, the position was the opposite: they already had their secretary, but they wanted a Home Rule parliament. Whether such groups should be seen in terms of the theory of collaboration developed to explain imperial stability depends on whether one sees Scotland, Ireland, and Wales as partners or subordinates in relationship to England.

Though power was in England's hands, influence on England on a wide range of subjects came from the other constituent parts of the United Kingdom: Scottish political economy, philosophy, and literature were determining intellectual forces in the first half of the nineteenth century; Scottish, Irish, and Welsh views on history and custom in turn contributed to the acceptance in the third quarter of the century of an historical and customary understanding of relationships in land tenure, and, though to a much lesser extent, with respect to industrial relations also. Historicism (the view that society and politics must be understood in terms of the changing historical experience of a country) was most marked where change was greatest. Scottish tartans and clan societies, with Lowlanders often to the fore, the Welsh National Eisteddfod (revived in 1819 and held regularly from 1858), and the Gaelic Union (from 1882) in Ireland are representative of a much more general historicist revival, and in the

1890s the Celtic revival linked, to an extent, all three. The revival was in part linguistic self-defence as English became the unavoidable general means of communication. Gaelic was discouraged by educational reformers but was monitored in the Scottish census from 1881; it declined markedly in the course of the century as a primary and even as a secondary language in Ireland and Scotland (though over 230 000 in Scotland—over 75% in the west Highlands and Islands— still spoke it 'habitually' in 1881). But in Wales Welsh remained a language understood by almost half the population.

Disunited nationalisms and the uses of history

These semi-separate historical traditions each contained within itself cross-currents sometimes as strong or stronger than the main tide: Highland culture in Scotland was as much damaged by Scottish Lowlanders as it was by the English, perhaps more. In Ireland, the predominantly Presbyterian Scottish-settled area of Ulster was to prove, as the century wore on, even more hostile to the political realization of 'Ireland' than the Anglo-Irish ascendancy (as the Anglican landowners of southern Ireland were known and of which Charles Stewart Parnell was a member, though not a characteristic one). The expanding industrial area of south Wales, with its cottages huddled in the valleys in the shadow of the coal tips, had little in common with the rural north, and transport between the two areas was poor. Compared to Ireland, Scotland, or Wales, England was, even allowing for her significant regional differences, a much more homogeneous country throughout the nineteenth century.

Scotland built the largest historical monuments, larger than those built in England to Albert or the Duke of Wellington: in Edinburgh in 1846 to Sir Walter Scott, her greatest novelist and most influential historian, and near Stirling in 1869 to William Wallace, the grandest of the many nineteenth-century monuments to that medieval hero; it incorporates a Hall of Scottish Heroes celebrating modern as well as medieval distinction. Both the Scott and Wallace monuments were paid for by public subscriptions (the Albert Memorial in Hyde Park was only finished by Parliament voting almost half of the money).

Dublin reshaped the city centre to commemorate Daniel O'Connell. In London, Trafalgar Square and Nelson's Column celebrated a British rather than an English hero (despite the fact that Nelson's famous message read 'England expects . . . '). Sir Walter Scott anticipated and shaped a good deal of nineteenth-century non-English nationalism by the way he arranged the visit of George IV to Scotland in 1822, famous for popularizing the restoration of tartan and the wearing of the kilt. The occasion is recalled in David Wilkie's portrait of the monarch, appropriately kilted in a costume designed by Sir Walter, (1829). The visit both encouraged local nationalism and associated it through the sovereign with the Union.

History was more obviously important to the 'peripheries' of the UK than to England, for it was a chief means of maintaining identity in the face of imperial politics and an increasingly United Kingdom-wide market in culture, dominated though not in fact controlled by England. But in England, also, history was a powerful and much-employed engine of national unity, with a continued stress on the importance of what were presented as the great moments of national achievement: Magna Carta, the Reformation, the defeat of the gunpowder plot, and a series of other, chiefly Protestant successes. In each of these separate but partially enmeshed cultural traditions, partly feeding off each other, partly juxtaposed to each other, attempts were made to introduce new 'national' (the word of course begged the question) celebrations, the most successful of which was Trafalgar Day, 21 October. It built on the success of Trafalgar Square (constructed 1829–45, with Nelson's Column erected in 1843) as London's place of popular assembly and was formalized by the Navy League (1894) to celebrate the Royal Navy, the 'Senior Service', always more highly regarded than the army despite the brutality of its serving conditions, but declining in status through a series of disasters in the last quarter of the century. It epitomized the United Kingdom's defiance of the Continent. In England, the mid-nineteenth century saw the foundation of the National Portrait Gallery (1857)—earlier than its Scottish equivalent (1889)—of many local history and archaeological societies, and, in 1868, of what became the Royal Historical Society. The *Dictionary of National Biography*—the term 'national' being studiously undefined—began publication in 1885. These initiatives were not, for the most part, promoted by academics, though they coincided with the start of history courses in some English universities.

The constituent parts of the United Kingdom varied in their affec-
tion (or disaffection) for it, and thus were rarely effective in presenting a common front to England. For the Scots, and especially the
Lowland Scots, the Union and the empire in the nineteenth century
offered considerable economic, social, and political advantages. They
gave the Scots a large context in which to develop, and they took good
advantage of it. They played a considerable role, considering their
numbers, in both Westminster and popular politics. Glasgow was for
a time the 'Second City of the Empire'. Scots were prominent in the
Indian army and administration and in the government, administration and politics of many of the colonies (especially Canada, Australia,
and New Zealand, and with Nyasaland (Malawi) practically a Church
of Scotland protectorate). Moreover, their professional class was left to
run Scotland without much interference—for in the second half of
the eighteenth century the English had taken full advantage in the
aftermath of the 'Forty-Five' to establish adequate compliance. The
National Association for the Vindication of Scottish Rights (1853)
attempted to defend Scottish values against anglicization but was not
an effective political force. Even in religion, where the disruption of
the Church of Scotland in 1843 was in large measure the result of the
carelessness of Westminster legislators, the Union permitted a quite
different pattern of religious development from that of the rest of the
UK. 'North Britain' the address given on many a Scottish letterhead
in the nineteenth century—exemplified the partnership many Scots
felt they had in the United Kingdom and its empire.

In Ireland, the opposite was the case: England persisted with an
established Church seen by the mass of the population as foreign and
hostile to Catholicism, and the two steps taken to alleviate this
situation—Catholic emancipation in 1829[2] and disestablishment in

---

[2] The Corporation Act (1661) and the Test Acts (1673, 1678), and other legislation,
required all those holding national and local public offices, including being a Member
of the Commons or of the Lords, or a magistrate, to be members of the established
church, that is the Church of England and Ireland, or the Church of Scotland, with
Roman Catholics the chief target of exclusion. Nonconformists were also thus
debarred, though to a lesser extent, as some also took communion in the Church of
England. In 1828 Parliament repealed the Test and Corporation Acts with respect to
Nonconformists, and in 1829 Roman Catholics were 'emancipated' in the sense that
they could now sit in the Lords, and be MPs, army officers, magistrates, mayors, and
other such officials (exclusion from some such minor offices had been diminished in
1793). But various other offices, including the Crown, the lord chancellorship, and the
lord lieutenancy of Ireland, remained confined to Protestants; members of Catholic

1869—seemed grudging, consequently failing to legitimate the Union to the extent hoped for. Even so, the Irish professional class flourished in the nineteenth century and the Union had more staying power than might have been expected. Daniel O'Connell's movement to repeal the 1800 Act of Union (not a wholly separatist objective) did not survive his death (1847). In the mid-century, the Irish Republican Brotherhood and the Fenians began a genuinely separatist movement, whose support in Irish elections was rarely measured. Isaac Butt's Home Rule League (later Association) (1873) was more limited in ambition than O'Connell's movement but more electorally successful; under Parnell's leadership it quickly became the dominant political movement in Ireland, and from 1885 hegemonic in all but Ulster. It offered the Irish the advantages of control of Irish domestic policy within the context of the United Kingdom and the empire, and, as the only constitutional nationalist movement to move outside the Liberal Party, was highly disruptive to the two main parties at Westminster. In Wales, the professional class had not the same national function as its equivalents in Scotland and Ireland, there being no separate system of Welsh law and administration, and the ministers of the various Nonconformist churches thus gained an especial national status. From the 1880s Cymru Fydd (Young Wales), with support especially in north Wales, promoted Home Rule for Wales, but from within the Liberal Party.

For the English, England and Britain were largely synonymous, and the English saw Westminster as 'their' Parliament. The pictures and frescoes in the new Palace of Westminster—a significant test of national taste—reflected, with barely an exception, scenes from the heroic moments of English or post-1707 British history, even though several of the artists who painted them were Scots. It was a curious irony of the United Kingdom, as well as an accurate reflection of the uncertainty of its identity, that a common name was never found for

---

religious orders were forbidden to enter the UK and convents were prohibited. Various other restrictions continued, including educational exclusion, notably at Oxford and Cambridge, where the Anglican formulas required of those matriculating at Oxford and taking degrees at Oxford and Cambridge were unacceptable to Catholics (and also to many Nonconformists and secularists). Catholics entering either House of Parliament after 1829 had to swear not to 'disturb or weaken the Protestant Religion, or Protestant Government in the United Kingdom'. The county freehold franchise in Ireland was raised in 1829 from 40 shillings to £10, with the intention of diminishing the electoral effects of the Act.

its inhabitants: 'English' was commonly used by the English and some Scots to describe the inhabitants of the British mainland, but, especially after the 1870s, this became offensive to the Scots and the Welsh; 'Britons' was taken by mainlanders to refer to the inhabitants of the British Isles, but was never accepted by the Irish as applying to them, and, of course, Ireland is not part of Britain (though it is one of the British Isles). Not surprisingly, 'United Kingdomer' never gained any ground, though it was the only technically correct term.

Competition between the constituent nations of the United Kingdom got under way almost as soon as the sports of association and rugby football had their rules agreed. The first 'internationals' between Scotland and England at rugby and soccer were played in 1871 and 1872 respectively, followed by the first 'test match' at cricket, between Marylebone Cricket Club (which claimed rather vaguely to represent England certainly and perhaps the rest of Britain) and Australia in 1877. These matches formed the basis of what in the next century became a worldwide peace-time form of international competition. It was not long before membership of one's national team became seen as the summit of achievement in the relevant sport and support for the teams became an important part of national consciousness in the constituent nationalities of the United Kingdom.

The United Kingdom was essentially a union of convenience laced with sentiment. This absence of system was not seen as a weakness, but rather as an example of the extent to which 'Britain' and her empire were a flexible and adaptable polity, in which absence of systematization was a strength. Nor *was* it in its day a weakness: for its purpose of conducting a liberal empire, the Crown in Parliament was an exceptionally fertile sovereignty, combining a strong but representative executive with a legislature whose full statutory powers were very rarely asserted. The mixed constitution of the United Kingdom represented a distinctiveness from the rest of the world, and this sense of distinctiveness was itself a powerful force for union, even for many of the Irish, whose demand was for Home Rule, not independence. It was only in the next century, when the imperial context vanished, that semi-systematic union began to seem disadvantageous for the nations of the mainland.

Many argued at the end of the nineteenth century that imperialists who wished to try to coordinate the various parts of the empire into a unified system were the empire's most dangerous friends. It was certainly the case that the complex mixture of constitutional union, economic integration, and a rather reserved, unbombastic patriotism was to prove a combination for which millions, including the Irish, were ready to die in the First World War.

Nowhere were the peculiarities and paradoxes of the Union more clearly exemplified than in the armed forces. The Royal Navy's structure ignored the subnationalisms of the islands it defended, and the navy was the most thoroughly unionist of all government departments in its organization, as well as being the most prestigious. But the 'British Army' not only reflected national variety but was an important means of sustaining it, for it comprised regiments whose names hallowed English, Scottish, Welsh, and Irish military achievements and traditions, and whose recruitment presupposed and required strong local patriotism. Though the officer corps was by temperament the most unionist of any of the sections of British society, the army which it led embodied and strengthened—through its uniforms, music, and flags—vital elements of Scottish, Welsh, Irish, and English nationalism. Indeed, before the days of regular sporting internationals, military parades were the chief, regular public occasions for the display of nationalism, whether Scottish, Welsh, Irish, or English. Gladstone's second Liberal government in 1881 (developing a Tory proposal of 1876) recognized the importance for the army of the development of local affinity and historical awareness, for in a shrewd recruiting stroke, regiments were given names which quickly became historic, if they were not so already (in the old numerical system, regimental names had only sometimes been attached to the official numerical name). Thus, for example, the 6th Foot, 72nd Foot, and 88th Foot became, respectively, The Durham Light Infantry, The Seaforth Highlanders, and The Connaught Rangers. Tartan trews were introduced for the Scottish Lowland regiments. The changes coincided directly with the new historicism.

The weather

For most of the queen's subjects, a concept as grand as the empire or the Union was one implicitly absorbed, but rarely directly discussed. At the opposite extreme was the weather, that daily eccentricity of

British life. From Keats to Kipling, the weather formed a topic of poetry, and the variety of the weather in the geographically small area of the British Isles, like the exceptional variety of their geography, related to the variety of habits and economic activities. To an extent, industrialization diminished this variety: for the first time in human history, most workers' work was routinely indoors. As living standards rose and people moved into the towns, the weather became of less immediate importance to daily life: a factory worker's work ignored the weather, whereas an agriculturist's work was conditioned by it. Even so, with agriculture still the largest industry, and with clothes, cooking, and eating the key elements of working-class family budgets, weather conditions remained a matter of concern, and the seasonal character of the growth of the leisure and holiday industry depended on correctly anticipating the weather.

The greatest impact of the climate was undoubtedly in Ireland, where the exceptionally hot and humid conditions of 1845 contributed directly to the spread of the potato blight fungus which caused the famine (which also severely affected the Scottish Highlands). For the United Kingdom as a whole, the wet summers of the 1870s and 1880s worsened the agricultural depression, and form the back-drop to Thomas Hardy's great novels of rural decline, whose span of publication (1872–96) almost exactly relates to the years of the agricultural depression. The British Meteorological Society was founded in 1850 (becoming 'Royal' in 1883), the meteorological department of the Board of Trade was established in 1855, and national monitoring and forecasting began. Storm warnings were sent out by telegram and newspapers began to carry rudimentary weather forecasts. From the 1850s, the records of phenologists (local observers of flora and fauna) were published nationally and there was a network of statistical recording centres, the observatory on the summit of Ben Nevis in Scotland being established in 1883.

The Victorians usually used the Fahrenheit scale to measure temperature. It was a period of extremes of weather: the highest temperature ever recorded in the British Isles was 100.5° Fahrenheit (38° Celsius) at Tonbridge, Kent, in July 1868, and the lowest was −23° Fahrenheit (55 degrees of frost, −30.6° Celsius), recorded at Blackadder, Berwickshire in December 1879 (the standard of measurement of the latter reading has been challenged).

Attempts to plan for the weather fitted naturally into a society where time was increasingly so carefully costed, and it fitted also into the nineteenth-century view that scientific knowledge was the essential preliminary to progress, and that with progress went in the long run control. For ordinary people, recollection of the weather was one way of establishing the timeline of their lives: the freezing, snowy Decembers of the 1810s, Hubert Lamb has suggested, provided the young Charles Dickens with a view of winter and of Christmas of lasting effect not only for him but through his writings for his own and subsequent centuries. The great floods in Scotland in 1829, in the north of England in 1866, in Wales and the West Country in 1875, in the Thames valley in 1874–75 (when the river rose 29 feet, flooding Blackheath and the Woolwich arsenal), 1877–78, and 1894, and in the UK generally in 1882, 1888, and 1890, reminded even urban dwellers that nature was harder to control than the river improvements of the century sometimes assumed. In 1879, the extreme rainfall in north Wales caused a service of humiliation to be held in parish churches, the end of a tradition of soliciting divine help with the weather. 1838, 1855, 1860–61, 1880, 1881, 1890–91, and the 1890s generally saw exceptional frosts, with over 30 000 people on the ice on Loch Lomond in 1895; but the last fair to be held on the Thames at London occurred in 1813–14 (a reflection more of the condition of the river than of the climate). Exceptional heat was a more local phenomenon; temperatures were measured in Camden Square, London, from 1858, and a temperature of over 90 degrees Fahrenheit (the traditional mark of extreme heat in Britain, 32.2° Celsius) was recorded there almost every summer in the mid-century. In 1857 it was so hot in London that Gladstone noted umbrellas being used as parasols in Piccadilly. The most famous political intervention by the weather was in 1858, when the smells of sewage in the Thames during the heatwave encouraged Parliament to legislate to purify the river. Clothing was in large measure conditioned by the weather's distribution of smoke: black—the predominant colour of clothes in the urban areas—being more a means of concealing coal dirt brought down by rain, drizzle, and gravity than an expression of mood.

Photography

Personal narratives were also conveniently recorded through one of the period's most striking innovations. In 1834, William Henry Fox Talbot took the first photographs in Britain and by 1844 was marketing them in books. David Hill and Robert Adamson photographed the participants in the Disruption of the Church of Scotland in 1843, thus memorably recording the central nineteenth-century occasion of Scottish life. By the early 1850s photographs of politicians were readily available and from 1859 hundreds of thousands of *cartes de visite* (small photographs mostly of public figures, also used by professional people as calling/advertising cards) were sold (cartomania or cardomania, the craze was called).

Possessing the past and perceiving the present took on many new forms. Owning a photograph of the queen or of your party leader gave a new, direct form of association with national life, and many cheap biographies had real photographs mounted as frontispieces to suggest an intimate relationship. Gladstone quickly appreciated the importance of ordinary people possessing photographs of him and insisted on photographers charging cheap prices for them. Representations of landscape in the thousands of cheap photographic postcards made by firms such as Valentines of Dundee had a powerful effect on popular perceptions and expectations. From the 1850s, any family with a little money could record in an album the narrative of family development, from birth to death (and both were photographed). The Kodak box camera (with a roll-film of 100 exposures) was invented in 1888, but until the introduction of the Pocket Kodak in 1895 (costing just over £1, with a roll-film of 12 exposures), the taking of photographs was still largely a matter for specialists. Sitting for photographs on important occasions became a part of normal life, and studios, travelling photographers, and booths at the seaside and other holiday places did huge business. Photographers such as Henry Taunt of Oxford and George Washington Wilson of Aberdeen became notable persons in their localities. Working families saved to record important family events, and the possession and display of such photographs became an important aspect of family status. The high mortality rate of children gave this means of permanent record an added urgency and poignancy. Some photographers, like Julia Margaret Cameron, used the camera to emulate or excel in psychological insight the traditional art of portraiture, and some developed new techniques of landscape art. But most took photographs in conventional poses, the convention being an important part of the record. The nineteenth is the first century for which we have literal visual narrative records, whether of a war, a city, a statesman, a family, or a pet.

Political narratives

Narrative—the sense of time passing in an ordered way—was important in the nineteenth century, a century acutely aware of change and the passing of time. The Victorians' enthusiasm for, and the publication of, statistics reflects this at a numerical level, and their many popular history books at the political. Charles Darwin enlarged the timeframe within which the world lived and developed, and made time so long as to be hard to comprehend; politicians used the timetable of parliaments and politics with considerable success to provide an understanding of national experience. No century so firmly remembered itself through political narratives. 'Time is on our side' said Gladstone in one of his most famous speeches; the Victorians hoped he was right, but often had a nagging sense that, for all their success and world dominance, time was slipping away.

In political terms, 1832, 1846, and 1886, set the narrative of the century. In 1832 the first Reform Act set the precedent for subsequent political change; in 1846 the repeal of the Corn Laws ended a long-standing debate on economic and fiscal relationships which had begun as the war with France finished in 1815 or even earlier; and in 1886 the proposal for Irish Home Rule epitomized the Liberal need to meet national grievance with a bold political solution. 1832 and 1846 resolved their respective crises, and in their different ways harmonized political, social, and economic relationships; but to the Irish question the British found no effective answer. 1832 was a particularly significant reference point for the rest of the century, soon superseding 1815, for the period of Tory rule from 1815 until 1830 became an episode to be set aside, except as a warning of what not to do. 1832 was linked, as the century progressed, to two other dates, the Reform Acts of 1867 and 1884, for the vote had for the nineteenth century a totemic status; it gave political power, but it also gave membership and implied the capacity for responsible behaviour in the community, and its exercise was, until the secret ballot of 1872, a public and accountable act, reported in the local press and recorded in poll books. For novelists as different as Benjamin Disraeli and George Eliot, the disintegration of the Tories in 1828–30 and the passing of the 1832 Reform Act by the Whigs was the start of modern politics. Disraeli's best known novel, *Sybil* (1845) is set in the aftermath of 1832, which, he remarks, 'set men a-thinking' and 'prepared a popular intelligence', and George Eliot's *Felix Holt, The Radical* (1866) and *Middlemarch* (1871–72) are both set in 1830–32. 1837, the accession of Queen Victoria, was close to 1832, and the absence of a change of monarch for the rest of the century allowed the public narrative to be associated with events essentially determined by the House of Commons. Even for many women this was also largely true, as their objective was participation in public bodies presently exclusively male, of which the Commons was the chief (if not their first target).

Other dates were significant in their spheres. The Crimean War (1854–56) was important and disruptive to the Victorians' view of themselves and their world as peaceful and orderly; but it was not important enough to be seen as a permanent point of reference in the narrative of the public mind. Attempts to promote the significance of imperial events were largely unsuccessful, though 'since the Mutiny' recognized the defining date in nineteenth-century Indian history and 1857 was a constant warning to every colonial governor and district officer throughout Asia and Africa. The famine in Ireland (1845–48), the Disruption in Scotland (1843), and the 1868 general election in Wales became points of national reference, the first two of which carried no resonance in England.

Race and the Victorians

The Indian Mutiny, as the Victorians almost always called it, roughly coincided with the development of a marked tendency to use racial terminology in a way which today seems more systematic than contemporaries achieved or intended. Sir Charles Dilke in his survey, *Greater Britain* (1868), saw Britain as central to a conflict between the 'dearer' and the 'cheaper' races; the 'dearer' race was the English (at home and overseas), the 'cheaper' races were the rest, including the Irish. Dilke expressed a confidence which was not widely shared:

> Everywhere we have found that the difficulties which impede the progress to universal dominion of the English people lie in the conflict with the cheaper races. The result of our survey is such as to give us reason for the belief that race distinctions will long continue, that miscegenation will go but little way towards blending races; that the dearer races are, on the whole, likely to destroy the cheaper peoples, and that Saxondom will rise triumphant from the doubtful struggle. (1885 edn, p. 564.)

Encouraged by Social Darwinism and later by the eugenics movement, the urge to categorize in racial terms and to use the concept of natural selection became commonplace in the second half of the century, sometimes used to support the division of labour within the UK and the empire. Alfred Marshall, for example, in his *Principles of Economics* (1890), the chief and highly influential work of economic theory of the period, commented that 'England's geographical position caused her to be peopled by the strongest members of the strongest races of northern Europe'. He also considered that 'England is the only country in which any considerable play has been given to natural selection', 'the natural selection of the fittest' being especially effective in manufacturing. On the stock market, however, according to Marshall, 'the subtlest financial speculation . . . is done chiefly by those races which have inherited the same aptitude for trading which the English have for action.'

Marshall's was a relatively restrained use of this common sort of categorization. There was, however, wide discrepancy as to which categories of racial distinction should be used. There was, at the least, a casual use of racial terms which carried with it the assumption of types of behaviour: 'the Celt', 'the Jew', 'the Hebrew', 'the savage', 'your African', 'your Boer', 'your Hindoo', 'your Highlander', 'your Irishman' ('he is rather a Jew' wrote Lord Salisbury of Bismarck, when the latter drove a hard diplomatic bargain in 1885). Such terms were used loosely and inconsistently. To what category such terms were juxtaposed was also unclear: was it the English, the Anglo-Saxons, the British? William Stubbs pointed out: 'it is the very diversity of the elements which are united within the isle of Britain' which gave it its 'strength and vitality'. Though often described as such by historians, an Irish person in Liverpool was technically no more an 'immigrant' than a Cockney in Cambridge or a Scot in Newcastle. But that there was a widespread sense of superiority and ethnic complacency among the English encouraged by imperial experience can hardly be doubted: it is reflected in Tennyson's notorious line in *Locksley Hall: Sixty Years After* (1886):

Ev'n the black Australian dying hopes he shall return, a white.

Free movement and free speech

A free market in labour, with no immigration controls was, however, a striking feature of the United Kingdom throughout our period (the Aliens Acts of 1793 and 1795 were largely mitigated in the 1840s and repealed in 1871). Passports were not in practice needed to enter the United Kingdom after 1815. British subjects travelling to European countries were advised to carry passports, though from the 1860s this was not required by most Western European countries. Partly recognizing the increase in tourism, the stamp duty on British passports was reduced from 5/- to 6d. (25 to 2.5 new pence) in 1858. The British prided themselves on their role as host to all-comers: Jews fleeing from the Eastern European pogroms, immigrants from continental autocracies, particularly Russia, the Hapsburg Empire, and, in the first half of the century, the various states of pre-unified Italy. Alexander Herzen, the chief critic of imperial Russia, lived much of his productive life in London, as did Guiseppe Mazzini, the leader of Italian republicanism (when, at Metternich's request, some of Mazzini's letters were opened by the Home Office in 1844, there was a major political row) and for Karl Marx Britain and the British Museum provided succour as well as the raw material for his analysis of capitalism (his friend and co-author, Frederick Engels, lived in a smart house in Primrose Hill, off Regent's Park in London). London was also the point of gathering and of pressure for critics of the empire, the first Pan-African Conference being held there in 1900. In the latter years of the century, demand grew for some control of immigration from Eastern Europe, but in our period none was enacted.

The empire, sport, and middle-class education

What in 1815 was an empire comprising a small number of settled colonies, some strategic bases for the navy, and those areas of India in which the East India Company ruled as a chartered company, had by the end of it become, in terms of its population, a vast area ruled for the most part autocratically. As fast as Westminster gave devolved parliaments to areas of 'white' settlement, it found itself occupying ever more extensive territories comprised of 'subject peoples' where security rested as much on military presence as on the collaboration of local elites: in India there was a vast army of British and Indian troops, largely for internal security. Rare was the family in Britain or Ireland (of whatever class) which had no contact with the overseas empire, through relatives who had settled in it (or been transported to it), or who were in the colonial service, imperial commerce, or abroad with the navy or the army (the 70 000 British troops in India in the 1870s—officers, non-commissioned officers, and other ranks— itself ensured a huge network of familial links). Imperial contacts were so omnipresent that they barely needed stating.

This was certainly true of the sort of families which sent their children to what were known as public schools. The Church of England failed in much that it attempted in our period, but it certainly succeeded in the reform, extension, and development of these schools, as distinctive an institution for the propertied class as the workhouse was for the working class. They were deliberately national—in the sense of removing children from their locality—and they were mostly boarding, removing them from their parents. They inculcated Latin and Greek, the virtues of sport, and an intense sense of hierarchy; individual initiative was encouraged, but within a rigid structure of order. The small proportion of children who attended them were predominantly from the governing class, and constituted a large proportion of that class. Intensely religious in purpose and method, public schools set out to inculcate a strong sense of duty and probity at the expense of imagination. Their powerful ethos also inculcated a strong sense of rebellion in some of their more imaginative products, and they thus created an important axis of thesis and antithesis in English culture. Initially reformed and expanded from the 1830s by the Broad Church movement in England—Thomas Arnold, the famous reforming headmaster of Rugby, was one of that movement's strongest exponents—the public schools developed their role as the century progressed. Thomas Hughes's novel of public school life, *Tom Brown's Schooldays* (1857), opens with a description of the squirearchical Brown family and coins a famous phrase: 'the great army of Browns, who are scattered over the whole empire on which the sun never sets, and whose general diffusion I take to be the chief cause of that empire's stability'. Hughes then focuses on Tom's gradual awareness of 'the meaning of his life: that it was no fool's or sluggard's paradise into which he had wandered by chance, but a battlefield ordained of old where there are no spectators, but the youngest must take his side, and the stakes are life and death'. It was to Thomas Arnold and his admirers, Hughes quotes *The Edinburgh Review* as remarking, that 'we owe the substitution of the word "earnest" for its predecessor "serious".'

As the empire and its armies expanded, so the schools' usefulness increased. Many in the public schools saw sport as an allegory of life, and some as almost more real than life itself. At the end of the century, Henry Newbolt's poem, *Vitaï Lampada* (1897), viscerally effective in its juxtapositions, caught these schools' remarkable blend of individualism, sacrifice, militarism, and sport:

> There's a breathless hush in the Close to-night—
> Ten to make and the match to win—
> A bumping pitch and a blinding light,
> An hour to play and the last man in.
> And it's not for the sake of a ribboned coat,
> Or the selfish hope of a season's fame,
> But his Captain's hand on his shoulder smote—
> 'Play up! play up! and play the game!'
>
> The sand of the desert is sodden red,—
> Red with the wreck of a square that broke;—
> The Gatling's jammed and the Colonel dead,
> And the regiment blind with dust and smoke.

> The river of death has brimmed his banks,
> And England's far, and Honour a name,
> But the voice of a schoolboy rallies the ranks:
> 'Play up! play up! and play the game!'

Tom Brown's arrival at public school coincides with a rugby match. When eight years later he returns to his old school on the occasion of Thomas Arnold's death, he finds it deserted save for 'a few of the town boys' playing cricket on the best school wicket: he considers chasing them off, but decides against it: '"They've more right there than I", he muttered.' The vignette reflects the close but awkward relationship which sport encouraged between the classes in nineteenth-century Britain. 'Playing the game' was a moral as much as a physical activity, its code marking the difference between a gentleman and the rest (and 'gentlemen' could be found in any class); failure to follow the code 'lowered' the character to the level of a wage earner, the sort of person who participated in sport for money rather than honour. But Victorian sport became a large leisure industry as well as a means of personal improvement, and by the end of the century was a major aspect of public life. The early 1870s marked with remarkable accuracy the moment when informal and mostly local sporting arrangements began to be formalized into national institutional arrangements, with national competitions (see Chapter 3). The sports which quickly spread through the empire—including football, golf, tennis, rugby, and cricket—were, ironically, to expand in the next century as the imperial structure contracted.

The moral innovations of educationists with their ethos of the amateur rubbed uneasily against the more general needs of an urban society with, for the first time, a significant proportion of the population eager for organized sporting entertainment, chiefly as spectators. The large crowds at race courses and football matches, rumbustious but not often posing a real problem of public order, reflected a disciplined and orderly workforce. That such crowds were increasingly assembling for purposes of watching others compete rather than for purposes of political demonstration was a matter for congratulation on the part of the propertied class; in Germany, France, or Italy, unless they had been brought out by the government, large crowds would almost certainly mean political trouble rather than a horse race or a football match.

The working classes and 'advancement'

The British working classes (contemporaries usually used the plural) kept their own counsel and a careful distance. To a considerable degree they were left alone to do so. Increasingly from the 1860s the propertied classes in the cities moved away from mixed housing into newly built suburbs. Churches in the towns became much less mixed in their congregations, and a critical element of Thomas Chalmers' parochial vision vanished. Though incomes rose and expectations of some element of leisure grew, even the more prosperous members of the working classes lived on the edge of financial danger, with the pawn shop at the end of the week the regular means of 'tiding over'. Working hours remained long and work conditions often hazardous.

The propertied classes worried over the working classes' ability to 'cope', chiefly because their failure to do so would mean an end to the adequacy of self-help welfare, and bodies such as the Charity Organization Society (1869) tried to advise the 'undeserving poor' on how to become deserving and thus more eligible for charitable support. But the improvement of moral behaviour (that is good household management) was a task well beyond a society whose educational provisions for the mass of the population were for much of the century rudimentary, and the swings of Victorian capitalism far outweighed any provisions that even a frugal and well-organized family could make. With some members of the clergy in the 1840s still regarding literacy as a dangerous encouragement to the reading of politically subversive newspapers, working-class literacy owed much in the first half of the century to the Sunday schools which members of that class themselves sustained. The move in the second half of the century to free and compulsory education ('elementary education' as it was called) through the provision of schools by school boards was painfully slow. But when it came in 1880 (available only for children to the age of ten until the 1890s) the working classes seem to have taken rapid advantage of it, accepting with little opposition what was a considerable change to a pattern of family life in which children contributed important supplements to the family income.

Universities

Children from working-class families could expect little change in their status unless they happened to find their way into one of the new expanding commercial sectors of the economy, such as banking, insurance, administration, or accountancy. Propertied families could progress to university, but this was, even among those classes, a rare step. In England, Oxford and Cambridge tried to maintain a monopoly of university education, with entry for Anglicans only. University College London emerged from a series of secular initiatives, inspired by Jeremy Bentham and his followers in the 1820s, with London University providing degrees by examination (but not instruction) for candidates from affiliated bodies in the British Isles and, from 1850, in the empire. King's College, London, Lampeter, and Durham offered Anglican education less expensively than Oxbridge.

In 1815, there were about 500 new students each year at Oxford and Cambridge combined; by the 1850s this had risen to about 800; reform of those universities by Gladstone's 1854 Act and by his first government's abolition of religious tests (1871) led to a slightly less Anglican student body and to the numbers rising to about 1800 by 1900; between 1800 and 1913, about 63 000 male undergraduates matriculated at Oxford and about 68 500 at Cambridge. Until the expansion of the 1860s, about two-thirds of these became clergy of the Church of England, and even at the end of the century fewer than 10% went into business. The latter figure casts some doubt on the view that Oxbridge 'gentrified' the entrepreneurial spirit of British businessmen; rather, it largely ignored them. The upper level of the civil service after 1854 in effect came only from the universities, but graduates among Members of Parliament were only in a majority in two decades of the century, the 1830s and 1840s (see M. G. Brock and M. C. Curthoys, *Nineteenth-century Oxford* (1997), Chapter 14). In the last third of the century, some provision for women was made at universities, and new universities began to be founded in the industrial cities, The Victoria University (1880) being intended to provide a federal structure for colleges such as Owens College, Manchester, which could not give their own degrees.

The ancient Scottish universities—mostly for students resident at home—saw a much greater proportion of Scots through higher education than was the case in England. Legislation in 1858 modernized their structures. In the 1860s, Scotland had one university place to every 1000 of the population, while England had only one place per 5800 of the population, and in Scotland a significant proportion of those entering university were the children of manual workers. But the Scottish entry was much less well-prepared for university-level study, the failure rate was high, and the higher education system was relatively static in Scotland in this period. A high level of graduation was important in Scotland given the exceptionally high rate of emigration by her professional class. The effectiveness of the 'lad o' pairts' tradition (that Scottish education equipped each person regardless of origin to make his way in the world) has recently been doubted, but, even so, Scotland was the only part of the United Kingdom where this egalitarian approach was the national objective with means in place for achieving it.

In Wales, non-sectarian university colleges were founded at Aberystwyth (1872), Cardiff (1883), and Bangor (1884); these were assisted by the Welsh Intermediate Education Act (1889), and were linked by royal charter (1893) as the University of Wales, Lord Rosebery, the prime minister, presiding over the first meeting of its council in 1894. Irish higher education was bedevilled by religious rows, but, even so, a promising start was made to countering the monopoly of the Anglican Trinity College, Dublin, with the founding of the 'godless colleges' of Cork, Galway, and Belfast in a federal university; these were foresworn by the papacy and many further governmental attempts to provide university education attractive to Roman Catholics failed. However, Cardinal Cullen and John Henry Newman successfully founded a Catholic university in Dublin, which later became the National University.

Because most Victorians saw education as inherently related to religion, they found themselves involved in a constant tug and tussle between the needs of the churches to instill their own varieties of Christian doctrine, the needs of an industrial society for more utilitarian teaching, and the needs of the various classes of society for schools reflecting the values of those classes. Tom Brown played frequently with 'village boys of his own age' (and that would regularly happen only in a village, not in a town). Bored with his private lessons and not yet sent to Rugby, he got into pranks disrupting the village school; but it did not occur to Tom, or to Squire Brown, his father, or to Thomas Hughes, the author of the book, that he might actually attend the village school. Religion and utility could with some difficulty be combined in schools, but the various classes of society could not be.

The nineteenth century in perspective

Though the political narrative of change of government—Grey's ministry of 1830, Peel's of 1841, Gladstone's of 1868, Disraeli's of 1874, Salisbury's of 1886—provided a time line much used by contemporaries and by twentieth-century historians, the passing of time and of controversy have diminished its use. The details of the political aspects of the Victorian era are joining those of the eighteenth century in distant, half-remembered complexity, though, as we have seen, certain political landmarks remain significant points on the map. An understanding of the nineteenth century is now more widely conceived and the contents of this volume are intended to reflect this diversity and to provide illumination of the era as a whole.

The nineteenth century is often assumed to be easy to understand because it is chronologically close, and because so many of its practices and innovations are with us still. But it was a phase, and a phase that is past. Though we live with its practical consequences, the period that gave them to us is now far distanced from us, and the nineteenth century, in terms of its mind-set, is in fact one of the centuries most alien to the modern mind. The nineteenth century's hold over the environment of the United Kingdom—political, urban, cultural, economic—has remained remarkably enduring, and the twentieth century 'modernized' less than it liked to think. But the mental categories which underpinned the nineteenth century's approach have in large measure been not only abandoned but replaced by a profound secularity which makes Victorian life the more complex and hard to penetrate the more deeply it is inspected. And the change from empire to offshore European island has for those living in the United Kingdom led to a narrowing of horizons and to a quite different set of priorities about the purposes of the life of the nation.

Many who lived in the nineteenth century hoped that they were establishing patterns of life and standards of behaviour that would condition the development of the world generally, for, though bewildered by the pace of change, the Victorians had a high view of the world-role of the United Kingdom. The economy drove nineteenth-century Britain and gave her the base for her distinctive role in world affairs. A rich public life, carefully nurtured and sustained by a strong sense of service at the local and national level, was remarkably uncorrupt and almost made a fetish of distancing itself from economic matters. Its counterpart abroad, the British Empire, by the end of the century owned a continent (Australasia) and a subcontinent (India) and was a major power in each of the other continents. More than in any other century, extra-European questions determined Britain's foreign relations. The definition of public life, and the Victorians' increasing tendency to make a sharp distinction between public and private life, made discussion of gender and the position of women an especially complex and revealing question, which has in recent years seemed of more significance than class to an understanding of the period. Victorian literary, artistic, and intellectual culture reflected at a high level the ambivalence of the many facets of the century, and have provided a more enduring base for worldwide interest in the British nineteenth century than political life: a result which would probably surprise and pain the Victorians, though they had a strong sense of providing what was already becoming the world's language. The chapters of this book describe these aspects of nineteenth-century life. They reflect the complex variety and cultural pluralism of the United Kingdom between the battle of Waterloo in 1815 and the death of Queen Victoria in 1901, a variety and pluralism the more striking given the dominant world role of the country within which they flourished. The differing perspectives of the chapters lead in some cases to the same person, event, or development—Alfred Tennyson, the Great Exhibition of 1851, the development of the railways—being discussed in different chapters from different points of view.

The term 'Victorian', used generally in this book, strictly refers only to the years of the queen's reign (1837–1901), and is a usage of convenience rather than a wholly consistent category. It is perhaps the least contentious (and the most widely used) of such epithets. 'Victorian' was used by contemporaries as early as 1839 to describe their epoch, and it was and is often—though not with respect to literature—taken to date from rather earlier: the reign extends backwards from 1837 but not forwards from 1901 (nobody then or now would include the 1900s as 'Victorian' and at least one authority, Maurice Reckitt, has argued that the Victorian age ended with the jubilee of 1887). Including the period after the French wars as part of what can be seen as the Victorian century indicates the extent to which those years led into the mid- and late century; they could also be seen as an appendage to those wars, to the revolution and counter-revolution that occasioned them, and even to the eighteenth century. Either way, they stand as a staging post, a *caesura* between one distinctive period and another. They certainly failed to establish a lasting identity of their own, as the economic and political crises which they contained but did not solve drifted on to fade as the Victorian economy and state evolved.

Plate 3 The Great Exhibition – transept of the Crystal Palace, looking north. Between May 1 and October 15 1851 the 26-acre site in Hyde Park was host to almost 14 000 international exhibitors and over 6 million visitors. With receipts topping £506,000, much of its substantial profit went towards the building of the Victoria and Albert Museum.

Society and economic life

Martin Daunton

The Great Exhibition of 1851, held in the Crystal Palace in Hyde Park, stands as a symbol of British economic power in the nineteenth century, a visible expression of the country's economic might. No other country, before or since, has achieved such hegemony in the world economy. The Exhibition was part of the mid-Victorian boom, during which Britain dominated world markets in heavy engineering products, supplying the world with steam engines and machine tools, railway equipment and ships. In 1880, the United Kingdom was responsible for 41% of all manufactures entering world trade, far exceeding Germany's 19% and the United States' puny 3%. Not only was Britain the 'workshop of the world', displaying consumer goods and machinery from its great manufacturing cities to astonished and admiring crowds; Britain was also the banker of the world. London had succeeded Amsterdam as the centre of finance and insurance, and Liverpool was one of the nodes of the Atlantic economy, linking the raw cotton of the slave South to the factories of Lancashire. Britain was the entrepôt of the world, with the exotic and mundane commodities of the world flowing through the warehouses of London, Liverpool, and the other great ports, both from the empire and other primary-producing areas of the world. Tea arrived from China, wool from Australia, cotton from the American South, sugar from the Caribbean, grain from the Baltic and Black Sea. This avalanche of goods was carried into British ports by the world's greatest merchant marine, increasingly powered by steam engines rather than sail, built from iron rather than wood in the shipyards of the Tyne and Clyde, and fuelled by the steam coal of south Wales. From the warehouses—amongst the most striking architectural feats of the early nineteenth century—commodities were dispatched to the exchanges, bought and sold by brokers and merchants for the cotton factories of Lancashire or woollen mills of Yorkshire. The exchanges attracted customers from the rest of Europe to purchase tea or spices for Continental markets; and foodstuffs were directed to the shopkeepers of London and the provinces. Not only was Britain the workshop and banker of the world, it was also a nation of shops and shopkeepers, an economy devoted to consuming as well as producing. The Crystal Palace displayed the wonders of production to thousands of visitors, who travelled to the Exhibition from far and wide, the first time that the railways permitted even the modestly affluent to make their trip to the capital, to join in the excitements of metropolitan display.

The Great Exhibition coincided with the decennial census, which was begun in 1801—in itself a symbol of the desire to measure, to count, and classify which became so characteristic a feature of Victorian society. The census of 1851 showed that Britain was an industrial society, and that most of the major structural change in the economy had been completed. In 1851, 43% of the entire population was working in the 'secondary sector' of manufacturing, mining, and building, and the proportion only rose a little in the next half century, to reach an all-time peak of 46% in 1911. The share of the 'primary sector' of agriculture had declined in the eighteenth century; the census for 1851 marked the onset of a new trend, of absolute drops in the population of rural counties. For the first time in the history of the world, more than half of an entire national population was living in towns. In 1851, London was the world's greatest city, eclipsing not only the cities of Europe but also Edo (Tokyo) which was as large as London at the opening of the century. London astonished the world; Manchester by turns repelled, shocked, and amazed travellers who came to inspect and analyse this vision—or nightmare—of the future. The census of 1851 indicated that the population was still growing and still moving into the cities—a process which earlier in the century was the cause of political alarm and foreboding.

The Great Exhibition marked a point of celebration of British economic success, and the census report also reflected pride in progress, social stability, and political competence in dealing with the problems of an urban, industrial society. But the sense of confidence was recent, and was celebrated with a degree of relieved surprise. The period since the return to peace in 1815 had been economically, socially, and politically strained, with the outcome in doubt. Would economic growth produce welfare for the bulk of the population, or a miserable subsistence in an over-populated rural south and in squalid industrial towns, with the threat of unrest and agitation in country and town from the machine-wrecking of Luddism to the rick-burning of Captain Swing and the demonstrations and petitions of the Chartists? The novels of Mrs Gaskell, Charles Dickens, and Benjamin Disraeli, the social comment of Frederick Engels and Henry Mayhew, presented an image of misery rather than well-being, a failure to share in the profits of economic change. Why was the situation so fraught between the battle of Waterloo and the erection of the Crystal Palace, and how did a new confidence in economic progress emerge by 1851?

The 'stationary state': the limits on growth in the early nineteenth century

At the end of the eighteenth century, Thomas Malthus predicted that the hare of population growth would outstrip the tortoise of food production. Was there not a possibility that population increase would force up food prices and reduce wages to subsistence level, increasing rents for land and so diverting profits to landowners and starving industry of funds? There was no expectation in the early nineteenth century of a breakthrough to a higher and constantly improving standard of living for the majority of the people. Was there not a danger that the unrelenting increase in the number of mouths to feed would lead to starvation? The massive *structural* change in the economy in the previous century had not allowed an escape into new levels of affluence. Even as late as 1848, John Stuart Mill assumed that Britain might reach a 'stationary state' in which further growth became impossible.

Britain's population reached unprecedented levels from the 1780s, breaking through the upper limit reached in the early fourteenth century and the sixteenth century, when further growth was checked by famine and disease. Instead, population continued to grow into the early nineteenth century, with the result that it became more difficult to feed. The productivity of the soil could only be raised by dint of considerable effort and cost, and it was not possible or sensible to rely on a supply of grain from overseas, which could not always be guaranteed. There might be a glut of foreign grain one year but not another, with dangers of fluctuations in prices and profits which would cause problems for British farmers, weakening their motivation to squeeze more from the soil by investing in new techniques. Lord Liverpool had witnessed the tensions caused by problems of food supply in France prior to the revolution, and large parts of Europe experienced a serious subsistence crisis in 1819. A policy of agricultural self-sufficiency, based on steady and profitable prices for British farmers, might therefore make sense to his liberal Tory administration.

Agriculture did succeed in feeding the British population, but at the cost of social transformation in the countryside. High demand for food meant that prices rose in the late eighteenth and early nineteenth centuries, and landowners were able to charge higher rents to their tenant farmers. The rights of villagers to common rights were eroded, and in the grain growing areas of the south and east, men were reduced to being seasonally employed agricultural labourers on low wages, and women were forced out of the labour market. The size of farms increased, and large numbers of animals were used to provide power and to manure the soil. Landowners and farmers invested in new buildings, in enclosing the open fields, and winning more land from the waste in the uplands. As a result, British agriculture was remarkably successful in supplying more food to the growing population, allowing an unprecedented proportion of the population to live in towns and to work in industry and services.

However, this structural change did not necessarily result in a breakthrough in the standard of living. The achievement of Britain at the start of the nineteenth century was that enough was done to *preserve* the income of a much larger population without a serious collapse of welfare but without a breakthrough to new levels of prosperity. Not only was agriculture itself more efficient, but some of the pressure on the land was removed by the use of coal in place of wood as a domestic fuel, and for various industrial processes which required heat, such as smelting iron or baking bricks. By dint of great technical ingenuity in overcoming problems of ventilation, pumping, and haulage, Britain had a significant lead in the use of coal per head of the population which provided a massive injection of energy into the economy, at a stable real price. There were also considerable improvements in the service sector. The construction of turnpike roads, canals, docks, and railways meant that goods could be taken to market more cheaply and speedily, ships could find cargoes more quickly, and manufacturers reduce the need to hold stocks of raw materials. Mine-owners produced coal at a more-or-less constant price; the ship-owners who carried the coal down the east coast to London were able to reduce their freight rates, by a considerable improvement in the efficiency of the ships, in the speed of turn-round in port, and in the productivity of the market for shipping space. Further, the replacement of fairs and markets by regular shops reduced the costs of retailing.

Britain's ability to maintain the larger population was also the result of the emergence of the social and legal institutions of a highly commercialized society based on credit, which relied on a sense of trust between businessmen throughout the country. A cotton manufacturer in Lancashire needed to obtain raw materials on credit from a merchant in Liverpool; the manufacturer sold the yarn or cloth on credit to a merchant, who in turn had to wait to receive his money from the customer on the other side of the world. The system operated by means of bills of exchanges, a promise to pay at the end of say, three months—and anyone holding a bill who needed money more quickly would obtain ready cash by discounting it with a bill broker. A rapidly expanding industrial economy such as Lancashire was hungry for credit, and turned to the London money market which drew on areas with spare funds, such as East Anglia where farmers and landowners were flush with money after the harvest. By the early nineteenth century, Britain had a highly sophisticated, commercialized and credit-based economy. Solicitors provided mortgages to industrialists to build a mill; local 'country' bankers provided credit and handled bills of exchange; merchants provided trade credit for raw materials. London emerged as a major financial centre, encouraged by the provision of loans to the government during the wars with France which came to an end in 1815. The great merchants and financiers, such as Barings and Rothschilds, turned to foreign loans and trade finance. The Stock Exchange initially dealt in government stock, and could now provide a market for shares in the new railway companies. Insurance companies offered protection against fire and shipwreck. Although the British legal system was satirized by Charles Dickens in *Bleak House* in 1852 as ponderous and costly, it created the instruments for an active, fluid, liquid economy. Of course, reliance on credit and trust posed its dangers, exposing the economy to financial collapse as in 1847 and 1866. Growth and uncertainty are inseparable. But the law accepted that business failure was understandable rather than culpable, and offered generous terms to bankrupts to pay off part of their debts before returning as active risk-takers.

By these means, Britain was able to ensure that the standard of living did not collapse in the early nineteenth century. But there was not a breakthrough to a new level of welfare. The structure of employment in industry provides a good indication of the limits to productivity. Trades may be split, very simply, into three categories with a greater or lesser chance of improvements in productivity. At the bottom of the scale were trades serving local markets, such as carpenters, masons, bakers, or shoemakers. These workers usually served a small, face to face market, with limited prospects for gains in productivity. In 1831, they still accounted for about a third of all adult male workers, and they were a massive dead-weight on the economy. The second category consisted of trades where productivity could be raised by a division of labour, a concept developed by Adam Smith in his example of a pin factory, where workers variously specialized in drawing the wire, making a point, fixing the head, and so on. He argued that ten workers each undertaking one task could produce many more pins than ten workers each producing an entire pin. Much the same could be said of the division of labour between towns and regions, each specializing in producing the commodity in which they had the greatest advantage. The limits of productivity increase by specialization and division of labour would soon be reached. A real breakthrough in output per head, which could be sustained and allow a continuing increase in incomes, rested on the application of steam power to production and the provision of more energy per worker. Only in the 1830s and 1840s did this sector start to grow sufficiently to affect the performance of the economy as a whole, overcoming the constraints on output and incomes per head.

The British economy in the first half of the nineteenth century was therefore on a knife-edge, with a precariously maintained level of welfare achieved at considerable social cost. The poverty-stricken rural population of the south, supported by poor relief in aid of wages, faced large tenant farmers across a gulf of suspicion. Deference to the squire and the parson was often a façade, masking constant challenges to authority by poaching and more explicit threats of rick-burning. The government's concern to maintain the food supply could easily be portrayed as class privilege. When food prices fell, from the heights of wartime back to the levels of the 1780s, farmers and landowners experienced financial difficulties in maintaining payments on their heavy investments. The government needed to ensure a steady supply of food, and to allow agriculture to adjust to lower price levels—a threat to food supplies would mean political and economic disaster. But the Corn Law could easily be portrayed as protection for land against industrial and urban interests which were left to fend for themselves. These complaints were not without foundation. After all, failure to renew the wartime income tax in 1816 meant that the tax system was more reliant than ever on indirect taxes which fell on production, trade, and consumption. Traders, industrialists, and working-class consumers had every reason to complain that they were paying heavy taxes to support idle *rentiers* who had invested in the national debt. As prices fell, the recipients of fixed interest payments on government bonds were better off at the expense of producers who had to work harder to meet their demands. Adjustment to peace was difficult, not least because the economic problems exposed the flaws in the political system in adjusting the claims of different interests.

Ireland was the great exception, where the precarious balance was not maintained and living standards did collapse into famine and disease. Rather than an agricultural and industrial revolution, Ireland experienced 'involution', a process by which the rural population always rises to the limit of available resources. The potato allowed the land to support more people. Small holdings could sustain large numbers of people spinning and weaving linen cloth at home, and farmers developed highly labour intensive forms of cultivation to produce grain for the British market. The failure of the potato crop in 1845–46 led to disaster. Starvation and disease killed about a million people and encouraged a massive migration of about four million people between 1850 and 1914. Indeed, Engels wondered whether 'there will be Irishmen only in America'. Although population losses can be made good very quickly, in Ireland population growth remained low for the rest of the century as a result of late marriage. Ireland provided an object lesson of the curse of Malthus—and the crisis of the 1840s contributed to the political problems which plagued relations between Britain and Ireland.

Remaking economic policy

Between 1815 and 1851, the government was forced to tackle the problems of adjustment to a peacetime economy, which was increasingly urban and industrial. The highly regressive and inequitable burden of taxes was rectified by a programme of retrenchment, and by the reintroduction of the income tax in 1842. The process was fraught, with bitter ideological conflicts and the prospect of economic ruin for important figures in the City when their privileges were removed. Despite the fear of farmers and landowners that the repeal of the Corn Laws in 1846 would lead to ruin, they experienced a golden age of prosperity for a further 30 years. Supplies of cheap grain from overseas were limited and transport costs high, so that prices did not collapse. Landowners and farmers invested in 'high farming', spending more money on drainage, animals, and fertilizers to raise productivity to new levels. Rather than collapsing into economic ruin and losing their political role after 1832, the landed elite entered a period of prosperity and confidence. The repeal of the privileges of the East India Company, the removal of protection of West Indian sugar planters, the abolition of slavery, the abandonment of the navigation laws in 1848–49, and a major revision in duties in 1860, meant that monopolies were replaced by free competition and the Commons was purged of economic interest. In the early 1840s, revenue from customs duties was 32% of the value of imports into Britain; by the early 1860s, the figure was down to 11% and by the late 1890s to 5%. The inequities of the taxation system had been removed, and trade, industry, and working-class consumers were confident that reform and retrenchment liberated production from the costly burdens of a militaristic state.

There were also tussles over monetary policy. During the war, the government suspended convertibility of banknotes into bullion, which gave considerable freedom to banks to issue paper money.

However, 'resumption' of convertibility would have serious consequences, for it would limit the supply of money and create deflation. Resumption was agreed in 1819, to take effect in 1821, but the
debate between an expansive and restrictive monetary policy did not
disappear, for much depended on the level of control over note issue
by banks. There was a tussle between the 'banking' and 'currency'
schools which mirrored the earlier divide between the opponents and
supporters of resumption. In the Bank Charter Act of 1844, the currency school won, and the power of banks to issue notes was
restricted: no further bank was to have the power of note issue; and
existing banks lost their power in the event of a merger or suspension
of issue at any time; and no bank could increase its note issue above
the level of 1844. The victories of the bullionists in 1819 and currency
school in 1844 were crucial events, on a par with the repeal of the
Corn Laws—the question of who controlled the money supply, and
on what terms, was absolutely fundamental. The opponents of
resumption and supporters of the banking school argued that a
buoyant source of money would stimulate the economy, creating
modestly rising prices to produce a sense of prosperity and reduce the
real burden of debt. It was a policy for production, which would at
the same time give more power to bankers. The proponents of the
currency school feared that the economy would face the risk of financial crisis, and that too ready a supply of money would tempt traders
into speculation rather than 'real' trade. The Bank Charter Act, like
free trade, was a theological as well as an economic policy. A generous
supply of money and protection from competition allowed businessmen to escape from the need for prudence and foresight, tempting them into sin with the prospect of escaping damnation. Free trade
and the automatic regulation of money supply by the gold standard
meant that the political system could be purged of interest, the role of
monopolists and financiers removed, and the penalties of economic
misbehaviour visited on those who had strayed from the paths of
prudence. Of course, the distinction between speculative and 'real'
trade was somewhat overdrawn, and the imposition of stricter controls on supplies of money and credit could drive many honest and
prudent traders into ruin in the serious 'crashes' of 1826, 1837, and
1847. But in the later nineteenth century, the benefits of financial
stability were more obvious, and Britain was not prone to the financial panics experienced in the United States, with its chaotic and

uncoordinated banking system. Meanwhile, the burden of the national debt was reduced. When Edward Hamilton, the private secretary to Gladstone and a leading Treasury official, published *Conversion and Redemption* in 1886, it was not a study of missionary activity and the saving of souls, but of conversion of the national debt to a lower rate of interest, in order to redeem it more quickly. The play with words was more than a private joke by the son of a bishop; economics and economic policy were about sin and salvation, creating a moral and prudent society.

Until the 1840s, there was a ceiling to growth, which condemned people to the misery of subsisting in crowded, insanitary cities or rural hovels. Here was the vision of life in Manchester and other great cities sketched by writers as diverse as Frederick Engels, Benjamin Disraeli, and Augustus Pugin, with their different solutions, of respectively communist revolution, Tory paternalism, and medieval community. The answer for the Whig reformers of the 1830s was to force the poor to become self-supporting, compelling them to work by the threat of the Poor Law and workhouse or the prison. Ireland, and then London and finally the provinces secured a police force to establish order. Charities and schools, churches and parks, all helped to 'civilize' or moralize the towns and their inhabitants, helping to forge an active middle-class society and to negotiate relations with the respectable poor. Perhaps more importantly, by 1851 the economic problems and crises of the first half of the nineteenth century were starting to fade. Was there anything to fear from a nation of day trippers and spectators, who came to gawp rather than to revolt? London and Manchester had not experienced the revolutions of 1848 on the Continent. The Luddite machine breakers, the rick-burners of Captain Swing, and the Chartists succumbed to the lure of free trade and liberalism, hoping to join in the benefits of economic growth and the political nation, rather than to overturn the economic and social order.

In the period from 1815 to the 1840s, economic policy was bitterly contested and central to politics. In the second half of the nineteenth century, these policies no longer caused division on anything like the same scale, and were largely taken for granted as part of the natural order, a set of cultural assumptions which helped to define the national identity. Economics was taken out of politics—or, more accurately, a particular set of economic policies adopted in the 1840s was defined as in some sense as being beyond politics. These debates over economic policy reached closure by 1851 not simply as a result of ideological tussles and political compromises, but also in response to changes in economic realities. By 1851, economic growth was at last moving ahead of population growth so that income per head started to rise. Until the 1840s, income or GNP per head was constrained, and the gloomy accounts of the 'condition of England' in novels and social commentaries were plausible—especially in the aftermath of the devastating depressions which hit the economy. When he produced his account of the condition of the working classes in England in 1844, Engels predicted that revolution might well start with the next serious depression. He was mistaken, for the welfare of the bulk of the British population was about to move to higher, unprecedented levels in the next half century.

Breaking the bonds: growth in the second half of the nineteenth century

Poverty and hardship continued to trouble social reformers and politicians in the second half of the nineteenth century, but there was a real change in emphasis from the sense of inescapable immiseration of the early nineteenth century. By 1851, the bulk of the population was, for the first time, sharing in the benefits of economic growth with a sustained rise in income per head. The census of 1851 reflected this new economic, social, and political confidence that the blessings of economic growth would transform the life of all Britons, and the political system was sufficiently responsive and flexible to solve all problems. The authors of the report on the census—George Graham, William Farr, and Horace Mann—expressed their amazement that the population of Britain had increased by ten million since the first census of 1801, which 'nearly equals the increase in all preceding ages'. But they did not dread an outcome of starvation and unemployment. They asked, as so many before them, 'can the population of England be profitably employed?' Their answer, unlike so many before them, was confident. The growth in numbers and movement into the towns was a source of liberation and progress. The towns were more than a sum of their individual factories, for they 'engage in a manufacture as one vast undertaking'. In the towns, people lived more closely together, so that firms could specialize and labour could be divided; industrialists could exchange ideas and compete; everyone was stimulated and dynamic. There was no need to fear towns as a source of disorder and degradation, for 'one of the moral effects of the increase of the population is an increase of their mental activity; as the aggregation in towns brings them oftener into combination and collision'. Graham, Farr, and Mann were confident of the future, predicting that 'the quantity of produce either consisting of, or exchangeable for, the conveniences, elegancies, and necessaries of life has, in the mass, largely increased, and is increasing at a more rapid rate than the population'. They did admit to one shortcoming in this world of progress and prosperity: the high, and increasing, level of mortality in the great towns. But their optimism soon returned, for they believed that 'extensive sanitary arrangements, and all the appliances of physical as well as of social science, are necessary to preserve the natural vigour of the population, and to develop the inexhaustible resources of the English race.' (*Census 1851, Population Tables, Vol. 1*, pp. lxxxii ff.) The 1850s marked a new confidence in the superiority of the British people, with a mission to rule and civilize.

By 1851, steam power was transforming industrial productivity sufficiently to make a marked difference to output and income per head throughout the British economy. The importance of coal was initially as a source of *heat* energy; now it was replacing human and animal energy, wind and water, as a source of *mechanical* energy. Steam engines were initially used for pumping water from mines and winding men and minerals up and down the shafts, or for blowing air in blast furnaces. In these ways, steam power helped to hold down the price of coal, and hence of iron and other metals smelted with coal. But it was only in the 1840s that the cost of steam power dropped significantly as a means of operating cotton mills, and as late as 1870 it had only made inroads into a few other trades. Even in the cotton, iron, and coal trades, hand labour was still endemic. Cotton cloth was turned into garments by poorly paid, predominately female workers in the sweatshops of the East End of London or by unwaged housewives for their families. In the iron industry, hard manual labour was still crucial for charging furnaces or dragging ingots around the forge. And, down the pit, men and boys still won coal from the seams by unremitting physical exertion. Nevertheless, the balance of the economy had shifted since the early nineteenth century.

It was not simply that the high productivity sectors of the economy started to have a greater impact in the second half of the nineteenth century, with a spread of powered machinery into more sectors of industry. The standard of living of most working-class families also rose as a result of plummeting prices. Prices fell at the end of the Napoleonic wars, but settled at a plateau in the middle of the century. Thereafter, between 1873 and 1896, prices of both industrial and agricultural goods fell sharply. A phenomenal increase in the supply of primary products occurred, with the extension of cultivation in the United States, Canada, and other areas of recent settlement; the integration of Asia and parts of Africa into the world economy; the construction of transcontinental railways; the drop in ocean freight rates with the adoption of steamships. All these factors contributed to a huge increase in the supply of primary products. Cheap grain, dairy products, meat, and raw materials started to flood into British ports from the 1870s. The world was opened up to trade and industry, with British iron, railways, ships, capital, and expertise in the fore.

Deflation, like inflation, has its winners and losers, and price trends are one of the major influences on the history of any period. The price index of all goods (where the average of 1867–77 is 100) stood at 77 in 1850 and 99 in 1870, rising to a peak of 111 in 1873, which was followed by a long period of decline to a low point of 61 in 1896, when a gradual rise set in. The fall in food prices hit some groups in society—most obviously the landed aristocracy who were forced to reduce rents by as much as 40% in the grain producing areas. Landowners had flourished as a result of high prices and rents in the late eighteenth and early nineteenth centuries. They completed the process of parliamentary enclosure; they eroded the rights of villagers; they replaced their tenants' long leases with short leases in order to force up rents and take more of the profit. Although prices dropped somewhat after the Napoleonic wars, British farming and landownership remained profitable. The repeal of the Corn Laws in 1846 did not spell ruin, despite the increase in imports from as little as 7.5% of total consumption in England and Wales immediately prior to repeal, to as much as 40% in the 1860s. Prices in Europe were no lower than in Britain, and freight across the Atlantic was expensive. The mid-Victorian period was a golden age for British agriculture, of 'high farming' and high profits, with investment in new farm buildings, drainage, and herds of animals to fertilize the soil. Land gave status and high income, and the landed aristocracy was a self-confident caste. In the last quarter of the nineteenth century, it was their turn to suffer.

Short leases allowed landowners to increase rents in prosperous times; now farmers could reduce their rents. Agricultural labourers were reduced to misery in the early nineteenth century; in the last quarter of the nineteenth century, it was their turn to get higher wages. Some landowners were fortunate to have land for urban or industrial development, such as the Bute family with its soaring royalties from the booming coalfield in south Wales and its ground rents from the flourishing port at Cardiff. Others were less well placed, and had to devise various shifts and stratagems to maintain their social and political position. The caste started to break down, and society to open up to new men of wealth. Landowners might manage to diversify their portfolio, investing in a wide range of home and foreign shares, like the second Earl of Leicester. When the first earl died in 1842 his grateful (or deferential) tenants erected a monument in the grounds of Holkham Hall to celebrate his encouragement of agricultural improvement. When the second earl died in 1909, he had invested almost a million pounds on the stock market. Others married into the financial wealth of the City of London, allying the status of land with the new plutocratic wealth of finance. Lord Rosebery, who succeeded Gladstone as prime minister in 1894, buttressed his position by a marriage alliance with the most plutocratic of plutocrats, the Rothschilds. Those less fortunate in the marriage market could join the boards of companies, lending dignity in return for fees, like the Marquess of Salisbury who served as chairman of the Great Northern Railway Company. The fall in agricultural prices therefore contributed to the remaking of the landed elite, the traditional political class of Britain. As Oscar Wilde's Lady Bracknell remarked in *The Importance of Being Earnest*, 'land has ceased to be either a profit or a pleasure. It gives one position and prevents one from keeping it up.'

The most obvious beneficiaries of falling prices in the last quarter of the century were the urban working people of Britain, who had more purchasing power than ever before. The gold standard, Bank Charter Act, and free trade now came into their own. Prices were falling, and the benefits of economic change were captured by the working class. The political and economic system achieved a high degree of legitimacy, bringing together classes in support of the blessings of the British constitution and a free trade economy. In the mid-Victorian period, money wages rose from an index number of 100 in 1850 to 159 in 1873, which was sufficient to deal with rising prices and produce a modest gain in real wages. During the ensuing period of falling prices, money wages still rose slightly (to 166 in 1890), and real wages increased by almost 2% a year. This was the longest and fastest rise in working-class consumption in the nineteenth century. Many industrialists were placed in a difficult situation, for their profit margins were squeezed by a combination of falling prices and rising wages, which was only moderated by the fall in raw material prices and interest rates. Labour's share of industrial income rose and profits fell between the 1870s and 1890s. Of course, industrialists—like the agricultural interest—complained of their plight and talked of a depression. Some talked of a need for a change in monetary policy to increase prices by making silver part of the money supply, so as to create a modestly rising price level. Others proposed retaliation against unfair competition from abroad, using tariffs to force other countries back to the true path of free trade. But these complaints had little chance of political success, for most workers and consumers—the bulk of the electorate—were benefiting as never before. There was no depression in the sense of a fall in output. Most industrialists could respond to their problems by cutting costs, speeding up work rates, and challenging workshop practices. Higher real wages were therefore achieved at the cost of tighter work discipline and an increase in the workload. More positively, the structure of work and leisure changed. The pace of work was more intense but the number of hours worked dropped in many trades in the early 1870s, from 60 to 54 a week. Work ceased on Saturday afternoon, and bank holidays were introduced. Although extended holidays were much rarer, largely confined to the textile districts where the traditional 'wakes weeks' survived, there were greater opportunities for regular recreation and leisure. The British were becoming a 'kindlier' people, less prone to violence and disorder. Their energies and emotions were displaced into domesticity, sports, hobbies, and consumption which became possible with higher disposable incomes.

Consumption and recreation

Of course, improvement in working-class standards of living offered new opportunities for many businesses catering for the domestic market, and gave more people a chance to share in the delights of a culture of consumption and leisure. Seaside resorts were democratized, catering for working-class as well as middle-class holiday-makers. Millworkers from Blackburn or Oldham could decamp to Blackpool for their week's holiday. Workers in other districts were more likely to go for a day trip, catching the train to Skegness to enjoy a brief respite from the mill and mine. The demotic culture of Blackpool would not appeal to the sedate visitors to Eastbourne, but a trip to the sea was in the reach of a larger number of people, and was usually a family, domesticated event. But on Saturday afternoon, the men could escape to the football ground. In the early nineteenth century, football was a chaotic, formless game, played on the streets with uncertain rules. In the later nineteenth century, sports were codified and professionalized. The Football Association was established in 1863, with the first admission charge for a football match in 1870, and the formation of the Football League in 1888. Sporting events, and support for the local team, were central to the creation of a regional or local identity within an increasingly integrated nation

Meanwhile, spending on alcohol peaked in the early 1870s at 15% of total consumption; by the First World War, it was down to about 8%. A higher standard of living allowed working men and their families to adopt a wider and more varied pattern of consumption. In the early nineteenth century, music halls were designed to encourage the customers to drink, which was the major source of profit. By the later nineteenth century, music halls charged for admission, with entrepreneurs such as Oswald Stoll constructing chains of lavish theatres with exclusive contracts for leading performers such as Marie Lloyd. Stoll needed to protect his investment, and ensure that he retained his licence and attracted a respectable clientele. Drink was removed from the auditorium and prostitutes from the foyers at the behest of town councils eager to create a moral, respectable environment—a change intensely disliked by the more hedonistic members of all classes. A process was completed which started with the movement for the reformation of manners at the very start of the century, when unruly fairs and the morally dangerous pleasure gardens were closed down. Leisure was pushed off the streets and fair grounds, into policed and regulated spaces, of music halls, sports stadia, and public parks with their by-laws, park keepers, and injunctions to keep off the grass. The British people had become polite and civil. Choirs and brass bands proliferated, bringing together workers in pits or mills, members of chapels, supporters of temperance, and those in search of sociable—and competitive—recreation. They gathered at the Crystal Palace—re-erected at Sydenham in south London—to compete for prizes as the best band or choir, in much the same way as football teams sought sporting glory, or leek growers and pigeon fanciers vied to produce the largest or the fastest specimen. In the suburbs, the middle class developed their own set of cultural institutions, of golf and tennis clubs, musical *soirées* and garden parties. British society became highly cohesive, with its plethora of clubs and societies, but did not integrate, or expect to integrate, people of different social classes. Class relations were both stable, and at the same time segregated.

A major exception to the fall in prices in the last quarter of the nineteenth century was a rise in house rents, to a large extent as a result of improvements in quality and amenity. In the early nineteenth century, towns became denser, with a subdivision of property and a crowding of poor housing into any available space. Members of the middle class tried to escape from the threat of disorder and squalor, but even they could not travel far until the middle of the century when they started to abandon terraced property and communal garden squares for suburban villas. The census of 1851 still showed a high level of overcrowding, most notoriously in the densely packed tenements of Scotland and the cottage flats of Tyneside. Even in 1911, over half of the population of Glasgow was living at a density of more than two persons a room, and a third of the population of Newcastle on Tyne. The housing stock started to improve from the 1870s, as disposable incomes rose, and some of the constraints on cities were removed. Horse onmibuses were expensive, confined to reasonably well-off members of the middle class, but the horse tram from 1870, and even more the electric tram at the very end of the century, allowed more people to live in the suburbs. The development of cheap bicycles in the 1890s provided both a means of recreation and escape from the city, and an effective way of getting to work. The Public Health Act of 1875 also empowered local authorities to impose by-laws on house construction, to monitor standards and facilities. Of course, the poorest could not afford this new accommodation, and many urban authorities were sweeping away the squalid slums on grounds of public health and safety. Most commentators were confident that the poor could move up the housing ladder into property vacated as the better-off moved to suburbia, and that the solution lay in reforming the feckless habits of undesirable tenants. More realistically, the problem was a mismatch between the cost of decent housing and the low level of wages in unskilled, casual jobs. Although some local authorities were turning to the provision of public housing, by no means all progressive opinion was agreed. Would it not be better to remove poverty, and allow working families to find their own accommodation without sinking into dependence on the state?

The housing conditions of most Britons did improve, both in town and country, and the home became the locus of a new pattern of domesticated consumption by working-class as well as middle-class families. The first expensive consumer durable and symbol of respectability, bought on hire purchase, was the piano. Gas lighting became ever more common in working-class homes, with the spread of the slot meter for easy payment from the 1890s. Mass marketed, branded soaps and scouring powders—Pears and Sunlight, Vim and Brasso—kept houses and their inhabitants clean, and made fortunes for entrepreneurs such as William Lever. At Port Sunlight, he built model housing for his workers, and in the Lady Lever Art Gallery displayed John Everett Millais's painting of 'Bubbles', an image used to sell his soap. Cheap food was dispensed to the masses by Maypole Dairies and Home and Colonial Stores, which made fortunes for grocers such as Thomas Lipton. Patent medicines were peddled by Thomas Holloway and his fortune was recycled into care for the mentally ill and the education of women, at the Holloway Sanitorium and Royal Holloway College. Department stores catered for the more elegant or status consciousness. Mass advertising for mass production and consumption became commonplace, and was closely linked with the development of a mass media. The beneficiaries of a more prosperous and literate urban consumer were press barons such as John Walter (father, son, and grandson) of *The Times* or Edward Lloyd who published cheap books and newspapers of a more popular nature—a line pursued with great success at the end of the century by the Harmsworth brothers, Alfred and Harold. They were responsible for creating the *Daily Mail* in 1896 with a readership of a million by 1900, and the *Daily Mirror* in 1903. In 1908, in what could be seen as a symbol of changing social relations, they took over the newspaper of the establishment, *The Times*. W. H. Smith, the newsagent who secured a monopoly on bookstalls at railway stations to supply news-papers and books to passengers on their journeys, encapsulates many of the processes of the second half of the nineteenth century. Here was the tradesman who entered Parliament in 1868, becoming first lord of the Admiralty in 1877, and leader of the Commons when the Marquess of Salisbury became prime minister in 1886. Smith repre-sented trade and 'villa Toryism'; when he died, his widow was created Viscountess Hambledon—a clear sign of the changing composition of the peerage.

The growth of a culture of consumption was central to the shaping of personal identities. It was also a highly political process, for con-sumption was shaped by the state in a variety of ways. Although the government stepped away from protection and moved to a policy of free trade with the repeal of the Corn Laws in 1846 and the reduction of customs and excise duties over the next half century, it is too simple to suggest a simple decline of involvement and a shift to *laissez-faire*. The government spent less, with a marked drop in its share of gross national product from a peak of 23% in 1810 to 8% in 1890—a remarkable and sustained fall in public expenditure. How-ever, the government could still regulate the activities of private enterprise and voluntary associations to whom so many activities were left. Indeed, the economy of free trade was not intended to lead to rampant individualism and destructive competition. Opening international markets to the blessings of comparative advantage was a means of moralizing economics, creating international harmony between interdependent nations. At home, the aim was to create a society of actively cooperating citizens. Domestic politics would be purged of interest groups vying for preferential treatment. But there was a danger that new interest groups could emerge in their place, with equally harmful monopoly powers. The railway, gas, water, and telegraph companies needed powers from Parliament or a local authority to get permission to dig up the streets or to run over private land. They usually had a hold over consumers within a particular area, with similar powers of 'taxing' to the old monopolies of the East India Company or West Indian sugar planters. They needed large sums of money to construct networks, which could not be provided by family concerns or private partnerships and therefore required some form of corporate organization and limited liability. The result, it was feared, might be irresponsibility and unaccountability, which would allow these large concerns to exploit individual consumers and small business concerns. By making limited liability and joint stock more readily available in 1855–56 and 1862, it was hoped to ease entry and to stimulate competition as a further step towards sweeping away barriers to enterprise. But there was also concern that limited liability posed dangers. Most manufacturing and trading concerns remained family firms or partnerships with unlimited liability, so that imprudent or exploitative business practices would soon lead to a loss of reputation and the failure of the concern. By contrast, the managers and shareholders of companies had less reason to be prudent, for they were protected by limited liability, and the customers could not shift to another supplier if they were dissatisfied with the quality of water or the reliability of the rail service. Consequently, the prices and profits of these utilities were tightly regulated. Consumers had the right to appeal to the courts to fix prices, or to refer charges to a commission; the public interest was protected by granting fixed-term licences with the right of public purchase, which was increasingly exercised by local authorities and, in the case of telegraphs in 1868, by the central government.

Regulation of the market did not stop there. The creation of the General Medical Council in 1858, for example, gave doctors more power to exclude 'quacks', and the sale of patent medicines was controlled. Indeed, the medical profession secured increased powers over the bodies of their patients in the middle of the nineteenth century, with compulsory vaccination of all children against smallpox, the right to confine lunatics to asylums, or to subject suspected prostitutes to examination for sexually transmitted diseases—a system of 'medical despotism' seeming to threaten civil liberty which was hotly contested in the later nineteenth century. Although the legal doctrine of *caveat emptor*—buyer beware—suggested that consumers were at the mercy of producers and shopkeepers, the market was in fact shaped by politics and the law. Medical officers of health and their staff tried to ensure that supplies of milk and meat were free of infection, and regulations were introduced to control food adulteration. Customs and excise duties defined goods as moral necessities or immoral luxuries in a way which shaped consumption: the most ardent Liberal supporter of low taxes did not object to high duties on beer and tobacco. Gambling was a popular pastime for men in the industrial cities, showing their skill and discrimination in judging football teams and racehorses. The emergence of the Football League with regular fixture lists and 'form' gave working-class men the chance to fill in their 'coupon', predicting the results of games which were transmitted over the telegraph wires to appear in the evening newspaper, to be eagerly checked and discussed. However, most working-class betting on horses was illegal, creating a flourishing 'black economy' in industrial towns of illicit bookmakers taking bets on street corners. The purchase of goods, and especially the more expensive consumer durables, entailed granting credit, which involved highly moral assumptions on the part of parliament and the courts. A working-class consumer who failed to pay could be taken before a small debt court by a shopkeeper, and dealt with in a summary manner with the assumption that poor consumers were feckless and irresponsible. Traders who failed to pay *their* debts were treated much more leniently as bankrupts, responsible and enterprising members of society who had met with unfortunate circumstances. Consumption was also gendered, for most purchases were made by women who pledged their husbands' credit—a potentially dangerous power to grant to 'irrational' women who might be seduced by the glamour of department stores and the wiles of salesmen. The courts therefore ruled that wives could pledge their husbands' credit for 'necessaries' but not for luxuries. Thus a husband could be sued by a grocer for any food bought by his wife for the household, but a department store could not sue him for the price of an expensive coat unless the husband had given a clear instruction that she was acting as his agent. The patriarchal head of household was therefore protected from the irrationality of his wife, and the male shopkeeper had to bear the risk. In the case of the poor, many judges showed sympathy with the plight of women forced to rent housing or buy clothes and food for their families with inadequate resources. Many judges articulated a form of moral economy, assuming that consumption was a female domain which needed to be protected from the full force of a free market. To describe the Victorian economy in the era of free trade as *laissez-faire* is far from accurate, for the supposedly free market was permeated by cultural assumptions and legal regulations.

Pollution and death

In 1851, the economy was at last starting to deliver improvements to the income of most people in Britain. But the authors of the census were aware of a grave shortcoming—all too often in a literal sense. Towns were becoming more unhealthy, poisoning themselves with their own human, animal, and industrial wastes. Coal might make Victorian cities warm and productive, but the skies were darkened and the atmosphere polluted, with serious consequences both for respiratory diseases and, less obviously, for rickets caused by a lack of sunlight. Industrial and human wastes fouled drinking water, turning the Thames into an open sewer whose stench drove Disraeli choking from the chamber of the Commons in the 'great stink' of 1858. As *Punch* pointed out, the organizers of the Great Exhibition were required to supply glasses of pure water, free of charge to all visitors; whoever was responsible 'must have forgotten that whosoever can produce in London a glass of water fit to drink will contribute the rarest and most universally useful article in the whole exhibition.' Water-borne diseases such as cholera and typhoid threatened rich and poor alike. Crowded housing encouraged the spread of tuberculosis and infectious diseases such as measles. The lack of adequate sanitation meant that human and animal wastes fouled the environment, creating ideal conditions for swarms of flies, with frequent outbreaks of food poisoning. Many towns in the early nineteenth century were virtual deserts, with limited supplies of clean water for drinking, or washing bodies and clothes. Lice could proliferate, leading to outbreaks of typhus. Bad drains and sanitation killed infants in the slums in their thousands, but even the royal family was not immune. The sanitation of Windsor Castle was almost as bad as the slums of London, with seeping cesspits polluting the water supply. Prince Albert probably died of typhoid in 1861—a disease which also struck the Prince of Wales in 1871.

The urban environment deteriorated in the second quarter of the nineteenth century. In large provincial cities of 100 000 and above, life expectation at birth fell from 35 in the 1820s to 29 in the 1830s, with an improvement to 34 by the 1850s. The great cities of Britain were desperately unhealthy. In 1851, a child born in inner Liverpool could expect to survive to the age of only 26, whereas a child born in the small market town of Okehampton could hope to live more than twice as long, to the age of 57. One of the great changes in the second half of the nineteenth century was to make the great cities almost as healthy as the countryside, so that by 1911 the expectation of life in towns over 100 000 was 51 and in the countryside 55. The resolution of this crisis of urban mortality raised major political as well as economic issues.

Investment in the urban environment in the second quarter of the nineteenth century was simply too low to maintain the gains of the eighteenth century. The unreformed municipal corporations were strongly criticized in the 1820s and 1830s, as self-electing, unaccountable, and corrupt. Although the charge had its point, Whig critics of Tory corporations overlooked the existence of an active civic culture, and the ability of a range of associations and commissioners for lighting and paving to cope with the problems of urban growth. Of course, problems were mounting as cities became larger and more complex, and new cities emerged without any existing tradition of urban governance. But the Municipal Corporation Act of 1835 did little to resolve the difficulties. It was, indeed, as much about containing expenditure as permitting effective action to deal with the alarming problems of a deteriorating urban environment. The franchise for local government was confined to a small number of householders paying the local property tax or rates, and many councils fell into the hands of petty-minded, cost-cutting tradesmen, with a clear self-interest in holding down the cost of government. Municipal reform might well replace a patrician oligarchy of local gentry and merchants, weakening collective action and undermining the corporate, civic culture. There was a massive problem of securing collective action. Industrialists polluting the environment, or slum landlords providing unhealthy housing, were 'free riders' who passed the costs onto other members of the urban community. Any attempt to make them pay for their actions faced the problem that they dominated the urban electorate.

The situation started to change in the 1850s and 1860s. In the second quarter of the nineteenth century, many members of the local elite avoided the borough councils, and concentrated on voluntary bodies to provide zoological gardens, hospitals, schools, literary societies. From about 1860, they diverted these activities into the municipal arena. The corporate civic culture was disrupted by the tussles over reform in the 1830s, and now re-emerged in the form of an active municipal culture, with a new form of patrician political leadership. Economic self-interest also played a role. Small tradesmen might have an interest in economy; prosperous businessmen might have an interest in municipal action, to create an efficient and competitive urban economy. Woollen manufacturers needed cheap, soft water for washing and dyeing; merchants wanted modern docks. The extension of the franchise in 1867 also weakened the hold of lower middle-class, penny-pinching 'economists', and made it possible to build a new form of cross-class alliance around municipal action.

Most of the improvement in urban health in the later nineteenth century was the result of investment in drains, water supply, better paving and street cleaning, in housing and hospitals—in short, in the infrastructure of a healthy and civilized urban society. A partial measure of the change over the second half of the nineteenth century is provided by the relationship between investment in utilities (water, gas, trams, and electricity) and in manufacturing industry. In 1850, utilities were no more than a tenth of the level of investment in manufacturing; in 1900, they were over a third. Investment in utilities rose tenfold, and in manufacturing not quite threefold. One symbol of the shift in attitudes and in the scale of investment was the passage of a private bill in 1855, giving Glasgow corporation power to construct a massive scheme to draw water from Loch Katrine, at an ultimate cost of almost £1 million. The scale of the investment exceeded any of the great engineering and shipbuilding works along the Clyde, and it was undertaken with great speed and efficiency. The works were opened by Queen Victoria in 1859, with elaborate pomp in a fusion of royalty and civic purpose symbolizing the restoration of natural balance in a dangerous environment. Sir Walter Scott's epic of *The Lady of the Lake* (1810) had been inspired by the loch and the great city of Glasgow was uniting romance with commerce, linking purity and economic power. Even more striking were the schemes in London, where over £4 million was spent on a new system of sewers designed by Sir Joseph Bazalgette for the Metropolitan Board of Works, with a further £2 million on the embankments along the

Thames in the 1850s and 1860s. Meetings of the Commons were no longer disrupted by the stench of the river and Londoners did not die from cholera.

The change was striking and important, for this investment helped to reshape the great cities, sorting them into residential suburbs, business and production, shopping and entertainment. Cities could be used in a new way, blazing with light in theatres and music halls and public houses. Department stores with tempting window displays provided a safe environment for women to visit, travelling from suburbs by tram and taking refreshments in Lyons Corner Houses. British cities were no longer such a threat to political stability and social order. This is not to say that cities had entirely ceased to be a source of anxiety and dread. The endless possibilities of the city could pose moral dangers of temptation and vice, of prostitution and degeneration, as well as rational recreation. The concerns over poor housing in Andrew Mearns's *The Bitter Cry of Outcast London* (1883), the murders of prostitutes in the East End by Jack the Ripper in 1888, the fears of physical deterioration exposed by recruitment in the South African War, all caused concern. Life in the inner city could, it was feared, lead to unfit, stunted men incapable of fighting for their country, and to women unsuited to breeding an 'imperial race'. The YMCA and YWCA tried to keep young men and women out of harm, offering safe havens in the city; supporters of purity crusades kept up pressure on councils and the police to restrict licencing of public houses and to control prostitutes. These concerns for the 'fitness' of the race became particularly acute as the birth rate started to fall at the end of the century. But the towns were also a source of civic pride, the centre of new patterns of consumption and a symbol of modernity, of fractured identities and endless possibilities. The most tangible result of the investment was a drop in mortality and an increase in life expectation so that by 1901 a resident of the great towns might hope to live as long as someone who stayed in the country. Urban life posed problems, but there was confidence that an efficient machinery of public health could offer a solution.

Marriage, sexuality, and births

The birth rate remained high in the first half of the nineteenth century, rising up to 1876, when it peaked and started to fall. In 1851, there were 34.3 births for every 1000 women aged between 15 and 44 in England and Wales, and in 1876, 36.3 The subsequent fall in the birth rate was one of the major social transformations of Victorian Britain. By 1911, the birth rate in England and Wales had dropped by a third, to 24.3 births per 1000 women aged 15–44. The birth rate fell more than the death rate in the later nineteenth century, with the result that the rate of population growth slowed down from the high level of the first half of the nineteenth century. In 1881, the birth rate exceeded the death rate by 15 per 1000; by 1911, the difference was down to 9.7 per 1000. It was not just a slowing down in the growth of the British population which led to debate and concern, for there was also fear of a deterioration in the *quality* of the British race. Could Britain rule a worldwide empire with a massive indigenous population, and compete in world trade with the Germans and Americans, if its population was increasingly drawn from the denizens of the great cities and slums? After all, the birth rate of the prosperous, educated middle class and respectable artisans had fallen more than the birth rate of the poor. The preservation of the 'British race' became a common trope in political discussion, not least as Queen Victoria's reign drew to a close at the time of the South African War. Was the solution to raise the standard of the poor, by improving the environment, ensuring that they were healthy and reasonably paid, and that ability and talent were found and nurtured? Or should the state intervene to control the fertility of the unfit and encourage larger families by better-off members of society? On the whole, the answer was found in environmental intervention and social reform, to make the most of the available population and to raise their standards. The triumph of British medicine in the later nineteenth century was in prevention and public health, rather than forceful intervention in the bodies of individuals, for 'medical despotism' was overcome by civil liberty with the repeal of both the Contagious Diseases Act in 1886 and of compulsory vaccination.

The fall in the birth rate provoked political debate about the consequences for the 'imperial race', but why did social and sexual behaviour change in such a fundamental way? The major influence on the spurt in population growth at the end of the eighteenth century was the age and rate of marriage: more women married and at a younger age, so they were able to bear additional children in their fertile years between marriage and menopause. Within marriage, most women had children throughout their entire years of fertility, so that women born in the first half of the nineteenth century had a median age of 39 at the birth of their last child. Marriage remained an important demographic factor up to the end of the century, with a much higher proportion of non-marriers than in the twentieth century, and a much wider spread of ages at marriage. In 1911, about 17% of women aged 45–49 remained unmarried in England and Wales. In part, this so-called 'spinster problem' reflected the skewed sex ratio of Victorian Britain, for men were more likely to emigrate and to die young. The plight of the governess, the liminal woman between family and servants, reflected the problems of middle-class women in finding a respectable position at a time when they were barred from 'male' professions. When positions did start to open up in school teaching or as typists and telegraphists, they could not be combined with marriage. Similarly, women in domestic service as housekeepers or parlour maids had to make a choice between work and marriage. Professional men married late, at an average age of 31.2 in 1884/5—a pattern explained by the need to complete training and build up a prosperous business before supporting a wife at the same level of comfort as her father had provided. Not surprisingly, prostitution was endemic in Victorian cities, and not only to cater to the needs of professional men with an unusually long period of bachelorhood. There was plenty of scope for Gladstone's efforts to rescue 'fallen women'. In some working-class communities, women had very few opportunities to work and therefore married early, such as in the coalfields. In other communities, such as the textile towns of Lancashire and Yorkshire, women were able to work and might therefore delay marriage. The contrast is clear in two towns in Yorkshire in 1861: in the heavy industrial city of Sheffield, 85% of women were married by the age of 30; in the textile town of Keighley, the figure was 69%. Entry into marriage therefore remained an important influence on social life but, with one exception, it no longer controlled birth rates.

The exception was Ireland, where the average age of marriage and rate of non-marriage were both high. The potato famine meant that the population of rural Ireland fell sharply as a result of death from starvation and disease, and a desire to migrate to a new life in American or British cities. In 1845, the population of Ireland was about 8.5 million; by 1851, it was down to 6.6 million and had fallen to 4.5 million in 1901. In relative terms, migration from Ireland was the highest in Europe, surpassing even the Italian south. Migration from Britain, and especially Scotland, was also surprisingly high in the nineteenth century, with a shift over the century from single men with some assets or skill to exploit in a new world, to predominantly poor families. This outflow from Britain was compensated by an inflow of poor Irish men and women into British cities such as London, Liverpool, and Glasgow. On the whole, they took casual, unskilled jobs and became the subject of bitter animosity as competitors in the labour market and as threats to the Protestant ascendancy. Meanwhile, the survivors in Ireland adopted a new demographic regime which kept the population at a low level. Rather than dividing farms into smaller units, holdings were kept intact and the children had the option of migrating or waiting for their inheritance, often leading to bitter family tensions. This approach to inheritance certainly led to delayed marriage: in 1901, 22% of women and 24% of men aged 45–54 had not married, compared with 13 and 10% in 1841. In many ways, the small farmers of Ireland were more prosperous than before the famine, for rents fell and they could supply the British market with meat and dairy products. But the famine left a bitter legacy of hatred which the efforts of Gladstone did little to remove, especially with the development of a new, prosperous, heavy industrial district around Belfast, linked with the Clyde and dominated by Protestants, where a much larger proportion of the Irish population was living in 1901.

The striking fall in birth rates in late nineteenth-century Britain cannot be explained by the very modest rise in the mean age of women at their first marriage from 25.2 in 1871 to 26.3 in 1911. Clearly, sexual behaviour was changing *within* marriage, which raises the interconnected questions of why and how. Economic calculation undoubtedly played a role, for children were becoming more expensive. The cost of a public school and university education was high for middle-class families, and there was increased competition for available openings in the professions. Similarly, employment of children was increasingly restricted and working-class families were obliged to send their children to school, with the introduction of compulsory education for which they had to pay until 1891. The cost of children was also affected by the impact on women's earnings. In the coalfields and other heavy industrial areas, few married women had paid employment outside the home, in contrast to the cotton and woollen textile districts of Lancashire and Yorkshire where pregnancy and childcare had a serious impact on family incomes. Rational economic calculation might encourage a reassessment of sexual activity, but cannot provide the entire explanation.

Sexuality and masculinity were redefined as a result of subtle cultural shifts within particular social groups, rather than a simple economic calculus. This point helps to answer the question of *how* the birth rate was reduced. Barrier methods of contraception were still rare, whether the condom used by men or sponges and pessaries used by women. Although women might, *in extremis,* seek an illegal and dangerous abortion, most of the fall in births can only be explained by a change in male sexuality and self-control. Quite simply, the best means of birth control was celibacy within marriage, or at least a reduction in the frequency of sexual intercourse. In the male-dominated culture of dangerous physical labour in coal mines, manhood was still expressed in terms of virility. In the textile districts, working wives had more sense of their autonomy, and there was a more domesticated culture. Indeed, the rise of patterns of home-based consumption and family-based leisure in place of a work-based culture, helps to explain a shift in male identity. Similarly, in middle-class households, the cult of domesticity and the 'separation of the spheres' of office and home, city and suburb, could empower women. The home and the suburb were female zones, arenas of sentimentalized domesticity. The empire was transformed from a playground for male fantasies and libidinous release; and public schools became havens of muscular Christianity and erotic yearnings. These cultural shifts cannot be explained simply in terms of occupations and class. Rather, new patterns of behaviour started to emerge in particular social networks or communities. New norms were established. The man with a large number of children was defined as irresponsible and feckless; and the man who assisted with childcare and gardening (and even housework) as a good husband rather than effete and hen-pecked. Manhood (or at least responsible and respectable manhood) was redefined as controlled and caring, repressed and restrained, engaged in hobbies and sport. Men found their identity in pigeon fancying and football, on the allotment and river bank, often socializing their sons into the lore of these pastimes in a new definition of fatherhood. Family and community, husband and wife, father and son, parent and child, were redefined in the later nineteenth century. Increasingly, the home became an escape from the stresses of work and an outlet for self-expression and consumption. Observation of the greater opportunities available to small families and their children in leisure, consumption, and education could encourage others to follow suit.

A decline in sexual intercourse was probably the main reason why fewer women had children in their later thirties and early forties when they were less likely to conceive. As a result, more women completed their families at a younger age, with a greater opportunity for life beyond pregnancy and childcare. By the early twentieth century, this pattern of early completion of the family was consciously pursued as a desirable pattern, marking a significant change from the early nineteenth century when many women were dead before their last child left home and married. For women born in 1891, the median age at the birth of the last child dropped to 32. Consequently, most women had finished with childcare by the age of 50, and their life expectancy was also greater, so that they might be able to offer assistance in looking after their grandchildren. The traditional working-class family celebrated by nostalgic social commentators in the 1950s was, like many British traditions, an invention of the late nineteenth century.

Poverty and welfare

The standard of living rose and opportunities expanded in the second half of the nineteenth century, but this is far from saying that the problems of poverty and social insecurity were resolved. The industrial economy was hit by periodic trade depressions. In the first half of the nineteenth century, prosperity soon led to speculative manias and spectacular crashes, with runs on the banks and financial crises. Although the financial system was more stable in the second half of the nineteenth century, many sectors of the economy were still prone to periods of depression, especially in the heavy industries supplying capital equipment. In the shipbuilding yards of the Clyde, Tyne, and Wear, for example, periods of frantic activity led to the construction of a large number of ships as shipowners scrambled to take advantage of high freight rates. As a result, the market was glutted, freight rates dropped, and yards were idle until the cycle was repeated again. In London, engineering workers were more likely to be in regular work, catering for a more stable domestic market—but the metropolitan economy was notorious for casual work on the docks and shipping industry, and for 'sweated' labour in the garment trades. The coal industry had its own dangers, of accidents and lung disease. Workers in all trades and locations were liable to ill health and loss of earnings, and had to face the certainty of old age. Many children lost a parent to an early death; many wives were widowed with few opportunities to make a decent livelihood. Nineteenth-century Britain remained, for all the improvements, a desperately uncertain place.

The old Poor Law of 1601 did provide a safety-net in England and Wales for at least some of these insecurities, helping the elderly and orphans to deal with 'life cycle' poverty with the proviso that they met the conditions of 'settlement' in a parish. But the old Poor Law was severely criticized in the early nineteenth century, above all for the payment of grants to men in employment in the southern counties, where the growth of population, loss of common rights, and dependence on inadequate, seasonal wages reduced families to poverty. Critics of the old Poor Law felt that these grants were counter-productive, simply allowing couples to have more children and forcing down wages still further. Scotland had always taken a harsher line, and seemed to offer a model to England. The New Poor Law of 1834 was based on the belief that men should be forced into the labour market and self-reliance, where they would earn a decent wage in a productive, efficient, free-market economy. Until they mended their ways, relief should be conditional upon entry into a workhouse, where conditions would be 'less eligible' (that is, worse) than independent workers. The workhouse complemented prisons, as part of a strategy of reforming the character of the poor. However, the construction of workhouses was costly, and depended on administrative and financial reforms which were not completed until the 1860s.

The threat of the workhouse did reduce applications for relief and held down the costs of the Poor Law, but even so the principles of 1834 were difficult to implement. The disruption of cotton supplies during the American civil war closed down most textile factories in Lancashire, and in December 1862 there were 270 000 applicants for relief. Clearly, they could not be sent to the workhouse, any more than unemployed shipbuilders in a trade depression. The answer of the government in 1863 was to provide public works schemes to employ the respectable, deserving poor so that the workhouse could then be retained as a deterrent to the feckless and irresponsible. A similar response was adopted in London in 1886, at a time of high unemployment. However, workhouses were also changing in character, offering treatment in illness, care for orphans and the elderly. The Poor Law authorities employed medical officers to treat paupers, and the workhouses were transformed into public hospitals and old people's homes—grim, institutionalized, impersonal, but without the punitive elements of deterrence of the idle poor.

In theory, the Poor Law deterred the feckless—and charity rewarded the respectable. British cities were honeycombed with voluntary societies, to convert the poor to Christianity of all denominations, to reform their manners, to care for their bodies in hospitals and dispensaries, to educate orphans, rescue prostitutes, prevent cruelty to animals, teach temperance, provide literary and philosophical societies—the list stretches on. These bodies were in competition with each other for the souls of the poor, but they had a basic similarity of purpose and often had little concern with complementing the Poor Law by restricting help to the 'deserving' poor. Saving the dissolute had its own virtue. The societies offered status and respectability to middle-class donors, creating reputations which had a real economic value in the business world. They helped to forge a middle-class civic identity, and also offered a means of mediating relations with the poor. A donor to a voluntary hospital might become a vice-president; he would also be given tickets to admit patients for treatment, and so create a sense of deference. At least, that was the theory. In reality, gratitude was as likely to be feigned as genuine, and by the end of the century middle-class philanthropists were under pressure from two directions. Doctors had their professional pride, and wished to control the admission of patients; and trade unions were starting to subscribe to hospitals, demanding their say in management. Philanthropy probably raised more money than taxation, but by the end of the nineteenth century attitudes were starting to shift.

Most people would, as far as possible, avoid the Poor Law, with its inquisitorial procedures, the threat of a 'labour test' and loss of civil rights (with the exception, after 1885, of those receiving medical treatment). Most working people attempted to cope with insecurity through their own individual or collective resources, and by exploiting a repertoire of survival strategies. A family could use the available resources of charity and the Poor Law to best effect, deciding where the most generous treatment could be obtained. A widow might be able to look after one child and send another to a charitable orphanage, or a couple might be able to look after their children, at the expense of placing an elderly parent in the workhouse. Resources could be spread over the year or week by credit from the local store or taking possessions to the pawnshop. Neighbours would help each other through crises. Increasingly, working people created formal institutions, using their modest incomes to cope with insecurities, as far as was feasible in the absence of political action to remove underemployment or the use of tax revenues to supplement their meagre resources. At the very least, they wished to avoid the indignity of a pauper burial. The Blackburn Philanthropic Burial Society, for example, was formed in 1839; by 1872, 130 000 members paid small weekly premiums to secure a death benefit to pay for a decent funeral. Life insurance became a profitable commercial venture provided by firms such as the Prudential. Most families also tried to insure themselves—or at least the male head of household—against sickness. The friendly societies provided sick pay and medical treatment, in a culture of sociability and mutuality. There was little point in individuals trying to lay aside enough in a savings bank to cover illness and disability, as Gladstone intended when he created the Post Office Savings Bank in 1861. It made more sense for families with minimal resources to come together and cover each other. The Manchester Unity of Oddfellows, for example, had 405 000 members in 1870 and 736 000 members by 1901. After sickness came unemployment. Skilled trade unions such as the Amalgamated Society of Engineers in the highly cyclical trades did what they could to provide relief during periods of depression. Miners tried to cope with their particular problems by establishing funds to compensate for accidents, and even to provide pensions in old age. Cooperative stores offered a form of saving by returning a 'divi' to members at the end of the year. The first society was formed in Rochdale in 1844, expanding to 1521 separate societies with 1.6 million members in the United Kingdom in 1899. These self-help organizations were an astonishing feature of the growth of an active civil society in working-class communities.

The nature of an industrial economy

The industrial economy of nineteenth-century Britain was highly fragmented, dominated by small units in the hands of families and partnerships, with a low level of integration between different stages of production. In the cotton industry, for example, most firms either spun yarn or wove cloth, which was in turn sent to an independent dyer and finisher. Only in 1856 was it possible for firms to become joint-stock companies with limited liability—and even then few industrial concerns took advantage of the legislation. Although railways, utilities, insurance companies, and banks were large-scale joint-stock companies, manufacturing industries were dominated by personal or family capitalism. These firms could usually raise their fixed capital by drawing on the resources of the family, and by ploughing back profits. They often needed a greater amount of working capital to pay wages or purchase raw materials, which depended on a reputation for trustworthiness and honest dealing. Social capital might therefore be vital to success, which was accumulated by involvement in religious and charitable bodies, family contacts, and civic responsibilities. Individual firms were small, but they were embedded in a wider urban and regional network for the exchange of skills and market information, which rested on formal, male institutions such as chambers of commerce, exchanges, and employers' associations. Here, businessmen could meet their colleagues in the town and wider region, bringing together different interests from banking, law, finance, and trade. They could, if necessary, provide a voice in national debates, such as the concern of the Manchester Chamber of Commerce in preserving an open market for cotton goods in India. In addition, the female world of family and sociability was important. Women were largely excluded from the world of the firm in the early nineteenth century, but they had an important role in the creation of social reputation, and their marriage settlements brought capital to the business and preserved it from the perils of failure. The talk of the town was almost as important as the smoke of the factory chimneys in creating a prosperous industrial economy.

Most industrial firms had weak internal managerial hierarchies. Railway companies or insurance and banking concerns, with their national branches, developed a stronger, bureaucratic form of management, with promotion hierarchies, pensions for blameless service, and hostility to unions. Few industrial concerns followed this pattern. Factories only slowly developed from outwork and workshop production in the first half of the nineteenth century, and they retained many features of the earlier method of production. The symbol of the new world of factory production was the large spinning mill in Lancashire, yet there was not a stark class conflict between a mass proletariat and a small capitalist class. In the first decades of the century, the spinning machines were semi-mechanized, and needed considerable strength to operate. In the 1830s, the millowners were eager to introduce fully mechanized spinning machines (self-acting mules) in order to replace expensive, unionized men by cheap, docile women. In fact, the men managed to retain control of the machinery, against the wishes of the employers. The onset of a boom meant that millowners were more eager to make profits while they could, rather than engage in a long strike—especially given the likelihood that greedy competitors would break ranks and seize the market. Subsequently, millowners made the best they could of their failure to wrest control over the machinery. On each set of mule spindles, a male adult 'minder' engaged two junior assistants or piecers. The minder was paid according to the output of the machines, so that he had an incentive to run them as quickly and efficiently as possible. He was responsible for disciplining and paying the piecers on a time rate, so he stood to gain from the increased pace of work. The employer could therefore leave labour recruitment and discipline to the minders, with their powerful trade union. The employers of the town or region would then negotiate an agreement with the union which specified that wage rates could only be varied within certain limits and at fixed times.

In highly competitive trades such as cotton or building, the employers were securing stability of at least one cost of production.

Organized employers and workers came together in boards of conciliation, creating a strong set of institutions at the level of the town or industrial district. On the whole, the government supported this institutional pattern by offering legal protection to trade unions in 1871 and 1875. Problems arose in two sectors. One was the railways, where large concerns developed a system of bureaucratic or military discipline. Workers were spread out along the line, dealing with customers and money, and taking huge responsibilities for safety as drivers and signalmen. Labour management rested on the creation of promotion hierarchies, and the offer of a pension at the end of employment, in order to create long-term loyalty and honesty. Trade unions had no place in this system, and would also threaten higher wages at a time when companies were suffering from pressure on their profits. The second area was unskilled trades, where there was a spate of unionization in the late 1880s and early 1890s with the formation of new organizations such as the Dockers Union and Gasworkers Union. In these cases, the employers saw no reason to cooperate with unions, and there was a surge of strikes or lockouts over the issue of recognition. Unlike in the cotton industry, the unions did not provide a means of managing the workforce; the employers preferred to hire workers at will for short periods, at low wages. However, the Royal Commission on Labour and the civil servants in the Labour Department of the Board of Trade stressed the virtues of unions in creating stability and order, and supported the spread of formal systems of conciliation. Although judges did sometimes impose damages on unions, most notoriously in the Taff Vale decision, what is more surprising is the considerable legal protection granted to unions by the Trade Disputes Act of 1906, and the widespread belief that unions were responsible and trustworthy.

Internal management within most firms was weak, and external institutions within the town were strong. British industrialists were slower than their German and American counterparts in moving to strong internal managerial systems with control of the shop-floor and more integrated firms. However, we should not overlook what they *did* create in the provincial cities and industrial regions of Britain. Indeed, it seemed to many commentators that these institutions offered stability, and integrated workers (or at least unionized men) into civil society. Alfred Marshall, the economist, linked economics with moral evolution, arguing that business life, and specifically free industry and enterprise, would lead to a virtuous, morally elevated society. It would stimulate energy and initiative; it would lead to rationality, frugality, and plain-dealing; and it would stimulate 'earnestness'. These virtues were exemplified for Marshall in the industrial economy of Sheffield, a city of small firms with cooperation in marketing, design, and technical education, where concern for a man's credit and reputation rested on honourable dealing. Free trade was not a simple economic model of individualistic competition; it was a cultural system based on hostility to monopolies, whether old chartered companies or new utilities; it stressed the formation of institutions such as friendly and cooperative societies, chambers of commerce, and professional bodies.

Marshall continued to be confident of the flexibility and efficiency of British industry, and was not impressed by concerns raised about Britain's competitiveness in the 1880s and 1890s. Dominance in world trade in manufactures in 1880 was, at least in retrospect, narrowly based. In the early nineteenth century Britain secured markets in textiles, especially cotton. The mid-Victorian boom was based on the production of semi-finished and capital goods such as machine tools, ships, railway equipment, and steam engines. By the end of the century, these sectors formed a declining share of world trade, and Britain was relatively weak in expanding consumer goods industries. Indeed, Britain was starting to import consumer goods from Germany and the United States. However, the situation was saved by two other features. First, Britain was exporting to the most rapidly expanding *areas* in the world economy, the primary producing countries from whom cheap food and raw materials were obtained. Second, the balance of payments was extremely strong. Britain had a deficit in physical trade from 1822, for it imported even greater quantities of food and raw materials than it exported industrial commodities. The only significant region of the world where Britain had a trade surplus was India. Vast quantities of cotton cloth and railway equipment were exported from Britain; India covered the cost by selling tea to other areas of the world where Britain had trade deficits. Above all, the deficit was covered by the profits from commercial and financial services, supplied by shipowners, bankers, insurers, and merchants to the booming world economy, and by the return flow of interest payments on British overseas investments. In 1890, for example, the trade deficit amounted to £86.3 million, but earnings on investments were £94 million and 'invisibles' £99.6 million This strong international position meant that confidence in the pound was high, and the government had few of the difficulties experienced in the twentieth century in maintaining a worldwide presence.

Debating British economic performance

Whether the pattern was entirely desirable became a major point of contention at the end of the nineteenth century, not so much because decline had started or was even imminent, but over the best way of preserving Britain's economic and strategic hegemony. Even in 1851, there were indications that Britain would not remain unchallenged, for the American goods at the Great Exhibition already indicated signs of a new form of manufacture, with standardized interchangeable parts. In Birmingham, guns were painstakingly assembled by time-consuming adjustment of non-standard gun stocks, barrels, and firing mechanisms. In America, Colt's revolvers could (at least in theory) be easily assembled from standard components, which led on to the Singer sewing machine and the model T Ford. By contrast, British firms continued with existing technology and practices. The institutional structures created by the organization of production in British industrial cities—the boards of conciliation, unions, and trade associations—might become a source of rigidity rather than stability. Millowners might wish to switch to newer, more efficient ring spindles, or engineering concerns to adopt new types of machine tools, to find that they were constrained by their agreements with the unions, which were firmly entrenched in institutional arrangements. It was difficult for them to mount an outright attack on the unions with whom they had worked so long, whose rights were protected by legislation and embedded in political culture. Although the Engineering Employers' Federation 'locked out' members of the Amalgamated Society of Engineers in 1898 in an attempt to introduce new forms of machinery, victory was more apparent than real. There was also a danger that regulations of railways and utilities designed to protect the consumer from exploitation could become a force for inefficiency. Not surprisingly, Britain's lead in manufacturing was challenged. In Germany, labour productivity in manufacturing was already 93% of the United Kingdom in 1871; by 1911, it had taken the lead, at 119%. Meanwhile, labour productivity in German utilities moved from a mere 31% of the United Kingdom in 1871, to 104% in 1911.

The picture was not entirely or even mainly one of gloom and decline. The institutional and social basis for a prosperous and dynamic economy still existed. German bankers were still moving to London, aware that the City was the centre of world commerce–men such as Ernest Cassel, a native of Cologne and crony of the Prince of Wales, who financed British schemes to modernize the Egyptian economy. In fact, Germany did not have a more efficient economy than the British by the turn of the century or even at the outbreak of the First World War. Gross domestic product per head provides a good measure of the relative position of the two economies. Taking the United Kingdom as 100, the figure for Germany was 63 in 1820, 59 in 1870, and 76 in 1913. Overall, Germany only passed the United Kingdom as late as 1973. Although German *manufacturing* productivity overtook Britain by the First World War, it was well behind in agriculture. British farmers were highly efficient with a small labour force; Germany retained a large, inefficient sector behind tariff walls, and forced labour was only abolished in 1871. The British lead actually widened in distribution, finance, and professional services up to the First World War. The Krupps might have surpassed British firms such as the Guests in producing steel, but there was no German equivalent to W. H. Smith. Although British banks did not invest within British industry to the same extent as their German counterparts, the financial sector should not necessarily be criticized for its failures. Merchant banks in the City provided trade credit to exporters, so relieving pressure on the funds of many manufacturing concerns, and banks provided money to a dynamic Stock Exchange. The development of the insurance market led to the creation of large-scale, bureaucratic, and efficient firms, such as the Prudential or Phoenix, providing life policies to pay for a decent burial for the poor, annuities for the middle class, fire insurance for industrial and commercial property. And the Kaiser was unwise to sneer that his uncle Edward VII went yachting with Thomas Lipton, the purveyor of bacon and tea to the urban consumer. An economy involves more than the production of heavy machinery and Dreadnoughts, for the experience of the war soon showed that victory also depended on efficient systems of distribution in order to get supplies to the front and feed the civilian population.

The British economy in 1901 was far from experiencing decline and decay, turning its back on the modern world in a retreat into a culture of rural nostalgia and regret. Britain was pioneering a new form of post-industrial, post-urban society. Cities were increasingly sites of consumption and display; and the country was consumed by urban dwellers in a new way, as day trippers and ramblers. The new technologies of flight or cinema or radio were not seen as threatening and disruptive at the turn of the century, for they could be linked with the imperial project and attract considerable government investment. In the early nineteenth century, as in the eighteenth, the British government was concerned with science as part of the imperial project—to map the earth and its geological and botanical resources, or to produce charts of the stars and of the earth's magnetic field to aid safe navigation of oceans. Charles Darwin's voyage on *The Beagle* was part of this enterprise, and the captain of the ship—Robert Fitzroy—went on to be governor of New Zealand and, in 1854, head of the meteorological department where he introduced storm warnings to help protect shipping from disaster. The government put money into the construction of the first submarine telegraph cables to the United States and to India, which rested on the expertise of William Thomson and other leading scientists in order to overcome the huge problems of manufacturing and laying cables and sending signals over vast distances. In the mid-nineteenth century, scientists stressed their role in creating peace and uniting nations as part of the world of free trade and cooperation; by the end of the century, they saw their main claim to authority and funding as being active participants in an imperial and militant nation. What stands out is their success in linking science to the needs of the state, rather than any cultural aversion by politicians to technological change—a point symbolized by Lord Salisbury, who was president of the British Association for the Advancement of Science in 1894 and deeply interested in electricity.

The long-term question was whether it was desirable to concentrate on services, allowing the manufacturing sector to lose its lead, and whether too much money was being diverted from domestic investment into imperialism. By no means everyone agreed that it was sensible. After all, this was the route followed by Holland, which had concentrated on commerce and finance, allowing industry to lose its competitive edge—only to surrender its role as a major financial centre. Did Britain wish to take this path to comfortable statis and an enervating stagnation? Perhaps Britain, like Holland, was falling into the hands of idle investors, sending their money overseas for safe returns, and neglecting opportunities to invest in productive industry at home which would have retained Britain's competitive edge. There is no doubt that British *rentiers* were investing massive sums overseas, starting in the 1820s with newly independent Latin America and the United States. There were subsequent peaks in 1872, 1889–90, and 1913, and investment overseas amounted to two-thirds of all British investment in the 1880s. In the opinion of J. A. Hobson, these investors treated Britain as a playground, a place of leisure and consumption, free of any concern with work and exertion; they starved producers of capital, so keeping workers in poverty and distorting the market for basic commodities. On this view, the plutocrats of the City had merged with the landed elite, to create a cosmopolitan and imperial economy which neglected national production and diverted funds from useful social investment in schools or hospitals. Free trade might be a desirable policy, but the distribution of income and wealth within Britain needed to be corrected so that the market did not produce socially undesirable outcomes. Significantly, Hobson wrote biographies of both Richard Cobden, the apostle of peace through trade, and of John Ruskin, the critic of materialistic competition and advocate of craft production. To Hobson, the free market could only lead to morally beneficial work and consumption which allowed men and women to develop their characters, if income and wealth were shifted to the poor and away from the rich who wasted money on luxurious expenditure and imperial schemes.

A case was made on the other side, that overseas investment created a prosperous, affluent society. British capital opened up Argentina and Canada, so that cheap meat and grain flowed into Britain; the dynamic world economy created markets for British exports, and demanded British shipping, insurance, and financial services. The income from these services meant that Britain could afford to buy more goods overseas, running a trade deficit so that British consumers could purchase more foreign commodities. On this view, free trade in a cosmopolitan economy remained a paying proposition. These debates were given a new force in 1903 by Joseph

Chamberlain, who argued that Britain's future should rest on a large, protected market such as in Germany and the United States. Britain might be developing the world economy, simply to provide the Germans and Americans with markets. Would it not be better to put a tariff wall around the British Empire, retaining it as a market for British manufactures, which would guarantee stable employment and high wages at home? Protection moved back onto the political agenda, from which it had been removed in the 1850s.

These debates posed the fundamental question of the purpose and point of economic growth, and the controversies over economic and social policy which had moved to closure around 1850 were now reopened. The census report and the Great Exhibition of 1851 offered the alluring prospect that Britain would become rich. They symbolized the point at which the British economy turned from concern about the prospects of growth—from the revolution foretold by Engels or the statis and stagnation of John Stuart Mill—to a greater confidence in the cornucopia of wealth. The alarms of Chartism died out, and the blessings of a liberal economy were celebrated for the next half century. As the nineteenth century drew to a close, a new phase of debate was opening. Britain no longer dominated the industrial economy of the world with the same assurance, and there was a concern to improve 'national efficiency'—whatever that might mean. Public expenditure had been reduced to low levels and the national debt redeemed and converted; perhaps expenditure could now be increased, and perhaps the rich should pay a larger proportion of their wealth and income to the poor in order to improve the general welfare of the British people. A new set of controversies emerged.

Plate 4 Lord Palmerston addresses the House of Commons during a debate on the commercial treaty with France, 1860. Mezzotint of a painting (1863) by John Phillips. Gladstone is seated on the left, behind Palmerston; Disraeli faces them to the right. Mr Speaker Denison looks on.

Public life and politics

Colin Matthew

Railways and a national community

Convenient national public life—and the nineteenth was the first
century to expect convenience—requires an infrastructure of reliable,
rapid, and widely available communication. This the dramatic technical inventions of the century provided. Transport improved markedly in the early years of the century through better roads, new
canals, and steamships for coastal traffic. From the 1830s to the 1890s
a national railway system was created, unplanned by government but
remarkably effective in connecting most communities in Britain,
especially on a north–south axis. The completion of the branch network was exemplified by the building of the Forth Bridge (1890), the
finest monument to the century's engineering achievements, and the
connection of the Western Isles of Scotland by ferry to the line which
reached Mallaig in 1901. The development of the railways had a transforming effect both on the nature and the extent of communication
within the British Isles and without. It was a catalyst for the development of the telegraph, the postal service, printing, travel, and leisure,
all of which had fundamental implications for the character of public
life, those complex social and political relationships which some
called civil society.

   With the railways went life by timetable and beside them went the
telegraph, introduced at first rather hesitantly by the railway companies from the late 1830s. Its value and popularity were dramatized

in 1845 through the capture of a murderer, police in Slough being alerted by telegraph from Paddington. The telegraph was national-ized by the Conservative government in 1868. It enabled almost instantaneous regular communication between members of the propertied classes, though for the majority of the population the arrival of a telegram signalled some personal calamity. From the 1880s the wealthy also had the telephone. Invented in 1877 by Alexander Graham Bell, a Scot, the telephone was much more quickly taken up than many such inventions: in 1878 the *Daily News* was already trying to relay Commons' debates to its printers by tele-phone. Until the turn of the century it was largely used for local calls, though London was connected to Paris by phone in 1891, the Prince of Wales and President Carnot exchanging greetings. Dublin and Belfast were connected to each other and to London in 1892 and a treasury minute encouraged the use of post offices in the development of a national phone network, achieved in outline by 1895.

The steam engine which made possible the railways also trans-formed printing. Especially after the abolition of the stamp tax on newspapers (1853) and of the paper duty (1861)—the latter initially rejected by the House of Lords—daily and weekly newspapers were founded in profusion. The Sundays had the largest circulations, with a lower political content. In the early part of the century newspapers with their high stamp duty had been the privilege of the elite (or of those willing to buy cheap but illegal papers evading the stamp duty). The duties on newspapers and on their paper came off in-between 1854 and 1861. Most towns came to have at least one newspaper, most cities at least two—one for each political party—and the capital cities of London, Edinburgh, and Dublin several. The Press Association (1868) made agency news nationally available by providing a central telegraphic agency for the new provincial press. News had discount rates when the telegraph companies were nationalized. Political news and speeches were fed electronically and instantly to an eager audi-ence, as were sporting news and results. The press's distribution on the whole remained local (few of the London newspapers attempted national distribution) but the news the papers carried was national as well as local. At the end of the century the *Daily Mail* (1896), using the completed branch-line network, quickly achieved national distribu-tion, undercutting many of the local papers. As Alfred Marshall noted, 'a nation can now read in the morning what its leaders have said on the evening before'.

Closely allied to railway expansion, but tightly controlled by the Crown, was the postal service: the penny post began in 1840, with a ½d postcard introduced in 1870 and a reformed parcel post in 1883. Pillar boxes were introduced in the 1850s, a suggestion of Anthony Trollope (a Post Office civil servant as well as a prolific novelist), and from 1861 the Post Office Savings Bank began the extension of services which linked the postmaster or mistress to the vicar and the policeman as representatives of the state in local life. In 1840, 46 237 letters were delivered daily in the UK; in 1890, 4 673 900.

This revolution of communication was perhaps more transforming than the process of industrialization to which it was allied, for it hugely increased the velocity of knowledge and the movement of ideas, goods, and persons. A person in Plymouth could reach Aberdeen or Aberystwyth in a day, and a person who did not wish to travel could be equally speedily in touch through newspapers, post, or telegraph. Even in 1830, rail travel between Liverpool and Manchester halved the coach time and almost halved the cost of a ticket. In 1833 the young W. E. Gladstone took 70 hours to travel (mostly by ship) from London to his father's house near Montrose; by 1847 he could do the journey in under 30 hours. The Cabinet heard the news of the disaster at Majuba Hill (1881) in South Africa in only 8 hours; before 1879 (when the telegraph reached the Cape) the interval would have been seven weeks. So the century saw a narrowing of distance in time, and hence an increase in speed of mind as well as in movement, which made possible a much more integrated national politics, a much better informed public (for fast news encouraged reporters) and, especially from the Crimean War (1854–56) onwards, the expectation of immediate statements and questions in the Commons on far-away events: speed of information made politicians more answerable, and imperial control became much more direct. The national excitement over the fate of General Gordon at Khartoum in the Sudan in 1884–85 was much the greater because the telegraph, which advanced with the relief expedition up the Nile, enabled reporters to provide daily bulletins.

National political debate could become a rapid interchange of ideas and responses, not much less fluent than their twentieth-century equivalents. These national connexions were chiefly to the advantage of those with money, but not solely. The 'parliamentary train'—a cheap daily train with a minimum speed of 12 miles per hour on every railway route—was imposed on the railway companies by Gladstone's Railway Act of 1844 and enabled, G. J. Holyoake noted, 'thousands to travel who otherwise could not travel at all'. Associations such as trade unions which flourished locally could, as the century progressed and as the House of Lords had feared, much more easily organize and campaign nationally. Ordinary folk as well as the wealthy could travel throughout the United Kingdom for sporting events and holidays (including Ireland where tourism developed after the famine of 1844–48 remarkably quickly). Cricket and football teams, and jockeys and racehorses, could travel to fixtures and races, and a national sporting calendar emerged side-by-side with national politics, as did the national hobby of betting. The Great Exhibition of 1851, coinciding with the completion of the primary elements of the railway system, brought many to London for the first time, though the great Chartist gathering in London in 1848 had shown the way. The Scottish Highlands became reachable in a day from London in the mid-century, and thus their development as recreational estates linked the wild to the urban with easy convenience. An understanding of this context of increasing ease of communication of people and ideas is vital to an understanding of the developing complexity of nineteenth-century public life.

Sport and national life

Sport and its organization offers an analogy for much that happened in nineteenth-century public life. Initially, individualistic sports, games, and pastimes inherited from the eighteenth century were pursued at a largely local level, though there was also the beginnings of national sport in horse racing, pugilism, and cricket. From the 1830s, formal games, mostly played between teams, and with increasingly codified rules drawn up by national bodies, replaced traditional local sports. Cockfighting and bearbaiting became illegal in 1835 by Acts of 1803 and 1835. Tom Brown in the 1830s moved from watching 'the noble old game of back-sword' in the Vale of the White Horse, whose two players' aim 'is simply to break one another's heads', to the codified team violence of rugby football. Rugby's *Laws*, presuming handling of the ball, were published in 1846. The same year, a meeting in Cambridge dominated by Etonians published the 'Cambridge Rules' by which the ball was kicked only. By 1863 a somewhat uncertain division between the different styles of football had clarified. Rugby clubs had developed in the schools, in Oxford and Cambridge universities, in London and in the northern cities, and in Scotland. In 1871 the English Rugby Football Union was founded and the first Scottish–English international was played in Edinburgh (Scotland won).

Association Football developed at much the same time, with a meeting in 1863 drawing together players from schools and universities and agreeing on rules and forming the Football Association, with similar associations being formed in Scotland (1873), Wales (1876), and Ireland (1880). Parallel to the cup, clubs in the Sheffield area formed their own association in 1867, the first of a series of what became county associations. In 1871 the knockout cup competition started, which brought together clubs of the very varied social backgrounds of those now playing the game. Until 1892 cup finals were played on the Oval cricket ground in London, with crowds of 25 000. From 1895 until 1914 the venue was the Crystal Palace, with a huge crowd of 110 820 in 1901. The cup encouraged preparation through other competitions and in 1888 the Football League was established with twelve professional clubs, including six from Lancashire, three from Staffordshire, and a Second Division from 1892, London still maintaining a separate organization, but eventually joining the Football Association in 1906. These sports were mainly intended for males, but there was a healthy women's cricket tradition in the nineteenth century, and lawn tennis and golf were also played by women, the Wimbledon women's singles championship being held from 1884, and the Ladies' Golf Union and its championship being established in 1893. From the 1880s, cycling was an important emancipating recreation for women.

The function of sport in middle-class character building was an important element in these developments, but there were also much wider influences. These team sports fitted the social division of labour and leisure patterns which the century saw develop. They were controlled, quick to play, and slotted into the timetables of schools, universities, and factory workers. They accommodated players and spectators in large numbers in fairly small spaces. The economy of sport fitted the requirements of an industrial society with disposable income available as wages rose from the 1850s. Soccer allowed local businessmen a stake in the town's prestige of a sort very different and probably more popular and certainly more profitable than building a library or a gallery—a trend mirrored in rugby when professionalism founded a separate league in 1895. Local prides and prejudices, and especially religious/ethnic prejudices, were reflected in the teams: Rangers and Celtic in Glasgow, Heart of Midlothian and Hibernian in Edinburgh, Liverpool and Everton in Liverpool, each drew passionate support from different elements of the community.

Other competitive games flourished: the first golf open championship (originally confined to professionals) was held in Scotland in 1860; lawn tennis became established as a popular game for clubs, hotels, and large houses in the 1870s, developed from the much older real tennis and Major Wingfield's game of 'sphairistike'. The first Wimbledon championship was held in 1877 and the international competition for the Davis Cup in 1900. In Ireland, the Gaelic Athletic Association, sponsoring Gaelic football, was founded in 1884 and Shinty rules were agreed in Scotland in 1880.

Cricket, of eighteenth-century origins or older, stood outside the time-pattern of these sports, which were designed to be completed in a morning or afternoon. Some of cricket's county clubs date from the 1820s, but most from the 1860s, and the game, whose rules were agreed in 1835, then developed at much the same time as football, with the County Championship established in 1873. The first international 'test' matches were against Australia in 1880, W. G. Grace scoring the first international century and establishing himself as the best-known sporting hero of the century.

Horse racing, the royal and aristocratic sport, was also transformed during the century, railways permitting easy movement of spectators and horses to courses. The Derby, run on Epsom Downs, was the national sporting event, linking the ancient concept of the fair with modern sporting organization and money. Its huge and largely peaceful crowds were a matter for national self-congratulation: W. P. Frith's famous picture *Derby Day* captured the Victorians at leisure as they liked to see themselves. The Grand National Steeplechase, as it was officially called from 1847, was run at Aintree outside Liverpool from 1836. It to some extent countered an increasing southern dominance of racing, its terrifying fences such as Becher's Brook and Valentine's becoming national names. The Prince of Wales was a highly successful owner, winning the Derby with Persimon (bred at Sandringham) in 1896 and the Grand National with Ambush II in 1900. Fred Archer, the leading jockey, almost matched W. G. Grace in national fame until his suicide in 1886, having won twenty-one classic races and ridden 2748 winners. Racing was the chief betting sport, the newspapers carrying detailed accounts of the odds and the results.

The third quarter of the century thus saw a spectacular expansion of organized sport and the establishment of patterns of leisure which dominated the next century. The 1870s was the distinctive decade, the organizational coordination of the chief spectator sports being matched by the establishment of a holiday system for industrial and commercial workers with the enactment of 'bank holidays' in 1871. Sport reflected the development of society generally, for the 1870s also saw the beginnings of modern forms of political organization, and a general movement towards more formal institutional relationships. By the end of the century, associationalism in sport was waxing as strongly as other forms of Victorian voluntary associations, such as friendly societies, were beginning to wane.

Reform and political integration: franchises and the political community, 1815–1901

The British financed the French wars of 1793–1815 and beat Napoleon with an unreformed political system, that is, a Protestant constitution with public office limited to members of the established church: the Anglican church in England, Wales, and Ireland, the Presbyterian church in Scotland. That the Protestant constitution had defeated the French, by arms and by its strong economy which paid other nations to bear arms also, gained it great credit which it took some time to dissipate. It also gave the Duke of Wellington, then victor of the battle of Waterloo, unusual stature in a nation which was suspicious of soldiers. The Duke, as he was known even to his opponents, cele-brated Waterloo annually at a great dinner attended by his surviving staff. The war had also ensconced politically a large business class that had done well out of it, and which favoured the political system within which it had prospered.

The quirky idiosyncrasies of the old constitution were held by its defenders to exemplify English virtues of pragmatism and tradition against the universalist principles and claims of the French revolution. But exclusion from representation, either through religion or through the absence of a seat for a growing town, was not merely a matter of indignity which could be balanced by 'virtual representation' (the idea that interests, churches, places, and classes could be represented indirectly). Private-bill legislation was the means of most local social and administrative change; legislation with national consequences, such as the Poor Law Amendment Act (1834), was rare and suspect, and most legislation for local services—a bridge, a park, a pier, a police force—needed a private Act of Parliament. Between 1800 and 1884, these outnumbered public Acts by 18 497 to 9556. A community which had no MP was thus clearly disadvantaged and legislation which was overseen only by Anglicans was bound to be seen as partisan locally as well as nationally.

At the end of the French wars, there was some expectation that the national effort would be rewarded by wider representation. Instead, Parliament voted to reflect chiefly the interests of its very limited and for the most part wealthy electorate, by repealing income tax (1816) and by imposing a Corn Law (1815), against the wish of Lord Liverpool's government and in the face of riots in the streets of London. The Corn Laws benefited, at least in the short term, the countryside at the expense of the expanding towns. By so legislating, the rural landowners set up a polarization of town and country which, as the century developed, their successors much regretted.

The aim of Lord Liverpool's governments (he retired in 1827) was to show that an unreformed, Anglican parliament could both incorporate growing industrial, commercial, and financial interests and also provide modest change, more through sound administration than dramatic legislation. Despite a strong radical reaction in 1815–19, the unreformed political system had more staying power than might have been expected, and the Church of England with which it was intimately associated has recently been shown to have had much greater capacity for internal reform in the 1820s than used to be thought.

Even so, the political system had become dangerously reliant on

Conservative majorities in the Commons, and when these became unstable, change became unavoidable: a non-Tory government by the late 1820s could hardly avoid introducing significant political change. Indeed, the Tories themselves recognized this, with the repeal of the Test and Corporation Acts in 1828 and Roman Catholic emancipation in 1829. With the political system weighed down by its own anachronisms and a strong Protestant reaction to the granting of Catholic emancipation by Wellington's government, the Whigs gained power in the general election of 1830 (required by William IV's accession to the throne). The post-war experiment of administrative and fiscal reform within an unreformed and sometimes repressive political structure came to an end.

The Whigs' legislation, eventually passed in 1832, reformed the franchises, redistributed seats on a large scale so as to give representation to many of the expanding towns, and introduced a national system of voting registration. They thus set up a framework for constitutional change, repeated with success in 1867 and 1884 (household franchise in urban and rural areas, respectively), and in 1918 (universal franchise for men, limited franchise for women over 30); each round of reform was accompanied by redistribution of seats and other changes.

Historians today play down the significance of these Acts considered individually. But considered as a process of change (though initially unintended as such), the Acts reflected the ability of the British government, legislature, and political system spasmodically to amend and renew themselves. This occurred without any fundamental reappraisal of the constitution, in the sense that new franchises were added (and old ones abolished) within the language of the constitution: there was no 'reform upon a system' on the Continental model: votes were still seen as privileges, not as rights of citizens, and the long series of changes in the nineteenth century known by the term 'parliamentary reform' essentially reflected a change in the numbers of voters rather than in the system within which they voted. More men became voters because more men fulfilled the widening statutory requirements for registration known as franchises, not because they were citizens with a right to participate. Thus, almost uniquely in Europe, the British constitution went through the century without any fundamental reappraisal, though the franchise changes made to it transformed representation while leaving undiminished the powers of the executive, derived from the royal prerogative but now largely exercised by the Cabinet.

Each round of political reform was the occasion or the result of a political crisis, unsurprisingly because political reform meant Parliament reforming itself, to the exclusion of some of its existing interests; thus for the Commons redistribution of seats was always as controversial as franchise extension. But each crisis was contained. Only in the first round, in 1830–32, did it look as if Parliament might lack the capacity to reform itself, when for a time the House of Lords seemed willing to push its opposition to the limit.

Initially, Ireland and Scotland had separate legislation and different levels and criteria of enfranchisement; but in 1884 there was a single Representation of the People Act for the whole of the United Kingdom, reflecting, perhaps, the moment at which the pluralistic legislative and government structure of the constituent parts of the United Kingdom was most fully unified. An important element of the 1884–85 package, the redistribution of seats in 1885, ended the traditional predominance of two-member constituencies in which two candidates from different wings of the same party (e.g. Whig-liberals and Radical-liberals) could run together without splitting the vote; a few two-member constituencies continued, in which Liberal and Labour candidates could run together. The 1885 redistribution also gave seats to the suburban areas on the edge of towns—'villa Toryism'—on which the Tories constructed the essence of their appeal for the next century. The new means of political communication to some extent balanced a marked tendency for constituencies to become more clearly defined by class and status. As F. W. Maitland observed, 'The ancient idea of the representation of communities . . . has thus given way to that of a representation of numbers.'

The extension of the franchise was a complex, important matter, global figures needing a good deal of detailed interpretation. Throughout the century, representation was chiefly achieved through the ownership or occupation of property, though education was also represented in the Commons through special seats for Oxford, Cambridge, Trinity College, Dublin, and the Scottish universities, and for London University from 1868. Businessmen were enfranchised through their businesses, being able to add as many votes (by 1900 about 500 000) as they had branches of their businesses, though they could only exercise one business vote in each constituency. Business votes could be easily created by members of the propertied classes, a tactic threatened with great effect by the Anti-Corn Law League in the early 1840s, though more usually employed by large landowners who created what were known as 'faggot votes' by issuing tenancies in time to register for the election and lapsing soon after. An Anglican clergyman, Washbourne West, was recorded as having 23 votes in as many counties, and of voting Tory in 17 constituencies in 1892, a formidable physical achievement made possible by railways and by the fact that general elections until 1918 spread over several weeks, with each constituency polling over two days.

The one-year residence qualification for registration meant that a male householder aged 21 or over—which came to be the largest of the franchises—moving into a constituency might not be eligible to vote for almost two years. A pauper (a legal category meaning a person receiving support from the Poor Law Guardians) was deemed civicly incompetent and lost his vote (if he had one). About 400 000 paupers (by the late 1890s), living-in servants (except in Scotland), male children and lodgers without exclusive use of their rooms, and the transient population of working people, which included not only labourers but such representatives of the middle class as Non-conformist clergy and army and navy officers, rarely met the residence qualification. The result was that enfranchisement was only partial, even for adult males (over 21), and even such franchises as existed were not fully exercised.

Before 1832, the electorate in England and Wales was probably about 440 000 (14%) (exact numbers prior to registration are unknown). Famous examples of tiny electorates—for example Old Sarum with its 7 voters—were more anomalous than has often been recognized. Even so, the pre-1832 electoral arrangements—it would be too much to call them a system—rested on ancient franchises with no standard of equality of treatment. Moreover, Parliament declined to reform itself gradually and despite the social changes of the previous fifty years no franchise and almost no redistributive changes were made in the 1820s. Conservative governments of the 1820s declined the path of step-by-step change. Delay ensured a major change when the political dam broke.

The 1832 Act abolished some of the ancient franchises, such as scot-and-lot voters and potwallopers, and introduced new franchises for the householder occupying a house whose rental value was at least

£10 a year, and several for the counties, particularly for the £10 copy-holders and £50 leaseholders and tenants-at-will paying £50 rental (the 'Chandos Clause'). The abolition of the ancient franchises, many of them held by working men, caused great resentment and narrowed the class base of the electoral system at the same time as the new franchises deepened it (in some constituencies the numbers actually fell: Stamford's 851 electors falling to 566 by 1852). Following the Act, about 650 000 (18%) men were registered (in itself an important innovation) as enfranchised. This was a modest numerical change, emphasizing that it was the precedent for change that was the vital feature of the 1832 Act, for all that some of its supporters pretended that it was 'final'. However, the Scottish electorate rose strikingly from about 5000 to 65 000. By 1866 population change and some inflation had increased the England/Wales total to 1 000 000 (18%).

The household suffrage for the boroughs in 1867 (which replaced the £10 requirement of 1832 with a simple requirement of occupancy) resulted in a borough electorate of about 1 200 000 (44%) in England and Wales. It was at this point that the real numerical break with the pre-1832 period was made. By 1892, borough enfranchisement had risen to 60% of adult males. Counties, which from the late 1860s often included suburban areas on the edge of towns, came to have relatively larger electorates, partly because the population was less transient—or moved only within the constituency—so that registration qualifications were more easily met. Thus, under the 1884 household franchise, counties in England and Wales had 73% of adult males registered by 1892. Up till 1884, and especially before the secret ballot of 1872, non-voters were in some constituencies well-organized and able to influence their enfranchised neighbours.

These percentages masked considerable differentials: in large cities, working-class constituencies often had very low registration levels, the seven seats of Tower Hamlets in east London, one of the poorest areas of England, having only 36% adult males enfranchised in 1911, the nine seats of Liverpool just under 50%, and the seven seats of Glasgow just over; and a significant proportion of the electorate in such constituencies were business voters. On the other hand, 69% of the adult males in Edinburgh were enfranchised. Thus the franchises worked through a maze of qualifications to enable men with steady jobs and settled domiciles to become voters. It would be wrong to see much of a rational pattern in the process by which this came about, but it was, even so, very much the result that Victorian propertied opinion came to welcome.

These complex franchises all had a single purpose: the election of constituency MPs to the House of Commons. In the course of the century many other bodies were created which reflected the value contemporaries attached to the idea that public life required representation through voting. In 1815, government below the national level was conducted by the justices of the peace at the Quarter Sessions, by the vestry chaired by the parish priest, and by the lords lieutenant. By the end of the century many of their powers had been given to representative bodies. A centenarian male ratepayer in 1900 who lived in Manchester would, in addition to his parliamentary franchises, have come to vote for the local Poor Law Guardians (1834), the Municipal Corporation (1835), the School Board (1870), the County Council (1888), and the Parish Council (1894), as well as various other local bodies.

Linked to the central activity of Parliamentary representation was a flanking range of pressure groups, associations, societies, and other campaigning bodies. Their enthusiasm greatly increased the depth of involvement in nineteenth-century public life, for the Commons acted as the central but by no means the only forum for the discussion of social development. These pressure groups were of a very varied character. Some were very large, such as the United Kingdom Alliance (promoting temperance and linking the many local temperance societies), the Liberation Society (campaigning for church disestablishment and religious reform), and the Peace Society; some were more elitist, such as the Cobden Club (promoting free-trade internationalism). Some had, at least initially, very specific aims, such as the Anti-Corn Law League. Such groups are often thought of as being associated with or trying to influence the Liberal Party; but there were important equivalents on the Tory side. Some of these, like the Church Defence Association and the Anti-League, were counters to their progressive equivalents, but others, especially in the imperial area, had their own agendas. Many of these bodies were United Kingdom-wide in their membership, but some, such as Cymru Fydd (Young Wales), related to one of the nations only. On the whole, the aim of such groups on the progressive side was to force the pace of change, and of those on the conservative side to slow or prevent it. At the end of the century, however, groups on the 'right' aimed to change fiscal policy so as to introduce protection. But it was not until the early 1900s that the Tariff Reform League began to use traditional liberal methods for a non-liberal objective. All these and many other bodies served to attach a very wide body of persons to what was essentially a debate on national policy focused ultimately on Westminster, and much, though not all, legislation will be found to have been earlier promoted by a pressure group. The group undertook much of the role in policy-making which in the twentieth century would be seen as the responsibility of political parties (the latter not then producing party manifestos). For some groups, the process of the promotion of the cause became a substitute for its achievement. But the capacity of the Commons to respond to campaigns was a vital element in maintaining its national legitimacy and in incorporating a rapidly growing and changing population into the United Kingdom's body politic.

At the limits of integration: radicals, workers, Irish, and women

This step-by-step incorporation of classes and communities into the working of representative government—never complete and certainly not homogeneous—was reflected in a similar change in those awaiting incorporation. With the government opposed to any constitutional change, the years after 1815 were the antithesis of most of what happened in the rest of the century. The Luddites of the years 1811–16, though chiefly concerned with machine-breaking, were thought to have a political dimension, and required an army of spies, informers, and troops to contain and transport them. Coercion Acts in 1817 produced a sharp reaction. Radical and republican cells planned revolution, focused chiefly in London, but also in the west of Scotland. An attempt was made to show the whole governing structure of the country to be corrupt, notable in John Wade's *The Black Book, or, Corruption Unmasked* (published in various forms and editions from 1819 until 1835), a formidable indictment, especially of the extent of political corruption and ecclesiastic pluralism. These linked the radical case for political reform with a much wider middle-class concern for probity and efficiency. The 'Peterloo Massacre' on 16

August 1819, at which 11 people were killed and over 400 wounded when a large radical reform meeting was broken up by the magistrates at St Peters' Fields, Manchester, showed the long-term danger to the authorities of careless use of power. Like Amritsar in India and Sharpeville in South Africa, Peterloo gave the dispossessed a rallying cry of great potency and encouraged a much wider concern. Poets evoked the popular sense of outrage. Lord Byron's *Vision of Judgment* was written in 1821, and perhaps the most savage attack in the English language was made by Percy Bysshe Shelley in *The Mask of Anarchy* (1819), satirizing Lord Castlereagh who was popularly held responsible for repression, and who cut his own throat in 1822:

> I met Murder on the way—
> He had a mask like Castlereagh—
> Very smooth he looked, yet grim;
> Seven blood-hounds followed him:
> All were fat; and well they might
> Be in admirable plight,
> For one by one, and two by two,
> He tossed them human hearts to chew . . .

The government and Parliament met the radical movement with draconian legislation of a sort normally used only in Ireland: the Six Acts of 1819–20. In 1820 in the Glasgow area, there were 85 indictments for treason following an attempted rising, with 24 capital convictions, three people being actually executed. Large numbers of radicals and dissidents were transported to Tasmania, New South Wales, and other colonial territories, for the British government had the power thus to export its dissidents and their views. Transportation was the companion of British public order, almost a silent companion in British history books. As 'encouraged' emigration was the safety valve for unemployment, so transportation enabled the clearance of crime. In all about 135 000 men and 25 000 women were transported to Australia, the proportion of political prisoners being hard to estimate. Large-scale transportation ended in the early 1850s. The last ship, the *Hougoumont*, reached Australia in 1868, 63 of her 280 convicts being Irish political prisoners.

Though superficially repressed, and with its cutting edge diminished by a successful economy, the radicalism of the 1810s did not disappear, but resurfaced in the Captain Swing riots in many of the rural areas of southern England in 1830–31 and the Rebecca riots in west Wales in 1838–44. These were the last throw of subterranean political radicalism in Britain, though in Ireland it continued through the century in the form of secret societies. Sporadic rural violence continued in Britain, especially in parts of the Highlands, where troops were used in the 1880s, but it lacked a national political context. The end of transportation partly marked a change in humanitarian views and partly the increasing resistance of colonists. But it also marked the end of the government's need for an imperial prison-house for serious dissidence in Britain.

In the 1830s, disillusioned by the extent to which the settlement of 1832 enfranchised property while abolishing old franchises which had previously allowed some working-class representation especially in the 37 'scot-and-lot' boroughs such as Reading and Newark, the Chartists, with their six principles, requested an extent of constitutional change which the propertied class was as yet unable to contemplate; nonetheless, it was change to the existing constitution which the Chartists demanded. Linked to a resurgence of trade unionism in the late 1830s, the Chartists, using the new means of speedy communication, briefly mounted a remarkable challenge, especially in 1838–39, 1842, and 1848. But, like Daniel O'Connell's 'monster meetings' in Ireland in the early 1840s, they were not able to sustain it long enough seriously to threaten political control, except in certain localities. The last great Chartist rally, in 1848 in London, though it attracted larger support than is often allowed, fizzled out. When the next round of major radical campaigning occurred through the Reform League in the 1860s, its limited demands could be accommodated within the developing Liberal Party: the Reform League sought participation in what was fast becoming the chief focus of national discussion, the political duel between Liberals and Tories in the House of Commons.

To an extent, the Reform League of the 1860s and those associated with it related to the trade unions, with an important overlap of membership. In the early part of the period, trade unions were seen as politically dangerous and were outlawed by the Combination Acts of 1799–1800. These proved ineffective against the growth of secret unions of skilled artisans and were repealed in 1824–25. Propertied opinion was, however, by no means reconciled to association as a natural aspect of working-class life, much though it was advocated for the propertied classes. In 1834 the transportation of the 'Tolpuddle

Martyrs' and other cases led to the transient but remarkable Grand National Consolidated Trade Union.

By the 1850s trade unionism in skilled crafts was a common feature of industrial life, sometimes active through strikes, more often fulfilling a welfare role through the provision of benefits in exchange for subscription. This tendency related to the cooperative self-help movement, whose best known branch was founded in Rochdale in 1844. These working-class movements emphasized the distinct quality and character of working-class life, but in a way that was relatively unproblematic for Parliament, which provided its reward, as it saw it, in a royal commission followed by legislation explicitly recognizing trade unions in 1871, modified in 1875. By this, trade unions could act as associations and conduct strikes, but, it was intended, without being liable for damages. In the 1890s, employers' associations were formed which both met and stimulated more energetic trade-union activity and membership; the employers on the whole got the best of a series of legal disputes in the 1890s, culminating in the Taff Vale case of 1901–02, in which the judiciary found that trade unions were, after all, liable for damages. This 'new unionism', as it was called, was more broadly based than the craft unionism of the mid-century. It was accompanied by a gradual change in expectation of what the state might do, and found the Liberal Party inadequate and exclusive. In this, it was spasmodically encouraged by the Fabian Society (1884), which espoused socialism but lacked the means of achieving it.

In the 1890s, several labour groups were set up outside the Liberal Party, notably the Independent Labour Party (1893), but these were not working-class parties on the Continental model. Rather, they asserted particular labour interests through a loose coalition with the Liberal Party, exemplified by the electoral pact of 1903 between the Liberal Party and what had become the Labour Representation Committee (1900) and by the continuing adherence of almost the whole labour movement to free trade and Gladstonianism in foreign, imperial, and Irish policy. There was, however, a considerable increase from the mid-1880s in a sense of working-class identity, which the electoral system did not as yet fully represent.

The nineteenth century thus saw the integration of the working class into the political system, not wholly, but to an extent which would have been thought miraculous in 1815. On the Continent working-class political action usually meant membership of a party which denied the legitimacy of the existing political order, and sometimes of the state itself, but in Britain until the South African War (1899–1902) the working classes were largely accommodated within the Liberal and Tory parties, a distinctive achievement much envied by the propertied classes on the Continent.

This was less so in Ireland, where the gradual integration that was characteristic of England, Scotland, and Wales was much more problematic. The Irish franchise initially had much less of an integrative effect than that of the mainland, intentionally so, for Catholic emancipation in 1829 was accompanied by a corresponding diminution of the Irish franchise. In the first half of the century, the Liberals always had considerably more than half the 105 Irish seats, with 68 in the election of 1835; but many of those recorded as 'Liberals' were really Independents or, between 1832 and 1847, followers of Daniel O'Connell (known as 'The Liberator') and his movement for Repeal of the Union. The famine of 1844–48, and the more general depopulation of the Irish countryside, superficially had little immediate political impact: the famine was so catastrophic as to make significant political response by its survivors impossible. Though the Tenant League and the Irish Brigade in the early 1850s encouraged Irish Liberal MPs to a degree of independent action, there was no return at the Parliamentary level to O'Connell's demand for the repeal of the Union, and in the 1850s and 1860s Irish agriculture enjoyed a deceptive revival. But the famine's long-term impact, especially through survivors who emigrated to the United States, was to provide a hatred of the English and an ideology of alienation which meant that Irish constitutional nationalism always had a rival on its flank. The Irish Republican Brotherhood (1858)—also known as the Fenians—denied the legitimacy of the United Kingdom. In 1867, the Fenians' explosion of a bomb at Clerkenwell gaol in London killed or wounded over a hundred people, thus focusing metropolitan minds on the Irish question.

Gladstone's mission in 1868 was 'to pacify Ireland' (*not* to liberate it). Though his government disestablished the Irish church (1869) and passed an important land act (1870), thus meeting the demands of middle-class Irish Liberals, it failed to deliver to the Catholics the Catholic university they wanted and the Land Act was soon seen as a disappointment. The Liberals lost ground in the 1870s to the Home Rulers led by Isaac Butt and, from 1881, by Charles Stewart Parnell (both Protestants). At the election of 1868 the Liberals had about 65 seats in Ireland, and were the dominant party; following the Reform Act of 1884, which enfranchised Irish small farmers and agricultural labourers, they had none, nor ever had again. However, after the Liberals espoused Home Rule in 1886 the Home Rulers normally voted with the Liberals and never sustained a Tory government; consequently, after 1886 the Liberals did not contest Irish seats held by Home Rulers.

The Unionists disputed that Home Rule was the extent of what the Home Rulers intended, and responded with a programme of coercion linked to land purchase. They aimed to 'kill home rule by kindness' but they signally failed to achieve this. Though they promoted social reform in Ireland with some success, their land-purchase programmes allowed the Anglo-Irish landowners (the basis of their authority in the south) to leave Ireland, without creating a new Catholic indigenous landowning class favourable to the Union, for the Home Rulers never lost a seat to the Unionists. In the north of Ireland, the question of the Union became the defining political issue, the Protestants of Ulster fearing 'Rome Rule' and a raiding of their industrial wealth by the poorer south. The story for the Unionists might have been very different if they had been willing to propose protection for Irish agriculture, for that might have considerably undercut the Home Rule movement.

Women were not included, at the Parliamentary level, in this integrative process. The respective attempts of J. S. Mill and William Woodall to amend the 1867 and 1884 Reform Bills failed. Some men saw women as already integrated, through the male heads of their households; others thought they had no case, seeing their role as 'private' as opposed to 'public', the distinction usually made by male and female opponents of women's suffrage. Gladstone, as leader of the Liberals, argued in 1884 that a female franchise clause would result in the defeat of the whole measure and later that the demand for female suffrage was not yet sufficiently strong. Some MPs, mostly but not exclusively Liberals, raised national consciousness of the question by an annual motion in the Commons. Mrs Fawcett's National Union of Women's Suffrage Societies (1897) campaigned in a spirit similar to that of the Reform League in the 1860s, but though attracting a large membership and constituting an effective cross-party lobbying platform found itself outflanked by Mrs Pankhurst's Women's Social and Political Union (1905). That women *were* able to vote for the Poor Law Guardians, for various local and school boards, and for county and parish councils, made the principled objection to their having the Parliamentary franchise the more difficult to understand.

The Union and the nations

Towards the end of the century there were, therefore, powerful pressures upon the Liberal Party. Even so, it continued to lead a broad-based class and United Kingdom-wide coalition which in terms of its constituent elements was not dissimilar to that which it led in the mid-century or even from 1830. In that sense, politics in the United Kingdom remained remarkably integrative. Broadening political participation had not meant, as many of its opponents had feared, a political system nullified by class interests.

Ironically, it was nationality, much more than class, which posed the problem, but even here the stated objective of the Irish Home Rulers was devolution not independence; republican independence parties did not become electorally significant in Ireland while Home Rule had a chance, up to the First World War. Though the Tories portrayed themselves as the party of national integration, and certainly used the cry of 'disintegration' to some effect in parts of England and Scotland, their position as a party in the United Kingdom as a whole declined markedly as the century proceeded and the franchise extended: 'Unionist', the title they used at the end of the century, was an assertion of hope rather than a statement of fact. In Wales, they were initially the largest party, but declined after 1867 as Nonconformists and labourers became enfranchised; in 1835, the Tories won 17 (53%) of 32 seats, in 1895 (a good election for them), 8 (23%) out of 34 seats. In Scotland they were always in the minority after 1832, though improving their position after the Liberal Party adopted Home Rule in 1886; they won 15 (28%) seats out of 53 in 1835, and 31 (44%) (including 14 Liberal Unionists) out of 70 in 1895. In Ireland, the Tories had some presence in the first half of the century, winning 35 (33%) of 105 seats in 1835; but after 1859, when they won over half the seats, they were largely confined to the north, winning 15 (15%) of 101 seats in 1895 (a worse result than when they lost the general election in 1892). Increasingly, therefore, the Tories became a party relying on supremacy in England, where in 1835 they won 200 (43%) out of 464 seats, and in 1895, 343 (75%) (including 51 Liberal Unionists) out of 456 seats. Unionism, in the sense that the term was used by the Conservatives, became essentially an English creed, codified by some south of Scotland ideology. Particularly in England, and particularly in areas of high immigration, the Tories had some success in attracting working-class votes; but their essential appeal was as the party of Anglican property. Of the 95 seats (in 89 constituencies) which may be regarded as predominantly working class, about 30 (31%) commonly went to the Unionists at the end of the century.

Reflecting on 'English' progress though the century, Gladstone wrote optimistically in 1877: 'We have all happily settled down into one homogeneous whole.' Compared to France and Germany, the United Kingdom for much of this period was a politically peaceful, integrated society, but integration did not mean uniformity. The United Kingdom was a curious hybrid constitution, a mixture of a homogeneous Parliament at Westminster side-by-side with different systems of government, law, and religion in the three kingdoms it governed (and in Wales strong distinctiveness developed without these institutional advantages). By avoiding the imposition of uniformity, government and legislature ensured a high degree of tolerance, despite J. S. Mill's fears about the tyranny of the majority expressed in *On Liberty* (1859) and *Representative Government* (1861).

Representative government implies the settlement of political differences by constitutional means, and it was the willingness of almost all groups to work within the constitution and of the ability of the governing class to respond and adapt to the priorities and demands of other classes and groups that was the key to Victorian political success: Peel's Tamworth Manifesto (1835) was a wise guide for all governments. We may note two striking examples. The Anti-Corn Law League (1839) represented a strong political and economic strand of the expanding middle class, chiefly in the northern cities and partially Nonconformist (though not to the extent that is sometimes suggested). Its vigorous pamphlet and newspaper campaign using all the new media received a quick response: seven years later the Corn Laws were abolished (1846) and the free-trading ethos of the League was represented at the heart of the empire. When Ireland demanded Home Rule through 86 of its 103 MPs, British politics again quickly responded: within a few years Home Rule was the chief (if unfulfilled) objective of the Liberal Party. First the Tories in 1846, then the Liberals in 1886 split their parties in order to incorporate these major demands. The expectation of flexibility and the hope of success retained the support of a wide and sometimes directly opposed range of groups at Westminster.

'A nation of public speakers'
(*The Times*, 23 October 1873)

Victorian public life was linked by what seemed an ever-growing flow of words, spoken and printed. The primacy of political debate in national life was exemplified by the new Palace of Westminster, built to replace the old House of Commons destroyed by fire in 1834. The vast new palace by the Thames was designed by Charles Barry with interiors by Augustus Pugin. Its imposing exterior and sumptuous chambers—the Lords opened in 1847, the Commons in 1852— proclaimed the dignity of politics and politicians. The House of Commons was the model for a network of debating societies, from the Oxford Union (founded in 1823) to the many town and city parliaments which mimicked the Commons in procedure and even in membership. The newspapers which so voluminously reported parliamentary and out-of-doors speeches provided cheap, swift dissemination of political information. Churches and denominations— and the clerical parties within them—followed suit with newspapers, and mirrored the Commons with their convocations and assemblies. They also in turn created an expectation of long speeches: the congregations of the churches of Scotland and the chapels of Wales (often used for political meetings) were accustomed to hour-long sermons. Much of the content of newspapers was political, for politics provided the regular drama of public life, and politicians ended the convention of only speaking (and then rarely) in their own constituencies. The provincial press, linked up by the telegraph, carried national news almost instantaneously, so that by the 1870s a political speech was available—verbatim if by a major figure—at breakfast tables throughout the three kingdoms. A national community of news and political discussion accompanied the growth of the Liberal

Party from the 1850s, which especially thrived, and indeed depended, upon political news being kept to the forefront. 'We are more than ever a debating, that is, a Parliamentary people' observed *The Times* in 1873.

As this national debating forum developed, so too did party organization, though less fully than might have been expected. Bribery and 'treating' (dispensing free drink)—which Victorians liked to think was 'reformed' by the 1832 Act—was common in most constituencies until the 1880s. There was an awkward balance struck between seeing a vote as a saleable asset like any other, and the concept of a healthy polity made up of citizens who voted rationally after weighing up the arguments rather than the bribes. Those who were least willing to support legislation to reduce bribery were often, paradoxically, those who supported proposals for 'fancy franchises' giving extra votes to university graduates or income-tax payers. As the new franchises expanded the number of votes, bribery became more expensive and harder to organize. Until the Secret Ballot Act of 1872, voters' decisions were publicly recorded in local newspapers or pollbooks, and political agents—often local solicitors working for the local magnates or businessmen who called the tune in politics—could check on the effectiveness of their expenditure. A series of Corrupt Practices Acts attempted to reduce bribery and treating, but none was effective until the bribers found their trade too expensive; the Act of 1883 recognized the consequences of the secret ballot and bribery of individuals was markedly reduced, but not extinguished, election expenditure going instead to party organization and propaganda. In the course of the period 1832–80, election petitions following general elections led to 161 elections being declared void; 1852 was the worst election, but from 1859 until 1880 the number void at each election was between 11 and 21. Between the Act of 1883 and 1901, only 12 elections were declared void, five of them being in 1892.

The size of the post-1867 urban electorate called for a novel approach to modernize and support the traditional face-to-face, very localized character of party organization. Both the Conservatives, through Conservative Central Office (1867) and the National Union of Conservative and Constitutional Associations (1868), and the Liberals through the National Liberal Federation (1877), tried to provide a national structure for their parties, to coordinate campaigning and perhaps even expenditure. Both proved fertile forums for disruption within the party, and neither was very effective organizationally. At the local level in the 1870s, party caucuses developed—most famously in Joseph Chamberlain's Birmingham. These were thought by Moshei Ostrogorski, the Russian political analyst whose *Democracy and the Organization of Political Parties* (1902) remains an important commentary and source, to be destructive of democracy; but in fact most caucuses were transient and only spasmodically effective. Local worthies—Lord Derby in Liverpool, Lord Rosebery in Edinburgh—remained almost as important at the end of the century as their equivalents in 1820. Parallel to the caucuses, the national party leaders were increasingly presented as exceptional personalities. Max Weber's famous identification in 1918 of the charismatic leader as the central figure of modern politics was derived from his study of Gladstone's Midlothian campaigns—Gladstone, Weber thought, was 'the dictator of the battlefield of elections'.

Party ideologies, traditions, and governments: Tories and Whigs, 1815–52

The primacy of politics and political life in the British Isles in the nineteenth century reflected important national priorities. The century began and ended with the United Kingdom government at war. But after 1815 governments and parliaments liked to see themselves as inherently peaceful, even though almost every cabinet fought a war. 'Defence spending', as it came to be called, accounted for a third of central government expenditure, and sometimes more, but Britain saw herself, partly through this high allocation, as the guarantor of world peace, her behaviour scrutinized by the 'peace movement', an active force in British politics from the 1840s, when the term entered the language.

We have seen that Lord Liverpool's governments from 1815 to 1827 pursued order with a hard ruthlessness and inflexibility which, on the franchise question, led to the erosion of the conservatism they preached. But Liverpool's liberal conservatism lasted better than might have been expected. The 'liberal Tories' (as posterity has deemed them) of the 1820s began the move to freer trade which in the mid-century became a rather un-British dogma. They attempted by tariff management to preserve a balance between agricultural and industrial growth and thus to harmonize rural and urban interests. However, the rather uneasy coalition which comprised the Tory Party of the 1820s crumbled. Liverpool's retirement in 1827, followed the same year by the death of his liberal Tory successor, George Canning, marked (rather more than occasioned) a disintegration of the Tory Party, confirmed by the failure of Lord Goderich's brief government of 1827–28. Politicians began to call themselves 'Tory' in the late 1820s; hitherto it had been an oppositional term of abuse.

The party had tried to combine a strong commitment to the established church with a commitment to order and an appeal to the broad interests of property. The Duke of Wellington emerged as the Tories' best hope of continued office. Faced with potential middle-class as well as peasant rebellion in Ireland in 1828–29 when Daniel O'Connell won a by-election but as a Roman Catholic could not take his seat at Westminster, Wellington and his lieutenant Robert Peel proposed and passed Catholic emancipation (1829), thus placing the priority of order and the safeguarding of property above the safeguarding of a Protestant parliament. In 1828, the Test and Corporation Acts of 1661–73, which similarly but in practice not so energetically excluded Nonconformists, had been repealed. The Church-of-England character of the Westminster Parliament was thus diluted (many contemporaries and some historians forgetting that the established church in Scotland was Presbyterian and that the Commons since 1707 had never been thoroughly Anglican). These changes, and especially that of 1829, had a powerful effect on sections of English conservative opinion, which concluded that Catholic emancipation had been carried by financiers who had purchased rotten boroughs and thus become MPs: a genuinely representative Commons, they thought, would have rejected Romanism. Such persons, who included the Marquis of Blandford, at least briefly supported parliamentary reform for the Commons, though little was said about the Lords, which had passed the 1829 Bill at Wellington's request. As George Cornewall Lewis wrote in his history of the period (1864), 'it required fifteen years of peace to exhaust the popularity which the Tories had reaped from the triumphant conclusion of the war; but the work was effectually accomplished.'

The Whig government of Earl Grey, elected in 1830, ended the long years of Tory administrations resulting from the split in the Whig

Party over the French Revolution and its war and the view, success-fully promoted by Liverpool over many years, that the Whigs were unpatriotic, unreliable, and irreligious. The latter point was met by the emergence of younger Whiggish intellectuals much interested in theology. Grey's government passed the Reform Bill in 1832 after King William IV had agreed to create enough peers to get the Bill through the Lords. The Whigs shifted the focus of cabinet government from administration to the promotion of reform by contentious legisla-tion, and thus set the pattern for progressive governments well into the twentieth century. The ending of slavery in the empire (1833), a Factory Act (1833), supported by inspectors, and the Poor Law Amendment Act (1834) were each highly controversial. However, the Whig Cabinet split over the question of religion and Ireland and were dismissed by the king, a brief Tory interregum following (1834–35) with Peel as premier; his Tamworth Manifesto (1835) accepted reform and provided for a more flexible conservatism which accepted 'the correction of proven abuses and the redress of real grievances'. The Whigs returned with Lord Melbourne as premier leading an uneasy alliance of Whigs, Radicals, Liberals, and followers of Daniel O'Con-nell, who sought distinctly Irish as well as Liberal policies, including repeal of the Act of Union. The government enabled reform of the larger urban areas through the Municipal Corporations Act (1835) and they encouraged the modernization of the Church of England. However, Lord John Russell's ambitious plan for an educational system foundered, as did all such, on religious dispute.

The Whigs in 1834 and 1839–41 also set a pattern of political dis-integration: every non-Tory government until the end of the century fell through self-defeat in the Commons, as loose party organization was unable to prevent the defection of MPs who felt that the Cabinet was proposing too much, or too little. Through the 1830s, as the towns and the population and the demand for cheap food increased, the balance attempted by the liberal Tories in the 1820s was clearly becoming very hard to sustain. The Anti-Corn Law League energetic-ally exploited the government's unease, and the threat that the League might join with the Chartists in a coalition of the new middle and working classes spread a cold alarm: it looked as if the political gains from the Reform Act might be squandered.

In 1841 Whig disintegration led to a general election won by Sir Robert Peel and the Tories—the last general election to be won by the

Tories until 1874. As in the 1820s, Peel sought a conservatism based on property, economic progress, and the discipline of the market; and, as in the 1820s, it was hard to use a party which was chiefly defined by its allegiance to the Church of England as the agent in this experiment. The Tory Party, keyed up by high expectations after a decade of Whig rule, soon became truculent. Peel's experiment in fiscal modernization—exemplified by his reintroduction of income tax (1842), his reduction of protective tariffs in a series of budgets, his Bank Act of 1844, and his proposal to repeal the Corn Laws (1845–46)—dismayed those in his party (such as the romantic 'Young England' group) who believed conservatism should be a bastion against modernization. They were further dismayed when the government moderated strict Protestant Anglicanism by such devices as greatly increasing the endowment of the Roman Catholic seminary of Maynooth, near Dublin. Opposition to Peel centred around the Tory agriculturalists (mostly small-to-medium farmers) and the hard-line supporters of the Church of England, the two groups to some extent overlapping. Disaffection coalesced in the votes on the repeal of the Corn Laws (save for a nominal 1/- duty) in May–June 1846 (carried by the help of the Whigs, with 222 Tories out of about 360 voting against their government) and the Conservative government fell in June when the Whigs withdrew their support over Ireland. Peel carried with him almost all the office-holding Tories, and none of significance again served in a Tory government. The split in the Tory Party in 1846 proved to be the most irreconcilable of any split in British politics. When the Tories fell out, they split irrevocably; when Whiggish governments collapsed, their party regrouped (this was even to some extent true of the split in the Liberal Party over Home Rule in 1886, certainly more so than with the Tories in 1846).

The Tories from 1815 until 1846 had tried to run an ordered society based on a managed economy and established religion. Population increase, industrial demand for unmanaged markets, the unwillingness of sections of the Party to make compromises, the articulation of a new ideology of political economy and progress, the evolution and expansion of the Nonconformist churches, had whittled away the Tory base. Peel's behaviour in 1846, summed up in his praise of Richard Cobden in the final Corn Law debate, reflected his painful and exasperated recognition that the Tories had lost the contest for the mind of the century. It was a notable and unusual defining moment in British history. The way was now clear for the gradual but inexorable assembly of a coalition built around free trade, the politics of the minimal state, a degree of modernization of institutions, and a greater degree of religious pluralism. Free trade represented both the moral autonomy of the individual in a free market and the cosmopolitan internationalism of a society of mutually interdependent nations. It was thus an ideology of peculiar power, and it entranced a nation which usually prided itself on being practical, not ideological.

A Whig government was formed led by Lord John Russell, brother of the Duke of Bedford and a member of one of the great Whig houses, and tacitly supported by Peel and his followers (known as the Peelites). It won the election of 1847 but was unable to recapture the reforming ethos of the Whigs in the 1830s. Repeal of the Navigation Acts in 1849 was largely a confirmation of Corn Law repeal of 1846. Conservatism revived with the dual leadership of Lord George Bentinck and Benjamin Disraeli, the former attempting a thoroughgoing alternative to Peelite–Whig free-trade capitalism, the latter much more accommodating to it than his baroque manner suggested. As in the early 1840s, the Whigs disintegrated. They were replaced by a minority Tory government in 1852 led by Lord Derby, who replaced the dead Bentinck, and accepted that protection, in the words of his chancellor of the exchequer, Benjamin Disraeli, was 'not only dead but damned'. For all their fuss in 1845–46, Tory finance under Disraeli's chancellorships (1852, 1858–59, 1866–68) was almost as Peelite as Gladstone's. The Tories had, rather unnecessarily, lost the free-trade flag to the Whigs, Liberals, and Radicals, and the composition of the government of 1852 (the 'Who? Who?' government, named thus from the Duke of Wellington's feigning not to know the names of his colleagues) showed that they had failed to attract back a single important member of the Peelites who had split from them in 1846.

Peelites, Liberals, Whigs, and Tories, 1852–74

In December 1852, following a general election in which they did quite well but by no means well enough to become the majority party, the Tories were ousted and replaced by a coalition government led by the Earl of Aberdeen. This comprised all the elements of what may be called positive free-traders, and embryonically embodied what became the Liberal Party: Whigs, Liberals, Peelites, Radicals. The government was Peelite in its emphasis on budgetary and administrative reform but, led by its chancellor of the exchequer, William Ewart Gladstone, it deliberately politicized measures which Peel would have presented in a low-key way, thus attempting to associate government with the much more general movement in middle-class and artisan society in favour of 'progress'. The Crimean War which began in March 1854 caused the temporary disintegration of the coalition in January 1855, but it was a government led by Lord Palmerston (1855–58), not by the Tories, which replaced it. Palmerston had been in and out of office since 1807, and was associated with the Whigs from 1830.

The Tories did much less well out of the Crimean than out of other wars in which they were initially in opposition, partly because Palmerston—by origin a Canningite Tory—was hard to outflank on the political right. Palmerston represented, more easily and more insouciantly than any other prime minister, that combination of progress and bombast of which so many Victorians approved, and he was a skilful exploiter of the new medium of extra-parliamentary speechmaking which allowed the national articulation of his views. After the brief interlude of the second Derby minority government (1858–59), Palmerston successfully resurrected the span of the Aberdeen coalition, with Gladstone again chancellor. Absence of dramatic legislation assisted in making Gladstonian finance the focus of politics, with the budget statement the centrepiece of the Westminster year. Gladstone linked free trade to foreign policy and radicalism through the trade treaty with France (1860), negotiated by Richard Cobden, and he made the cause of financial retrenchment a centrepiece of what had become the Liberal Party.

The Palmerston–Gladstone government of 1859–65—stormy though the relationship between the two men often was—successfully drew together many aspects of mid-Victorian social and political life. Its MPs were mostly Anglicans, but it attracted also Roman Catholics, Nonconformists, Jews, and secularists. In class terms, it retained the great Whig landowners, it represented the industrial and commercial middle classes, and it was supported by most of those artisans who had the vote. It confirmed its success by a triumph in the general election of 1865, the only post-1832 government to succeed in being re-elected. Palmerston died shortly after the election, Disraeli having said of his involvement in a sexual scandal: 'The Palmerston escapade! It should make him at least ridiculous; perhaps it may make him even more popular.'

Palmerston's death was a caesura in British political life, much more so than an individual's demise could usually be. He left behind him a conundrum which he had been careful not to try to solve: he had shown that the existing voting system was one in which the Liberals always won, yet the Liberals, as the party of progress, in principle favoured extension of the franchise. Why change a winning formula? was Palmerston's view. The Conservatives in effect agreed: why conserve an electoral system in which they could not win?—and their minority governments consequently contemplated a further reform Bill.

Russell, who succeeded Palmerston as prime minister, and Gladstone brought forward a modest Liberal reform Bill in 1866, and the party and the government disintegrated, radicals thinking the Bill did too little, more numerous cautious Liberals and Whigs that it did too much. Derby's third minority government, formed in July 1866, could only stay in office with Liberal support. It wished to change the system on Tory terms, and to show that it had the governmental competence to do so. The Tories were in an odd position: though instinctively hostile to political reform, they could only gain a majority by promoting it. A series of proposals was reshaped by the Liberal majority in the Commons, the result being the 1867 Representation of the People Act (with Bills for Scotland and Ireland in 1868), accompanied, as in 1832, by an important redistribution of seats. A new household suffrage in the boroughs extended the vote to the heads of all households, though with a stiff residency requirement. The Liberals were likely to lose from any change, but they probably lost less from this than from the alternatives on offer. The Tories gained from the redistribution. It is possible to see Disraeli—the coordinator of the Tories during the passing of the Bill—as moving towards the sort of universal franchise which in France resulted in mass support for the right-wing government of Napoleon III; but the extent of borough enfranchisement (to nearly 50% of adult males in 1868) stopped well short of this. Not many of the 'residuum', as John Bright described what Karl Marx called the lumpen proletariat, reached the registers.

Benjamin Disraeli 'climbed to the top of the greasy pole' in 1868 when he succeeded Lord Derby as prime minister of the minority Tory government, but he quickly slipped down it again. The new electorate showed little gratitude to the Tories. The general election of 1868 produced a Liberal government led by Gladstone, after a campaign focused on Irish disestablishment, which skilfully integrated all the religious forces that made up the Liberal Party, including moderate Anglicans who concluded that the Anglican church in Ireland was an embarrassment to the general case for established churches.

Gladstone's government combined Peelite financial and administrative reform with a return to the Whiggish idea of the 1830s of the centrality of reform by statute. Gladstone favoured 'big bills', as he called them, as a way of keeping the party together and of legitimizing the central role in national life of the House of Commons. This technique worked well initially: the Irish church was disestablished in 1869 (a formidable technical and legislative operation), an Irish Land Act was passed in 1870, and the Elementary Education Acts of 1870 (England and Wales) and 1872 (Scotland) achieved what governments of both parties had been reluctant to attempt since the 1830s, a national system of elementary education. It was based in England on a compromise by which state schools were provided where there were no church schools, a system which has lasted into the twenty-first century. Religious tests at Oxford and Cambridge were abolished (1871) and the secret ballot was enacted (1872), the Lords having obligingly rejected both these proposals in previous years, enabling the party to unite around them.

The elements comprising the Liberal Party coalesced on short- and medium-term objectives, but disagreed on ultimate objectives. Secularists wanted religious reform as the first step to a secular society; liberal Anglicans welcomed religious reforms as a means of securing the establishment; only free trade was a point of undisputed party allegiance. The trick of leadership was to keep several issues running at once and to persuade the party to expect legislative failures as well as successes. Temperance, religious, and educational measures all occasioned sharp disagreement within the party, and in 1873 the government's Bill for Irish university reform was defeated and Gladstone offered his resignation. Unlike Derby in 1852, 1858, and 1866, Disraeli with cool calculation declined to form a minority government in 1873 and the Liberals limped on until defeated in the 1874 general election: the first Tory electoral victory since 1841.

Over the 28 years since the fall of Peel's government in 1846, the Tories had held on. Disraeli had resisted the attempts of some of his party faithful to make the Tories a solely Anglican party. He had tried to attract prominent Roman Catholics and Jews, and to use the concept of property to countervail his party's otherwise rather restricted base, excessively reliant on Anglicanism and the country gentlemen. At the same time, he encouraged the party cry of church defence, but saw to it that on questions such as church rates, Irish disestablishment, and Oxbridge religious tests, there was protest but eventual accommodation. His aim had been, not to 'dish the Whigs' but to sideline the ultra-Tories. Though the Liberals led the way of using the new medium of political communication, the Tories kept up quite well, while also developing anti-immigrant politics especially in Lancashire, the Forth–Clyde valley, and London. Disraeli's speech tour in 1872, in Manchester and at the Crystal Palace, hit its target. The Tories worked to establish a countervailing force to the Liberals' enthusiasm for rationalistic speeches and debate, depicting the Liberals as a threat to empire and a danger to property. They attracted many of Liberal disposition who found it hard to make their political way in the tightknit Liberal constituency organizations: the Tory revival probably owed as much to this generational change as it did to improved party organization. Such persons were chiefly Anglicans, but the days when no non-Anglican would vote for a Tory were passing. New Tories were mostly free-traders, but free trade was a Liberal goal already achieved: as long as the Tories did not threaten it, it was a less effective Liberal cry than a decade earlier. After Disraeli's death, the Primrose League (1883), an unofficial Tory organization, played with some effect on Tory voters' anxieties about status and encouraged support for a hierarchic society.

Tories, Liberals, Liberal Unionists, 1874–1901

When Disraeli began his second premiership (1874–80), he was old and quite often ill, leaving the Commons for the Lords (as Earl of Beaconsfield, in 1876): 'Power! It came too late', he remarked. His government's reforms were in many cases left-overs or developments of Liberal initiatives, but these were skilfully presented as a Tory 'social reform' alternative to the Liberals' more constitutional approach. After an initial flourish of legislation in 1875–76, especially dealing with health, housing, and urban conditions, the government became increasingly preoccupied with foreign and colonial questions, with many of the Liberal opposition happy to move the ground of debate into that area, campaigning against Tory iniquities in their Eastern Question policy (the Bulgarian atrocities campaign from 1876), South Africa, and Afghanistan. Gladstone's Midlothian Campaign (1879–80), a severe agricultural, and to an extent trade, depression, and improved Liberal Party organization carried the Liberals to comfortable victory in the 1880 general election.

Gladstone intended, in his second government (1880–85), to remove and correct the evils of Beaconsfieldism, as he called it, and then retire from politics. He was, however, drawn into a series of complex political problems, especially related to South Africa and Ireland, and stayed in office as long as the Liberal government. The second Gladstone government was the last of any party to have a majority of seats in each of the constituent parts of the United Kingdom. Paradoxically, this broad base of support increased the difficulties of the government, for it had to meet the expectations of an exceptionally wide range of political interests. In Ireland, agricultural distress fused to an extent with constitutional and other forms of nationalism in the Land League to produce what seemed to many a quasi-revolutionary moment, including to his alarm Charles Stewart Parnell, the leader of the Irish Home Rule Party and also president of the Land League. The government broke the Land League by a combination of incarceration of its leaders and conciliatory legislation (the Land Act of 1881), but Liberal Ireland was 'dead and gone', the Home Rule nationalists awaiting their moment. This they got in the 1884 Reform Act, which extended household suffrage to the counties and to Ireland and, for the first time, was a Reform Act applying to all parts of the United Kingdom. Ironically, this attempt to treat the UK as a single political unit occasioned the first of a series of Liberal attempts to provide a devolution of parliamentary power from Westminster that would match the administrative and legal devolution which already existed for Ireland and Scotland.

Gladstone's government disintegrated in 1885 over the future of Irish government. A minority government led by Lord Salisbury played footsie with the Home Rulers, the start of a long exploitation by Salisbury of the Irish question for party advantage. His lord lieutenant for Ireland, Lord Carnarvon, favoured Home Rule, and there were other signs of possible Tory support. Parnell advised Irish voters on the mainland to vote Tory in the election of November 1885. But when the Liberals won the election, Salisbury declined Gladstone's offer of a bipartisan approach to Home Rule, and in January 1886 Gladstone formed his third cabinet on the understanding that it would inquire into Irish Home Rule.

In April 1886, Gladstone introduced a further Land Bill for Ireland (to buy out the Anglo-Irish landowning class) and a Home Rule Bill devolving domestic affairs to a parliament in Dublin. His party split and Salisbury, supported by the Liberal Unionists (as the anti-Home Rule Liberals were called), stabilized conservative politics on the basis of opposition to constitutional change, reflecting the position of Lord Liverpool in the 1820s. Despite the discrediting of Parnell in the O'Shea divorce case of 1890, the Gladstonian Liberals, supported by Irish Home Rule MPs, replaced the Tories in the election of 1892 and in 1893 the Commons passed an Irish Home Rule Bill. The Lords immediately rejected it by a huge majority, and also mutilated many of the other Liberal measures passed by the Commons. The aged Gladstone finally retired, his Liberal successor, Lord Rosebery, soon finding the Liberal Party more than he could handle. In June 1895 the Liberal government resigned, defeated in the Commons over a vote on cordite, and Salisbury's Conservative Party, now formally in coalition with the Liberal Unionists with Joseph Chamberlain as colonial secretary, began a term of office which carried them into the next century. Known as the 'Hotel Cecil' from the number of Salisbury's relatives it accommodated, the administration kept Home Rule at bay but was otherwise strikingly inactive until it rather casually provoked war with the Transvaal and Orange republics in South Africa in 1899. The government's conduct of the war discredited it almost as much as the Crimean War had the Aberdeen coalition, but, on Joseph Chamberlain's urging, a general election was held in October 1900 when, the army having captured the Boers' towns but not the countryside in-between, the war seemed all but won: the 'khaki election' handsomely returned the Unionist coalition for a further seven years, but it came to be seen as a greedy exercise in jingoism. Lord Salisbury resigned the foreign secretaryship in November 1900, but continued as prime minister until 1902, dying soon thereafter. He thus saw out

Gladstone, who died in 1898, and Queen Victoria, who died in 1901. This clutch of deaths epitomized the end of Victorian politics, the South African War occasioning major changes in foreign policy, in the national finances, and in the assumptions about voluntaryism and the minimal role of the state which had underpinned so much of Victorian endeavour.

Late-Victorian politics

Superficially, British politics at the end of the nineteenth century differed remarkably little from those at its start. Oxford and Cambridge Universities educated almost all the members of the Cabinet, who were almost all members of the established Church of England or (occasionally) Scotland. Henry Matthews and Lord Ripon were the only Roman Catholics to be Cabinet members (and the latter was a convert). Members of other churches—John Bright the Quaker, Henry Fowler the Methodist, Joseph Chamberlain the former Unitarian, H. H. Asquith the former Congregationalist—represented a slight loosening of Anglican dominance but scarcely reflected the extent to which late nineteenth-century Britain had become a religiously plural society. But in the Commons more generally change was noticeable. Consequently, religion remained the chief stuff of politics and the Anglican elite to an important extent ruled on sufferance.

This prominence of religion in politics was in part the result of the extent to which free trade, broadly interpreted, took economics out of politics. Free trade and low central government expenditure largely removed government—especially in England, Scotland, and Wales, but to a lesser extent in Ireland—from the sort of pork-barrel politics which followed the return to protection in other trading economies—particularly Germany and the USA—from the late 1870s. In the British case, though agriculture was in severe depression from the mid-1870s to the mid-1890s, even Conservative governments did not suggest tariffs or interference in prices (apart from some relief from rates, particularly agricultural rates in 1896).

In this sense, the free-trade movement which developed so strongly in the first part of the century proved remarkably enduring. 'Fair

Trade' and ideas about a managed imperial economy received attention and some popular support, and also some government action
through the encouragement of public works, either directly or
through commissioners, in what economists would call the micro
sphere. There was no intervention in the macro sphere of protective
tariffs or management of bank-rate. For the Liberals, their identity
was organically defined by free trade, and on this the Liberal Unionists, with the exception of a small group round Joseph Chamberlain,
were at one with Gladstonian Liberals; for the Tories, scepticism at
the dogmatism of the free-traders was insufficient to outweigh the
priorities of an urban electorate and of the banking and commercial
class on which Tory support increasingly relied. Moreover, the intellectual case for free trade remained a dominant doctrine, even for
those who wished to diminish it, who mostly argued that the free-
trade case was temporarily inconvenient, rather than inherently
wrong. From the mid-1840s the idea of a managed economy was
foreign. A *National System of Political Economy*, the title of Friedrich
List's handbook of German economic nationalism which was published in 1841 just as the British free-trade movement gained ascendancy, represented the Continental antithesis of what most Victorians
believed to be the foundation of Britain's greatness in their century.

Monarchy and the monarchs

Juxtaposed to this widening of democracy, but of some importance
to the idea of integration, was the monarchy. 'Monarchy' comprised
three rather different elements, the person of the monarch, the
powers of the Crown, and the function of the Court. The powers of
the Crown were of vital importance, for much foreign, military, and
imperial authority derived from them. Nineteenth-century parliaments made little attempt to reform or limit these powers and the
century ended with the executive at least as powerful as at its start,
cabinets of both parties finding the Crown's powers in commission to
them highly convenient. It was, of course, a question as to how far in
practice the Crown's powers were in commission, and how far still
with the monarch.

In 1815, George III was mad, deaf, and blind, all his powers and duties seconded (but by Act of Parliament rather than by royal volition) to his son, George, Prince of Wales. George III provided for the succession by fathering nine sons and six daughters. But these only produced one legitimate heir, Princess Charlotte, daughter of the Prince of Wales. Her death in childbirth in 1817 caused national mourning on an exceptional scale, with George III's unmarried sons being rapidly married off to German princesses. Only the youngest brother, the Duke of Kent, produced a legitimate heir: Princess Victoria (1819–1901, named rather unpopularly after her mother, Victoria being thought a foreign-sounding name).

On his accession in 1820, George IV was probably as unpopular as a new king with undisputed succession could be. His estranged wife, Caroline of Brunswick, returned to be queen and became the focus of a widely diffused campaign, led by Radicals but attracting more general anti-Tory feeling. The government's Bill to annul the marriage had to be withdrawn in November 1820. Caroline attempted to attend the coronation in 1821 but was locked out of Westminster Abbey. Her death shortly afterwards, conveniently for the king and the government, removed the immediate problem. The episode burnt the government's fingers and even George IV somewhat moderated his behaviour.

George IV and his brother William IV (1830–37) both saw themselves as active elements in the process of executive decision-making, the former doing what he could to delay Catholic emancipation, the latter taking advantage of a set-back to the government to dismiss his prime minister, Lord Melbourne, in 1834 and install a Tory government led by Peel, the last occasion on which the royal prerogative has been thus asserted by the monarch. Melbourne's victory in the subsequent election pointed up the danger. Queen Victoria, who reigned from 1837 until 1901, was only 18 at her accession. Tutored, perhaps infatuated, by Lord Melbourne, she associated herself initially with the Whigs, declining in the 'Bedchamber Crisis' to replace Whig courtiers with Tories when Peel tried to form a government in 1839. Her marriage to her first cousin, Prince Albert of Saxe-Coburg-Gotha, in 1840 (he was not made Prince Consort until 1857) maintained the dynasty with a plethora of heirs but created an ambivalent political situation, for Albert was a very Victorian reformer, keen to use the powers of the Crown to do good.

The monarchy was seen actively promoting popular events, such as the Great Exhibition of 1851, and associating itself with the progressive elements of the age, patronizing museums and galleries, music, science, the arts, and architecture. But cabinet ministers soon noticed that this active deployment of the monarchy included active involvement in the areas of foreign and military policy, where, moreover, the Duke of Cambridge, the queen's cousin, was commander-in-chief of the army from 1856 until 1895, a fertile source of reaction and Court patronage and intrigue. After Albert's early death in 1861, the queen became a recluse, declining public duties such as opening Parliament and living whenever possible away from London—at Windsor Castle, or at Osborne House or Balmoral Castle, the houses designed by Albert on the Isle of Wight and Deeside in Scotland. Her refusal to carry out public duties meant that a small republican movement in the early 1870s gained more general support, ironically in part from people who wanted the monarch to do more, not less.

The queen's reclusiveness masked a determined behind-the-scenes defence of her prerogative. She developed a fascination for Disraeli not far short of her friendship for Melbourne and she also developed a suspicion of liberalism and a hatred of Gladstone, and especially of the policy of Irish Home Rule. She publicly rebuked her liberal ministers over the death of Gordon in the Sudan (1885) but this was a rare public sally. For the most part, her interventions—on ministerial appointments, foreign and Irish policy, her leaking of information to the Tory opposition about the dissolution of Parliament, and the like—were secret and thus in a literal sense irresponsible. From about 1870 the monarch was in no sense politically neutral and Victoria's partisanship would have discredited the institution of monarchy had Gladstone and the Whigs in his cabinets chosen to make a public issue of her behaviour, or even let the Cabinet radicals know of it. However, much as she came to loathe Gladstonian liberalism, the dismissal of even a weak government was beyond what had become politically acceptable.

The Court under George IV and William IV was one among several points of social pre-eminence, with the great Whig houses almost equal to it: Whigs in the early years of the century still saw the Court in eighteenth-century terms, as a corrupt antithesis to aristocracy. But during Victoria's long reign, as the country became more democratic in temper and the House of Commons more confident of its representative role, a congruence of interest between court and aristocracy developed. Moreover, the importance of the great Whig houses was diminished by the large-scale creation of peers in the nineteenth century, a great benefit to the Tory Party, for Tory creations were already Tories, and Liberal creations tended to cease to support the Liberal Party in the Lords in the next generation. If the aristocracy's power was declining, this was countervailed by a heady increase in the number of hereditary peers (the Lords rejected in 1847, 1869, and 1888 proposals for life peerages). Membership of the Lords increased from 372 (excluding bishops) in 1830 to 562 in 1900, much of the increase being Tory nominations after 1885. Court appointments were a fertile source of political patronage, Lord Salisbury having an especially sharp sense of its utility and of a man's price: in the jubilee year of 1897, 520 peers, privy councillors, baronets, knights, and members of orders were gazetted, 100 more than in 1887.

Though they had their liberal elements, members of the Court and of the Lords, encouraged by their burgeoning numbers, took the view that in some way they represented true national opinion better than those elected to do so, and that they represented 'permanent' interests rather than the supposedly transient 'fads' of the Commons. In the first half of the century the Lords regularly threw out measures, including financial measures, which its Tory majority disliked. But, after the experience of 1831–32, when the Lords came close to destroying the constitution, they usually knew when to stop. However, after about 1884, despite the more representative character of the Commons, the Lords, led by Lord Salisbury, began a more systematic curtailment of liberalism. The liberals, wedded to a historical view of the constitution which implied that the Lords should evolve into insignificance, lacked the will and perhaps the intellectual categories to redesign the constitution. Gladstone, however, bequeathed them the issue of the Lords in his final speech in the Commons.

From the coronation of George IV on, members of the Court perceived the opportunity and the need for well-orchestrated state occasions. This took time to achieve—Wellington's state funeral was an impressive fiasco, the gun-carriage being so heavy that it broke up the surface of the road, and so large that it could not pass through the gate at St Paul's Cathedral—but Court ceremonial was systematized, and the royal family's obsession with correctness of uniforms became a national amusement. Ceremonial increased when the queen became Empress of India by the Royal Titles Act of 1876, passed by

Disraeli's government at her own request, against strong liberal opposition. The title confirmed the monarchy's association with imperialism and Unionism, to the short- and medium-term advantage of it and the Tory party. With the queen reclusive, the Prince of Wales lived an almost separate and very public existence, his boisterous enthusiasm for women, sport, and travel giving royalty an illusion of modernism. Despite his misdemeanours, the Prince of Wales maintained something of Palmerston's raffish popular appeal, and provided a bridge to liberalism which his mother did her best to break down. The wide participation in the jubilees of 1887 and 1897, and the national mourning at the queen's death in January 1901—all of them marked by military processions emphasizing imperial power—showed the extent to which the idea of monarchy had replaced the presence and authority of the individual monarch. Few British monarchs were less known in person even to the political class, or appeared less frequently in public, yet none gave her name more readily to her epoch than Victoria.

George IV broadened the appeal of the Hanoverians by his visit to Scotland in 1822, choreographed by Sir Walter Scott, the first such visit since the Stuarts. He also visited Ireland. Neither William IV nor Victoria added Scottish or Irish state visits to their coronations, but Victoria and Albert developed George IV's initiative by the building of Balmoral, bought in 1852, and by a general enthusiasm for rural Scotland, reflected in the Queen's deceptively naive publications, *Leaves From the Journal of our Life in the Highlands* (1869) and *More Leaves* (1883). The annual movement of the Court to Balmoral popularized the idea of the Highland estate as a holiday hobby and of the organization of rural society and economy around shooting and fishing. In a curious way royal patronage was held to legitimize the clearances of the Highlands, so savage a movement that it left no immediate political legacy, only an oppressive emptiness and sense of absence in the glens which even the queen herself sometimes felt. By the end of the century, over three million acres of the Scottish Highlands had been cleared as sporting estates. Balmoral, integrative though in some respects it was, was to have no Irish or Welsh equivalent. Victoria visited Ireland three times, in 1849, 1851, and 1861, and then not until 1900. She vetoed plans for a royal Irish residence and for a restructuring of Irish government to establish a court in Dublin led by the Prince of Wales.

The Cabinet and the civil service

The Cabinet linked the Crown, the civil service, and the legislature. With many strong, independently minded personalities, and with ministers still personally responsible for much of the content of government legislation, the nineteenth century was the Cabinet's golden age. The Cabinet had no secretariat, and Gladstone was the only nineteenth-century prime minister to keep regular, detailed records of its agenda and decisions. The structure of Cabinet government formally changed remarkably little in our period, though some existing domestic offices—notably the chancellorship of the exchequer—became much more important (even here, Gladstone was twice (1873–74, 1880–82) his own chancellor while prime minister). Changes were chiefly in the running of the empire: the colonies got their own secretary of state in 1854, when the War Office was also reorganized, as did India in 1858 when the East India Company was nationalized by statute following the Indian Mutiny. In 1885, a secretaryship for Scotland was established, an important step in administrative devolution. The Scottish secretary was a more important official than the chief secretary for Ireland, though the latter was secretary to the lord lieutenant for Ireland (sometimes called the viceroy), who had no equivalent in Scotland. The prime minister—an office not recognized by the constitution—had little direct power but much influence through the convention that he could demand the resignation of Cabinet members and determine the date of dissolutions of Parliament; the premier was increasingly expected to lead the party in extra-parliamentary speechmaking in general elections, and perhaps to range more widely: Gladstone twice addressed the Welsh cultural festival, the eisteddfod. The prime minister exercised much patronage, especially in the Church of England, for all major and many minor positions in the Church were filled on his recommendation, but also through the appointment of lords lieutenant for the counties and Crown representatives on many boards of trustees and the like. When in the Commons, the premier was normally leader of the House and responsible for the passage of government business there.

The civil service which supported the government comprised

about 25 000 persons in 1815 and almost 80 000 by 1891, many of these being custom and excise and income tax inspectors. Though housed in sumptuous buildings in Whitehall from the 1860s, the chief ministries had remarkably small staffs. In 1830 and 1880 the respective figures for permanent staff were: Foreign Office 39 and 109 (including the House Keeper), Home Office 25 and 60 (excluding inspectors), Colonial Office 31 and 60 (excluding Crown agents). The small scale of civil service departments allowed great power to strong characters within them and in several departments legendary permanent secretaries—'statesmen in disguise' as they have been aptly called— were in office much longer than the ministers they served: 'Mr Over-secretary Stephen' (James Stephen of the colonial office) was perhaps the best known, but James Kay-Shuttleworth in education, Sir John Simon and Sir Edwin Chadwick in health and social welfare—were commanding presences in their fields and often saw themselves as the equal or superior of their ministers.

In 1854 the reforming chancellor of the exchequer, Gladstone, commissioned through the Treasury a series of reports on the working of government of which the best known is the Northcote–Trevelyan report on the civil service. It led to a distinction between the administrative grade, made up of graduates, who wrote the policy papers, and clerks, who implemented them. A Civil Service Commission (1855) and entry to the administrative grade by examination (mostly in languages and classical culture) was by stages introduced, greatly to the benefit of Oxford and Cambridge Universities, for the examination questions reflected their liberal arts syllabuses. The civil service became less flamboyant but more reliable. The treasury, by better accounting, by parliamentary audit through the Public Accounts Committee (1864) and the Audit Act (1865), and by a public ethos which in general favoured government's disengagement from the economy, tightened its grip on most branches of civil service activity through its control of expenditure. Scotland and Ireland, however, with their separate centres of government in Edinburgh and Dublin, to some extent escaped the treasury's detailed scrutiny and in those kingdoms government intervened more in the economy.

Government expenditure, welfare, and taxation

Central government expenditure was remarkably small once the burden of debt consequent on the French wars had been diminished; it still took over half of the budget in 1836–40. Navy and army costs were, across the century, much the largest item of the budget, and central government spending on domestic affairs was, in proportion, small.

The highest expenditure on the war occurred in 1815 (£113 000 000); sharp deflation followed, with expenditure falling to £57 000 000 in 1820, and then remaining roughly constant until the Crimean War, expensive in itself and as a stimulous to expenditure, for budgetary levels rose gradually from £70 000 000 in 1860 to the first £100 000 000 budget in 1885 (if we include a special Vote of

Table 2.1 As percentage of total gross central government expenditure

	Debt charges	Army and navy	Civil government
1815	27	64	5
1816–20	46	39	8
1821–25	55	27	10
1826–30	54	29	10
1831–35	57	28	9
1836–40	58	25	10
1841–45	55	26	10
1846–50	50	30	12
1851–55	49	30	12
1856–60	37	40	12
1861–65	38	39	15
1866–70	38	36	16
1871–75	38	33	17
1876–80	35	33	20
1881–85	34	31	22
1886–90	29	34	21
1891–95	24	35	20
1896–99	21	37	20
1900–03	12	57	20

Note: (Compiled from B. R. Mitchell, *British Historical Statistics* (1988); the total to 100 is made up by administrative costs, Post Office, etc.)

Credit of £11 million to pay for the army in the Sudan and a possible war with Russia in Afghanistan); by the late 1890s the budget normally balanced at over £100 000 000, rising to over £200 000 000 during the South African War. Some contemporaries worried much over these gradually rising figures, but in fact the increase in public expenditure was far slower than the increase in the population and in the wealth of the country. Relative to population and wealth, the British in peacetime paid lower taxes in 1890 than in 1820.

The nineteenth century developed a crafty device for dealing with potentially expensive items of domestic expenditure such as social welfare and education: Acts of Parliament laid down a national policy, but the costs and implementation were passed on to the localities. In many cases the statutes were permissive rather than compulsory. This was partly because central government lacked the means of enforcing its wishes and partly because there was widespread resistance to centrally imposed measures which were paid for locally. The belated arrival of modern representative government at the county and local level (save for some urban areas from 1835) is one of the most remarkable features of a century which saw itself as reforming. County councils were introduced in 1888–89 for England, Wales, and Scotland, and for Ireland in 1898, and local/parish councils in 1894 and 1899, respectively.

The absence of general provision of local government meant that

Table 2.2 Proportion of central government gross expenditure to gross national product

	Expenditure £ million	GNP £ million	%
1853	55.3	642 (1855)	8.6
1860	70	702	10
1865	67.1	846	7.9
1870	67.1	953	7.0
1875	73	1136	6.4
1880	81.5	1101	7.4
1885	88.5	1120	7.9
1895	100.9	1459	6.9
1905	149.5	1814	8.2

Note: (Compiled from B. R. Mitchell, *British Historical Statistics* (1988) and C. H. Feinstein, *National Income, Expenditure and Output of the United Kingdom 1855–1965* (1972).)

various representative bodies were set up to deal with particular questions. The Poor Law Amendment Act (1834), followed in Ireland (1838) and in Scotland (1845), established a national system of workhouses and the Elementary Education Act (1870) and other legislation established in due course school boards to provide board schools where there was no voluntary school, most voluntary schools being Church of England schools. Elementary education was compulsory for children aged from 5 to 10 from 1880 (raised to 11 in 1893 and 12 in 1899), and effectively free from 1891. Attendance during the period of compulsory fee-paying was remarkably high. But these programmes were to be paid for by local taxpayers, taxed through the rates due on houses, farms, factories, and offices.

The workhouse has been called by Anne Crowther 'a place of unresolvable tension', (p. 3) responsible both for deterring the able-bodied poor and for providing a humane refuge for the helpless. The Poor Law was initially famously draconian, though no other country in the world then provided a last resort by right to all of its inhabitants. But what was striking was that guardians were rarely as draconian as they were meant to be. From 1834 until 1847—its most controversial period, which established the Dickensian stereotype of callous discipline famously etched in *Oliver Twist* (1837–38)—the English Poor Law was centrally overseen by commissioners, with Edwin Chadwick as their zealous secretary, and from 1847 until 1871 by the ineffective Poor Law Board. Ironically, Dickens' depiction was of the pre-1834 workhouse, though it was opposition to the 1834 Act, as well as the author's genius, which gave the book iconic status. The Poor Law never lost its stigma, but in certain areas of the country it developed quite effective medical services and the number on outdoor relief (that is, receiving help without entering the workhouse) certainly never fell to zero as the 1834 Act intended. Concern about excessive local spending led to the Local Government Board taking over central responsibility in 1871, but the board's attempt to restrain expenditure had only temporary effect. Even so, workhouse conditions continued to shock, especially as the standard of living for the employed was rising markedly.

The price of the voluntary character of most of such legislation as there was on social questions was a wide divergence of standards and a wide reliance on philanthropic giving to fund what by the end of the century were being seen as essentials. Some towns used their powers to eliminate what William Cobbett had called 'Hell-holes', most did not; some cities had excellent, voluntarily funded hospitals, many did not; one town would have a police force, another not. The Charity Organization Society (1869) saw the problem—that rich areas funded good, and poor areas deficient, services—but was more effective at identifying the problem than solving it. Ironically, from the 1880s opinion was beginning to take the view, in stark opposition to the COS, that more involvement and supervision by the state was the fairest solution. When the question was order, Parliament acted, police forces becoming compulsory in 1856–57; but when the issue was welfare, Parliament usually held back.

The pretence that central government did not fund local services, while in fact supporting them by annual 'grants', and the plethora of local boards, meant that no proper financial relationship between central and local was developed, and by the end of the century there was a serious deficit in local finance. Education funding was a mine-field of complexities, with a variety of grants and other monies, including in Wales the support of technical instruction from the 'whisky money' (tax on liquor licences, one of the few hypothecated taxes). But even taking these grants into account, central expend-iture in civil government remained tiny, proportionate to what it became in the next century. Perhaps because it was so small, it was contested and controversial far beyond its twentieth-century equivalents.

Our period began with income-tax abolition in 1816 sharply increasing the proportion of government income raised by indirect taxes, chiefly on food and items of daily living. Partly from Peel's reintroduction of income tax in 1842, paid only by those with incomes of over £150 (£100 from 1853), a gradual but clear movement towards direct taxation occurred, direct taxes being chiefly paid by those on good office wages or better. But at the end of the century about 50% was still raised from indirect taxes, especially those on tea, coffee, spirits, wine, beer, tobacco, and sugar duties. These were not protective and thus acceptable to free-traders. They were held to be 'voluntary' taxes, but in fact fell on the staples of working-class con-sumption. This was intentional, for the taxes on other similar articles were repealed as insufficiently productive. This was a regressive tax system, but less regressive than that of any other industrialized country.

Table 2.3 Percentage of UK exchequer revenue contributed by indirect and direct taxation

	Indirect	Direct
1811–15	60	40
1816–20	67	33
1821–25	74	26
1826–30	77	22
1831–35	77	33
1836–40	79	21
1841–45	75	25
1846–50	70	30
1851–55	69	31
1856–60	65	35
1861–65	65	35
1866–70	67	33
1871–75	65	35
1876–80	65	35
1881–85	59	41
1886–90	56	44
1891–95	56	44
1896–1900	52	48
1901–05	49	51

Note: (For details of compilation, see H. C. G. Matthew, 'Disraeli, Gladstone and the politics of mid-Victorian budgets', *Historical Journal* (1979).)

The income tax of 1842 was intended to be temporary, funding the move to free trade; but it was never repealed and contributed an ever-increasing proportion of the government's income. A campaign by the professional middle class to differentiate income tax, (that is, impose it more heavily on those with 'unprecarious' incomes such as money from land rents) was unsuccessful, as was the Cobdenite campaign to make all taxation direct, with heavy taxes on landed wealth. Legacy and succession duties, introduced by Gladstone in 1853, were light, though increased by stages, but in 1894 a more effective, graduated death duty was introduced, much hilarity subsequently occurring when a quick succession of deaths in his family hit hard the responsible chancellor, Sir William Harcourt.

'A kindlier people'?

Concluding the famous third chapter of his *History of England*, Thomas Babington Macaulay observed in 1839: 'it is pleasing to reflect that the public mind of England has softened while it has ripened, and that we have, in the course of ages become, not only a wiser, but also a kindlier people.' Most of those involved in Victorian public life in the rest of the century would have agreed with Macaulay. Victorians congratulated themselves on improvement, on reform, and on avoiding the mistakes of the post-1815 years which after 1830 quickly came to be seen, more than the eighteenth century, as the model of what to avoid; and the French Revolutions of 1830 and 1848 showed the possible penalty.

The treatment of capital punishment is always a useful indicator of the character of a society. The ending of capital punishment for crimes other than murder and treason by Peel's Acts of 1824–29 and the statutory ending of public executions in 1868 reflected a marked change. In 1817–20, there were 312 executions in England and Wales; between 1847 and 1890, the annual number was always less than 25, with 1871 the lowest year (3). The dissection of corpses following execution was prohibited in 1832. Death had ceased to be a significant weapon of state control and deterrence (however, unlike some Continental countries, capital punishment was not abolished, nor was there an effective campaign for its abolition). William Cobbett was imprisoned in 1810 for campaigning against flogging—the 'English vice' as it was known—in the army; Parliament eventually abolished it for the army in 1881, and much reduced it in the navy.

The Irish would hardly have seen 'Bloody Balfour', as they called A. J. Balfour, the Irish secretary of the late 1880s, as representing a kindlier people, nor the Skye crofters Sir William Harcourt as he sent in the troops in 1882 to quell agrarian unrest, nor the Welsh slate-quarrymen Lord Penrhyn in the strikes and lock-outs of 1896–97. Rural life remained quite violent, but urban crime fell remarkably, perhaps the only instance in world history of intense urbanization and rapidly rising population being accompanied by a falling crime rate. As Vic Gatrell has shown, between the 1850s and 1890 serious offences fell by a third, the Criminal Registrar noting in 1901: 'We have witnessed a great change in manners: the substitution of words without blows for blows with or without words; an approximation in the manners of different classes; a decline in the spirit of lawlessness.'

The public life of the British Isles was a complex kaleidoscope of differing traditions fitting roughly, and sometimes being forcibly shaped, into a parliamentary and orderly pattern. The small towns of Scotland, Wales, and Ireland contrasted markedly with their rural hinterlands where relationships between landowners, tenants, and labourers were a sharp antithesis to urban egalitarian aspirations. The great cities of midland and northern England—not only the largest such as Liverpool, Manchester, Birmingham, and Newcastle upon Tyne, but also the many medium-sized urban centres—developed and maintained their own public life in defiant resistance to the integrating embrace of London—which Disraeli called 'a nation, not a city'. But their ability to maintain anti-metropolitan centres of real political power declined as the century progressed.

Throughout the British Isles, Christianity in all its varieties was as important and as devisive a factor as class in public life, and a more complex one: the Church of Scotland and the Free Church; the Church of England, the various Nonconformist denominations; the Anglican Church of Ireland, the Ulster Presbyterians; and the Roman Catholics, central to Irish public life and a growing presence on the mainland. And each had its own parties and conflicts, further complicating the making of public policy. Moreover, the secularists, as militant as any of the churches, were effective far beyond their limited numbers; and between them and the churches, especially among those articulate in public life, were the agnostics, anxious but unable to reduce the intensity of religious controversy in Parliament and in local affairs. This plurality of opinion flourished much more easily at the end of the century than in 1815.

Plate 5 This extract from Fred. W. Rose's cartoon map of 'John Bull et ses Amis' (1900) neatly captures the ambiguity of Britain's empire, as a major source of strength and military support, but also of vulnerability and danger, indicated here in the shapes of Ireland and the warring Boer republics.

3

The empire and the world

Andrew Porter

By 1815, Britain was firmly established as one of the world's great imperial powers alongside France, Russia, and the Chinese and Ottoman Turkish Empires. In Europe, she stood out among the Great Powers which made peace at Vienna after the defeat of Napoleon. Domestic difficulties notwithstanding, her commercial and financial strength had sustained the European military alliances necessary to restore Continental peace, and since her victory at Trafalgar in 1805 her navy had secured her global supremacy at sea. Outside the home islands, themselves only recently consolidated by an Act of Union with Ireland in 1801, Britain's empire was made up of three elements. Although seriously reduced by the Americans' victory in the War of Independence, the colonies of white settlement were once again beginning to expand, in British North America (the Canadas), South Africa (Cape of Good Hope), and Australia (New South Wales). Since the beginning of the Seven Years War in 1756, an enormous empire had been created in India, the product of Britain's continuous involvement both in Europe's worldwide struggles and, through the East India Company, in Indian states' own internal conflicts or commercial competition. Finally there were long-standing West Indian colonies like Jamaica and Barbados, to which had been added a further miscellany of predominantly tropical territories. Many of these, conquered during the French wars of 1793–1815, were retained in the peace settlement, including Trinidad, Ceylon, Mauritius, and Demerara. In West Africa British possessions were limited to the settlement of Sierra Leone, and trading posts on the Gambia and Gold Coast.

Peace in 1815 marked for Britain the end of the latest stage in a global war which had continued intermittently since the 1740s. That experience had taught her governing classes some important lessons. Just as the war had demonstrated that European rivalries and imperial competition were closely connected, so the peace confirmed that imperial possessions and Great Power status went together. Nevertheless, diplomatic recognition of Britain's worldwide pre-eminence did not remove the possibility of new international challenges and a resumption of conflict. Throughout the nineteenth century imperial issues and foreign policy remained inseparable from each other.

The pattern of expansion

The growth of formal empire, that is, of overseas territory and peoples under Britain's direct and sovereign political control, continued to be an outstanding feature of the nineteenth century. The development, especially, of the white settlement colonies proved both striking and valuable. Canada's provinces were steadily extended westwards through Alberta and British Columbia on the Pacific coast, and were gradually incorporated into a federation, the core of which was set up under the British North America Act (1867). The slow emergence of six colonies on the Australian continent was the prelude to their political consolidation in the Commonwealth of Australia (1901). Expansion in Southern Africa, already a fact of Dutch settler life, continued after the final British occupation of Cape Town in 1806 until the conquest of the Afrikaner republics of the Transvaal and Orange Free State brought the country under imperial rule in 1900. Local lawlessness and pressures to settle New Zealand after about 1820 provoked imperial annexation under the Treaty of Waitangi made with North Island Maoris in 1840.

Almost everywhere the pattern of white expansion was the same. Much of its dynamism came from the British Isles themselves, but local 'sub-imperialisms' were also of great importance: Australia's port cities steadily extended their hinterlands, and Cape Colony settlers' restless penetration inland was a central feature of South Africa's development. Indigenous peoples were everywhere steadily displaced and often violently dispossessed of their lands by the intrusion of emigrants and local-born settlers. Local cultivators were frequently compelled to exchange the rhythms and relative security of customary or peasant life for the uncertainties of wages, limited contracts, and allotted reserves. Colonial governments' support for an infrastructure of roads, harbours, and railways, encouraged private investment and economic development, and duly transformed small, insecure outposts of expatriates into self-governing, self-confident 'settler capitalist' societies. Something of the often cocksure insouciance of this aggrandizement was captured by Cecil Rhodes, prime minister of the Cape Colony and mining magnate, in 1895, in reply to Queen Victoria's question as to his recent doings: 'I have added two provinces to your Majesty's dominions'. The empire's white settler population of perhaps 550 000 in 1815, and an equally limited trade with Britain, were completely transformed. The census of 1901 recorded 11.5 million people, and customs returns a trade valued at £118 million (1901). Profit and growth rates in the empire of white settlement compared well with those at home, and it accounted for about 13.6% of Britain's total overseas trade.

Not all parts of the empire flourished. The trade of the West Indian colonies, including the recent wartime acquisitions of Trinidad and what became British Guiana, was worth £15.4 million, an impressive 17.6% of Britain's trade in 1815. At the end of the century, affected by slave emancipation (1833–38) and the impact of free trade, their stagnant economies generated trade with Britain of only £4.99 million or 0.57% (1901), even though their population, boosted by the organized recruitment of Indian indentured labourers, had risen from 877 000 to just under two million (1901).

In the midst of these transformations, India retained her central position in the empire. Successive governors-general of the East India Company—for though closely controlled, the chartered company remained the government of British territory until after the mutiny of 1857—had by 1820 carved out the heart of what was to remain British India. Thereafter military conquest carried British control into the north-east in the first Burma War (1824–26), and further still into Burma in 1852 and 1885. In the north-west, Sind and the Punjab were conquered during the 1840s, and more Indian states were

annexed by Lord Dalhousie (governor-general, 1848–56). This consolidation of British control gave her unrestricted access to India's
immense resources and, especially after 1870, gave India an important
role in the balancing of Britain's international trade. Annexations
and natural growth brought British India's population from about 40
million to 294 million (1901). In 1815 her world trade stood at only £8
million but grew to £62.4 million with Britain alone by 1901.

India always overshadowed in importance Britain's other scattered
colonial accessions in Asia. Hong Kong was acquired from China as a
result of the first Opium War in 1842, and was extended in 1898 with
the 99-year lease of the mainland 'New Territories'. Although its
population grew, as an entrepôt for the China trade it was soon
outstripped in importance by Shanghai. In similarly sporadic fashion,
the Malayan mainland, Singapore, and parts of Borneo (Sarawak,
Labuan, and North Borneo) were all incorporated into the empire's
political and economic networks.

In Africa the growth of territorial empire occurred later in the
century and impressed observers far more than that in India and
other parts of Asia. On the west coast Britain's tiny footholds of 1815
were virtually unchanged by 1865; only Lagos had been annexed in
1861. In the next fifty years, however, colonial expansion forged ahead
in every quarter of the continent. By 1901 British Africa claimed 2.8
million square miles and a population estimated at nearly 40 million.
Economically, however, these African colonies were relatively
insignificant. By contrast, their trade at £32.6 million (1901), of which
the territories about to form the Union of South Africa (1910) provided some £27.2 million, accounted for a mere 3.7% of British overseas trade, and only 14.9% of the empire's trade with the metropole.

As the century progressed, the economic significance of these
imperial connections grew. Their relative importance and Britain's
ties with the wider world were conditioned more and more by Britain's rising population, industrialization, and urban expansion. Raw
materials for her industry and food for her people increasingly had to
be imported. From the tropics Britain purchased sugar, cocoa, tea,
Malayan rubber or minerals such as tin, and West African vegetable
oils; from the temperate areas of recent settlement came American
cotton, Canadian timber and increasingly wheat, Australasian wool
and later meat.

Even before 1815 Britain's economic demands had outgrown the empire's capacity as supplier and market, and this remained the case despite continuing colonial expansion. Britain therefore became a supporter of free trade in order to maximize her access to the basic commodities she required. Both the imperial and colonial governments were willing to encourage the movement of emigrants, British technology, and capital on which so many of her suppliers depended; subsidized passages and guaranteed prospects of land or employment were often available, making distance less of an obstacle. The result was the migration from the British Isles of some 22 million people in the century after 1815. England, Wales, and Scotland, for example, together saw 735 000 of their people leave for Canada between 1853 and 1901, and more than that number in each of the next two decades. Colossal numbers left Ireland in the wake of the famine, and more than one quarter of Australia's immigrant population by the 1870s was Irish. Migration and the export of capital moved in similar directions. By the turn of the century, 60% of Britain's overseas investment had been placed in the empire, some 40% of it in the white settler colonies. Much of the non-empire emigration and investment found its way to similar settler societies in the United States and Latin America; from 1853 to 1900, 56% of all migrants from mainland Britain went direct to the USA.

Within the tropical world, following the abolition of colonial slavery between 1833 and 1838, the expansion of British trade, investment, plantations, mines, and public works was accompanied by a similar movement of labour. However, apart from small groups of expatriates—like the Scots who ran so many of the great British mercantile firms east of Suez: Mackinnon Mackenzie, Jardine Matheson, and James Finlay—little of that labour was white. It was composed above all of Chinese and Indian workers, both free and indentured. Between c.1840 and c.1920, almost 1.5 million Indian contract labourers were recruited, above all for Mauritius, British Guiana, and Natal, and a further 5 million free workers moved to Burma, Ceylon, and Malaya. Indians also established themselves in East Africa; moving inland in the wake of colonial authority, many of them were from the beginning monied traders rather than labourers. More than 5 million Chinese immigrants entered the Straits Settlements in the period 1888–1915; others went overseas under contract, 120 000 to Australia (1854–80) and 64 000 to the gold mines of the Transvaal (1904–07).

Britain's global economic and territorial system depended on rapid advances in communication. There were regular and reliable postal services from the 1840s, long-distance steamships and telegraphs from the 1850s, and extensive railway building outside Europe especially after 1870. In India, for example, almost 25 000 miles of track had been opened by 1900. Many of these developments were assisted by imperial or colonial government subsidies and loans. Integration was also aided by a host of less tangible but no less vital developments, including the spread of the English language, and more competitive and efficient business practices not least in banking and company organization. Although in 1830 imperial communications and commercial practice were much as they had been a century before, thereafter they changed rapidly out of all recognition. The extension and declining cost of the telegraph revolutionized the provision of commercial information, marketing, and financial calculations, as well as metropolitan control of events. The opening of the Suez Canal in 1869 had a major impact on Britain's links with India and the Far East. Improved ship construction helped reduce voyage times: the outward mail service between England and Cape Town fell from 42 days in 1857 to 19 in 1893. Just as transport costs for commodities fell, so migration itself became more affordable for individuals and their families, and its organization therefore overwhelmingly voluntary.

There is no doubt that such ties did much to enhance and cement connections between all regions of Britain and her colonies overseas. However, it is more difficult to assess the relationship they helped to establish with other parts of the globe. British demands for open access and their exploitation of commercial privileges often produced conflicts with local governments and their subjects in parts of Asia, the Middle East, and even Latin America. In some cases, such as Egypt in 1882, the outcome was the forcible imposition of imperial control over the country. The Chinese government maintained its independence, but not without being forced to accept a system of 'unequal' treaties and concessions extorted as a result of war or military intervention in 1839–42, 1856–60, and 1900. Argentina has often been seen as critically dependent on British finance and commerce, and her political and social elites shaped by British ideas and customs. In these and many other cases, it has often been argued that the extent of Britain's presence, influence, and intervention, while falling short of annexation, nevertheless compromised local governments' exercise of sovereignty or independence to the extent that such countries have to be regarded, perhaps for long periods, as part of a British 'informal empire'.

The mainsprings of British empire building have always been argued over vigorously. Contemporaries were often—and rightly—impressed by both the uncoordinated expansiveness of trade, settlement, investment, and culture, and by the aggressive, systematic power-seeking of individuals such as Lord Palmerston or Joseph Chamberlain. Industrialization, urban population growth, and international competition pushed expansion forward, but economic interest and motivation not only varied immensely from one corner of the empire to another, but often eschewed formal imperial control altogether. From J. A. Hobson's *Imperialism. A Study* (1902) onwards, attempts by economic or political theorists and historians to attribute persistent causal primacy to one or another feature of capitalism—industry, finance, the City of London, particular business, or social networks—have all proved generally unsatisfactory. Much more progress in understanding the processes of imperialism has come from the investigation of overseas societies themselves, and how British interests of many different kinds became steadily more deeply enmeshed in local affairs.

Britain's concern to protect her status and to secure her growing presence overseas had led by 1901 to the imposition of direct rule and the creation of an immense range of imperial commitments, economic and political relationships, in Asia, Africa, and the Pacific. In many places, the formal empire often merged imperceptibly into a much wider range of global British activities where trade and investment in particular transcended any narrowly territorial view of the world and sources of power or wealth. These two categories of expanding interests—the empire of formal control, and regions of significant but informal British influence—were not only difficult to manage and maintain, but proved in their turn as likely to multiply Britain's international problems as they were to increase her strength or resources.

Modes of imperial control

The means by which Britain sustained her influence and managed her empire at the level of individual colonial territories were not only varied but changed greatly during the century. In Britain itself, these tasks were shared among several government departments.

The economic and political significance of India had long caused it to be regarded as a place apart, and to develop its own structure of government. Subject to the oversight and increasing direction of a British cabinet minister, the president of the board of control, India was administered by the East India Company. With its headquarters in the City of London and a governor-general at Calcutta to organize its territories in the subcontinent, the company represented an uneasy and ill-controlled combination of military, administrative, and steadily declining commercial concerns. As a consequence of the great Indian Mutiny and civil rebellion of 1857, the company was abolished. The India Act (1858) placed under formal imperial rule the area the company had administered (with a significant proportion of India, the Princely States, under informal rule, each prince or maharajah having a British political adviser, whose 'advice' was in practice not to be declined). The Act established a single system in which a secretary of state for India and his council in London watched over the viceroy and his council at Calcutta. Indian administration was essentially despotic; it was directed by an elite corps, the Indian Civil Service, which despite being opened to competitive entry in 1853 became increasingly conservative and routinely bureaucratic. Although dependent on large numbers of Indian employees at its lowest levels, the Raj did not encourage the advancement of Indians in its ranks, though this attitude changed somewhat in the 1880s. The possession and government of India was thought to confer great prestige on Britain, and Anglo-Indian connections permeated British social and political as well as economic life.

The affairs of other colonies, concentrated in 1801 in the hands of the secretary of state for war and colonies, were only allocated to a separate Colonial Office in 1854, one reflection of their comparative lack of importance for politicians at Westminster. Although occasionally young Members of Parliament, like W. E. Gladstone or Lord

Selborne, anxious to place their feet on the ladder of promotion, might start as a junior colonial minister, rarely were capable and well-informed secretaries of state such as Earl Grey (1846–52) drawn to colonial affairs. Even fewer continued in office for long; more often, biddable, ageing colleagues such as Lord Derby (1882–85) occupied the Colonial Office as a berth *en route* to retirement from active politics. Joseph Chamberlain (1895–1903) alone was sufficiently widely known, weighty, and determined a politician to keep the office and its affairs in the public eye.

The reasons for this state of affairs were several. Colonial issues were rarely of much interest to the electorate, and in Parliament they were useful weapons for the opposition rather than ministers. Only occasionally, as with the controversy resulting from Governor Edward Eyre's handling of disturbances in Jamaica in 1865 or the scandal of the Jameson Raid into the Transvaal in 1896, did colonial questions become a major preoccupation of the Westminster Parliament. Vocal critics of government policies overseas, like Richard Cobden in the 1840s and 1850s, or eccentric nuisances like Sir Ellis Ashmead-Bartlett and the outspoken Radical Henry Labouchere in the 1890s, made more play than most with colonial questions. More fundamental still were the amorphous and unwieldy nature of Britain's colonies; the virtual impossibility of getting to grips with their distant and bewildering detail; the consequent necessity reinforced by precedent for the delegation of authority to local figures on the spot; and Parliament's insistence on self-sufficiency or at least the utmost economy in their administration. Few politicians were sufficiently brave or foolhardy to think that they could do much more than react to colonial events. Lord Carnarvon failed spectacularly when he tried to engineer a regional federation in South Africa between 1874 and 1878. Normally it seemed safer or at least more prudent for London to avoid taking the initiative in the colonial empire.

Nevertheless, certain overarching developments are discernible in this period. First of all, imperial expansion went together with a growing divergence between the empire of white settlement, in which subjects successfully claimed rights of self-government by virtue of their British descent, and the empire of dependent or protected peoples, including India, who were generally denied such rights.

The development in this respect of the white-settler empire was influenced by Britain's own constitutional experience (in which parliamentary authority grew at the Crown's expense), together with North American, West Indian, and eventually, in 1791, Canadian precedents for locally elected assemblies. Appeals to the tradition and institutions of representative and responsible self-government became almost everywhere a central feature of white-settler politics from 1820 onwards. 'Representative government' made formal allowance for the influence of colonial opinion on a colony's administration. This was achieved by the nomination of prominent colonists to the councils which advised the governor, for example in Van Diemen's Land in 1825, as well as by the introduction alongside the councils of elected assemblies, as in Lower Canada in 1791. 'Responsible government' entailed colonial internal self-rule. Day-to-day control and decisions by imperial officials or councils were relinquished to a local prime minister and his cabinet drawn from the majority grouping in an elected colonial assembly, as first happened in Nova Scotia in 1847. French Canadians, Irish nationalists under the Union, and Afrikaners, as well as Scots and English emigrant settlers all pressed their claims to participation and control.

From the 1840s, when Britain's abandonment of imperial protection in favour of universal free trade removed one of the remaining significant arguments against devolution, the question became less whether but when the imperial authorities would concede responsible government. Concession followed less as a result of settled policy than as a consequence of London's assessment of the likelihood that such a move would foster both internal stability and the preservation of imperial ties. In both the British North American provinces and the Australian colonies the loosening of formal political controls was readily approved between 1846 and 1851. In South Africa, however, the equation was different; smaller white communities and complicated, often violent relations with the local African states meant that the Cape Colony only became internally self-governing in 1872 and Natal in 1893. Although imperial politicians miscalculated their ability to retain control over matters such as colonial tariffs and land policy, there remained both a sense that there was little alternative if good relations were to be maintained, and, in the background, an awareness that continuing emigration and economic development would at the same time nurture powerful informal connections. In all cases, political calculation and administrative convenience entailed progressively less stringent scrutiny by the Colonial Office of settler governments' legislation.

The contrasting authoritarian tradition, of 'Crown colony' government, developed from the Quebec Act of 1774 with its denial of an elected assembly in circumstances where it might either be unworkable or had no foundation in local custom. This preserved imperial and colonial executive authority in the hands of imperial ministers and administrators, and was widely applied to territories conquered during the Anglo-French wars before 1815. Dictated in part by convenience and military habits of command, it was also influenced by concern for security, allowing for local custom in theory at least to remain relatively undisturbed. In cases such as New South Wales and the Cape Colony such locally centralized and authoritarian forms of control began to be relaxed in the 1820s, but in the dependent or 'non-white' empire they became the norm. Increasingly they chimed in with the racial and cultural stereotyping which became so much a part of imperial life after the mid-century, and which cast doubt on the fitness of 'native races' for self-government of any kind. As a reflection of this, the Colonial Office relied increasingly for legislation in the Crown colonies on Orders-in-Council based on advice from the Law Officers of the Crown in London rather than on any consultation of local unofficial opinion.

Strangely anomalous among Britain's possessions was Ireland. Although it was nominally an integral part of the imperial British metropole, many Irish regarded the Union of 1801 as an act of colonial annexation, and the country was in significant respects governed in a manner akin to that of India or any Crown colony. Colonial status was embodied, so it seemed, in the offices of the lord lieutenant or viceroy and his chief secretary at the head of a distinct Irish administration in Dublin Castle. When set alongside the 12 000-strong paramilitary police force of the Irish Constabulary, the large number of troops stationed in the country (25 000 in 1881) might be represented as an army of occupation rather than a legitimate proportion of the home garrison. Long after the abandonment of 'anglicization' as official policy in respect of French Canadians and Afrikaners, it remained a central feature of national education in Ireland, its necessity presumably enhanced by the racial stereotyping and denigration routinely directed at the Irish. Indian parallels were noticeable in the Irish land legislation of 1870 and 1881. Unionists, of course, dismissed such 'colonial' analogies, even while Lord Salisbury compared the Irish to the 'Hottentots' of South Africa. For them the fact of Union justified not only the responsibility of Whitehall departments for many aspects of Irish affairs, but resistance to the disestablishment of the Irish Church, and the refusal of even the limited concessions to self-government included in the Irish Home Rule Bills of 1886 and 1893.

An enormous diversity of colonial conditions thus had to be managed by the imperial departments in London and by the local agents responsible for the day-to-day conduct of Britain's colonial rule. Official preoccupations also shifted as the century passed, from slavery issues which attracted enormous public concern in the years to about 1845; to 'responsible government' for white settlers in mid-century; to the gradual reconstruction of Indian government after the Mutiny; and to the territorial consequences of colonial partition in Africa and the Pacific after 1875. However, amidst their kaleidoscopic concerns, officials' activity was everywhere aimed at achieving an ultimately sustainable balance of interests between the British and the local communities. Although, as the Lower Canadian rebellion (1837) and above all the Indian Mutiny (1857) demonstrated, the empire's existence might depend in the last resort on overwhelming force, under normal circumstances that force was limited in extent and thinly spread. In the second half of the century, civilian police or limited local militias rather than troops also became the principal agents of law and order. It was thus essential for empire to rest in large part on a blend of inertia and consent, on the collaboration— active or passive—of influential local leaders and their followers.

Imperial officials therefore adjusted constitutional devices to colonial conditions, ranging in their inventiveness far beyond representative institutions and 'Crown colony' arrangements. Despite the ignominious demise of the East India Company, for example, the model of the chartered company was revived to provide a basic form of administration in parts of Africa and South-East Asia during the 1880s. It provided a sufficient measure of British control and influence together with the inestimable advantage of enabling the imperial government to avoid the heavier costs and responsibilities of outright annexation and direct rule. In promoting the Royal Niger Company (1886) and the British South Africa Company (1889) for this purpose, businessmen such as George Goldie and Cecil Rhodes tried to exploit government's predicament for their personal entrepreneurial advantage. The 'protectorate' was another device, based initially on negotiation or treaties between nominal equals and including promises of advice and protection, which was exploited to facilitate a wide and flexible range of imperial interventions and ultimate annexation.

Imperial authorities also used their powers of patronage or appointment, the mechanisms of taxation, and the provision of public works, to the same end. Nowhere, perhaps, were they more versatile than in India. In their deployment of the display and ritual associated with the great imperial durbars, beginning with that of 1877 to declare the queen empress of India; in the invention of new orders and decorations like the Star of India; in the passage of legislation to prevent the dispossession of indebted peasants; in the provision of irrigation and the recruitment of soldiers in favoured districts of the Punjab, the British won friends and influenced people.

Empire and the diffusion of British culture

Migration, trade, and investment were the most important agencies of British expansion; likewise, adapted institutions, law, the habits, or necessity of political accommodation, and the formal resources to impose authority when necessary, were very prominent means of imperial control. Nevertheless, significant additional contributions to the construction and management of the nineteenth-century empire were made by a host of what may be broadly labelled 'cultural' activities.

Of particular note in what should be seen as a great age of religious expansion was the part played in various ways by Christianity and the churches. In the early years of this period, imperial and colonial governments still held the view that state authority benefited from the support of organized religion. In response to public insistence, the renewal of the East India Company's charter in 1813 was associated with the establishment of an Anglican diocese and bishop at Calcutta. After the Demerara slave rebellion of 1823, bishoprics were set up in Jamaica and Barbados to support the improvement of slave conditions through providing churches and education. The Church and Schools Corporation was created in New South Wales in 1825 to administer the public lands set aside to finance Anglican churches and schools. However, this policy quickly became unpopular. Scottish Presbyterians, Irish Catholics, Baptists, Methodists, and others of no denominational allegiance resented above all the exclusive privileges which it gave to the Church of England; even Anglican churchmen came to resent the political difficulties of their position and the parsimonious or fitful nature of official backing. On all sides, and especially in Australia, organized pressure grew for the separation of state and church, as it did in Britain itself; in the settler colonies by the 1860s separation had been largely achieved, and elsewhere the principle of religious neutrality—as between, say, Christianity and Islam or Hinduism in India—was commonly appealed to by the colonial authorities. Thus, on the one hand acknowledgement of the strength of settlers' religious sentiments, on the other at least a prudent consideration for the principal non-Christian religions of colonial peoples, made colonial governments more acceptable and demonstrated their growing awareness of the complexity of the societies they ran.

Religious expansion, however, was far less the preserve of churches and governments than the responsibility of voluntary lay societies and individual believers or converts. Here Christian missionary bodies working with non-European peoples were of particular importance. Organizations such as the Church Missionary Society and the Baptist Missionary Society, originally founded in the 1790s, were by the 1840s quite widely respected, and with the aid of growing numbers of converts were entering a second major phase of expansion in different parts of Asia, Africa, and the Pacific. Their contributions to the life and structures of the empire were both many and many-sided. Their employees, such as David Livingstone, Scottish missionary with the London Missionary Society in South and Central Africa, and epic explorer of that continent from 1852 until his death, embodied for many contemporaries the heroic ideals and 'civilizing mission' to which Britain seemed peculiarly dedicated.

Again and again, missionaries eased the early encounters between indigenous societies and the incoming British. They were frequently welcomed as intermediaries, as sources of aid and protection in the face of invaders whose skills, wealth, and knowledge local peoples wished to acquire for their own advantage, but whose power and ambition they feared. Missionaries, already familiar figures and knowing at least something of local languages and protocol, thus played key roles in negotiations, from the Treaty of Waitangi (which led in 1840 to New Zealand becoming a colony) to the agreements which paved the way for Cecil Rhodes and his 'pioneers' in Central Africa in the 1890s. With hindsight they can be seen as having contributed substantially to the extension of colonial rule. Their common preference for 'modernity' and 'progress' defined in essentially British terms frequently went hand in hand with the assumption that colonialism—especially if amenable to missionary influence—was quite the best way forward for all concerned.

In many settings, however, they had also much to offer of direct advantage to indigenous communities. 'Modernity' and 'progress' were often associated with the eighteenth-century enlightenment's concepts of happiness and benevolence, as well as notions of trusteeship and utility. A concern to avoid exploitation fed directly into the humanitarianism frequently associated with the approach of many missionaries to colonial rule, as witnessed in the careers of Dr John Philip and John Mackenzie in southern Africa during the 1830s and 1880s. Missionaries' work with vernacular languages, to many of which they gave a written form for the first time; their schools, printing presses, workshops, and later their hospitals; all brought knowledge and skills at least capable of easing local hardship if not of opening up entirely new worlds and opportunities. Nowhere was this more evident than in the cases of the poor and persecuted—the freed slaves or 'recaptives' who were settled at Freetown in Sierra Leone, the Khoi people struggling against the oppressive labour demands of Cape settlers, or members of depressed castes and bonded labourers in south Indian villages.

Sierra Leone's creole society was especially notable but by no means alone in welcoming the missions for the education they brought, fully recognizing its value for far more than evangelism. Fourah Bay College in Freetown became affiliated to Durham University in 1876, conferred British degrees, and opened the way to professional careers for many West Africans. The career of the Yoruba freed slave, Samuel Ajayi Crowther, led him via Freetown and a tutorship at Fourah Bay to consecration at Lambeth in 1864 as the first African bishop in the Anglican church. Mission schooling to a lower level provided the basis for a host of other occupations—for example, in trading, clerical work for commercial and government offices, and school-teaching. This British education provided the social cement for a colonial African middle class throughout West Africa. The educated elite itself not only contributed to the functioning of colonial society. By the end of the century its members were of crucial importance in defining new local identities and in organizing political opposition to British rule, such as was articulated by the Aborigines' Rights Protection Society on the Gold Coast.

Similar patterns were discernible in British colonial Asia, not least in commercial and administrative centres from Bombay to Hong Kong where knowledge of the English language was at a premium. If Scottish missionaries like Alexander Duff took the lead in promoting English-language education in India, they were very soon followed by Indians themselves and by the government of India. However, Christian beliefs played a far smaller part in directly shaping responses to British rule in India than was the case in colonial Africa. Converts were relatively few, and explicitly Christian teaching was often deeply resented. Educated Indians, both Hindus and Muslims, instead often turned their acquaintance with Western learning and Christian ideas towards the reform and revival of their own religious beliefs and practices. However, in British India as in British Africa, albeit in different ways, religious encounters were thus similarly instrumental in encouraging resilience and self-confidence on the part of indigenous peoples in the face of colonial control. Britain's religious expansion not only provided the language and additional opportunities for collaboration between rulers and rule; it also offered further means, and stimulated the capacity, for resisting imperial authority.

Closely linked to questions of religion and education in the colonial diffusion of British culture was the position of women and children. When they left Britain, whether as permanent migrants or as temporary expatriates, most men probably wished, and many women expected, to recreate metropolitan patterns of gender, class, status, and occupation in their new colonial settings. This was more easily achieved by some than others, for instance by white settlers in colonial towns relatively untroubled by indigenous populations, or by officials or businessmen and their families living within a more or less closed community of their own. However, colonial conditions inevitably both imposed their own limitations and created new opportunities, everywhere modifying 'British' ways of life in the process.

In white settler societies, the relative youth of the population and the disproportionate numbers of men immediately transformed the circumstances of families and women; the scarcity of servants, the cost especially of skilled workers, and the variable availability of consumables, rapidly challenged assumptions as to necessities and standards of living, or broke down conventional divisions of responsibility by age or gender. Non-European societies were frequently judged by the manner in which they appeared to treat their women. Few survived the comparison with British—predominantly middle-class—ways: the seclusion and restraints imposed on Muslim women, the inordinate labour required of African women by their 'idle' menfolk, harems, and polygamy were seen as highlighting their lack of 'civilized' standards. Yet in setting out to change indigenous ways, through education, religious conversion, or the promotion of government-sponsored social reforms, British women often found themselves taking on initiatives and responsibilities far in excess of anything they might have contemplated at home.

British capacity to understand and work with the grain of local societies increased with time, albeit patchily. This arose both from the growth of their own knowledge and familiarity with those they ruled, and as indigenous people themselves came to understand the British better and either adopted Western ideas and attitudes or adapted them to their own advantage. A nineteenth-century explosion of colonial information contributed to this process in myriad ways, more readily perhaps in colonial Asia than in Africa. It did so through the increase in exploration and travel; by the spread of scholarly investigation of languages, religions, and cultures; from the mapping and survey of colonial landscapes and resources; with the development of anthropological classification aided by the ten-yearly censuses; and in every case by the dissemination of this information via books, periodicals, and learned societies. Even as the spread of knowledge slowly enriched British understanding, it also made possible the tightening of colonial controls.

From time to time, of course, the British miscalculated in pursuit of their ruling ambitions, and even when they did not, there were continually changes beyond their control which had to be anticipated and accommodated. This was true no less of white settler colonies than the tropical dependencies. People in Britain were slow, for example, to appreciate the nineteenth-century growth of local patriotism and distinct or separate identities in settler societies. There, professions of continued attachment to Britain as 'home' were perfectly compatible with a 'nationalistic' pride in their own achievements—in Australia's greater democracy and New Zealand's advanced social welfare provision, for example—or with a sense of their modernity when compared with the customs of the 'old' country. In these settings, such misunderstandings easily caused offence; in others, more culturally or racially charged, offence could rapidly lead to serious violence. Failure to grapple effectively with Canadian troubles in the 1830s left the imperial government with a rebellion on its hands in French-speaking Quebec. At the same time Afrikaners shook off the dust of the Cape Colony in their Great Trek northwards, and later twice went to war to ward off imperial controls. In the non-European world, colonial incomprehension or refusal to respect local customary rights frequently led the British into armed conflict. For a start, they provoked the great set-piece struggles of the century: the Indian Mutiny (1857), the Morant Bay rebellion in Jamaica (1865), the Zulu War (1879), the Irish land war (1880–82), the Sierra Leone Hut Tax War (1898), and the Boxer Rising in China (1899–1901). Furthermore, beneath these lay a host of lesser engagements, above all on the frontiers of settler societies in southern and central Africa, but also in the east and west, where 'pacification' euphemistically followed scramble and partition.

External challenges to the British position

It would be easy to conclude, from the comparative absence of major European conflicts in the nineteenth century, that Britain faced no significant external challenges to her dominant position or to her basic interests. But such casual hindsight should not be allowed to obscure the real worries of the day. To British governments the rapid recovery after 1815 of their old enemy, France, was cause for concern; suspicions based on ancient hostility were stimulated by the continuing volatility of French domestic politics and the propensity of her leaders and elite groups to indulge in adventures overseas. Flurries of French expansion occurred in the 1840s, not least in the Pacific; in Central America in the 1860s; in sub-Saharan Africa, especially from the late 1870s onwards; and in Indo-China. The European balance of power and French imperial ambitions were also interwoven in her perpetual preoccupation with the condition of Italy, and in a desire to control the Mediterranean by promoting her interests from Morocco to the Levant. As France felt herself increasingly threatened in the second half of the century by the rise of Germany in Europe, so the challenge she seemed to pose to British interests became steadily more serious.

If British observers were inclined to suspect the French of concerted plans to undermine or upstage them, they took them the more seriously because of similar threats from other quarters. Russia's own lack of sympathy with Britain and the collapse of their temporary collaboration were plain by 1820. Thereafter Russia's own designs rapidly emerged as no less a challenge to Britain's position than were those of the French. In British eyes the Russians were aiming at control of Ottoman Turkey in order to establish their presence in the eastern Mediterranean, and were encroaching on Persia and Afghanistan with a view ultimately to threatening Britain's possessions in India. To some extent Russian goals constituted a challenge to French interests as much as British, and so contributed to Anglo-French cooperation against Russia in the Crimean War (1854–56). More often, however, Britain had little choice but to counter her European rivals individually—France, especially in Egypt starting from the crisis of 1839–41, and Russia on numerous occasions both in Turkey and in Central Asia, beginning with the First Afghan War of 1839–42.

After 1870, Britain found the containment of these traditional rivals very difficult. France, humiliated by Prussia in the war of 1870 and feeling embattled and frustrated inside Europe, not only looked for compensation overseas but in the process increasingly aligned herself diplomatically and economically with Russia. Russia not only continued to confront Britain in the Ottoman Empire and in Central Asia, but emerged as a powerful competitor in the Far East. The Franco-Russian alliance, finally completed at the end of 1893, in effect confronted Britain along a line running from the English Channel via Gibraltar, the Mediterranean, the Near East and India's North-West Frontier, Siam (Thailand) and southern China, to Manchuria. It generated crises in 1885, 1891, 1893, and 1898, which were the more disturbing given the possibility that British entanglement with French interests elsewhere, in Africa or the Pacific, might also have repercussions for Britain in threats to her interests at almost any point along this divide.

New states also entered the field after 1870. Germany, Italy, and even an atavistically aggressive if ultimately feeble Portugal, not only impacted on the European balance by reinforcing the Franco-Russian alignment but developed their own imperial and colonial ambitions in competition with Britain, especially in Africa.

The range of her commercial and strategic interests made it impossible for Britain to ignore either the growing reality of Great Power aggrandizement or the possible consequences of weaker powers' fundamental fragility. For example, the Ottoman Empire's perennial weakness and, from the mid-1870s, its anticipated collapse, attracted the attention of France and Russia, both anxious to strengthen their power over Britain's Mediterranean trade and to threaten her communications with the East; Russian penetration into Persia and Afghanistan seemed likely to destabilize India's frontiers and, it was feared after the Mutiny, even British India itself. Spanish imperial decline and Portuguese bankruptcy might end in the establishment of new French or German spheres abutting on British territory in various parts of Africa. Few British politicians in the 1880s were as equable as Gladstone in his feeling that Africa offered room enough for all comers.

Britain's distractions evidently provided other powers' opportunities. This the United States demonstrated by intervention in Samoa and Venezuela, as well as by her territorial gains in 1898 in the Caribbean and parts of the Pacific Ocean. The Germans exploited British isolation in 1898 to their own advantage in Portuguese Africa and the Far East. Intervention in regions of British interest outside Europe itself was attractive to Britain's rivals. They saw in Britain's material strength something which made her influence and support desirable, with the result that at different times France and Germany both tried to edge Britain into their own alliance system in order to tip the balance of power inside Europe in their favour.

The defence of Britain's position

It remains conventional, as it was at the time, to regard Britain's empire as a source not only of considerable wealth but of world power. In reality this was only partly true, for empire also made her appear to others as a threat, an object of fear and envy. Ultimately Britain was also open to attack in Europe and at home because her major imperial interests were themselves at risk from being so far-flung. The need to acquire and to defend overseas colonial territory was frequently indistinguishable from the protection of the commerce and trade routes on which the United Kingdom itself depended, and the costs of defence were high. For much of the century more than one-third of the imperial government's expenditure went on defence. The difficulties of drawing on colonial forces even for comparatively local operations were at all times considerable. Inescapably both a Continental European and a global power, Britain was therefore constantly facing awkward decisions as to where her forces should be concentrated, and vulnerable to the fact that their concentration in any one theatre might leave her dangerously exposed elsewhere.

Diplomacy offered the first line of defence, and responsibility for the peaceful adjustment of international rivalries, security issues, and economic competition rested with the Foreign Office. The imperial government operated directly through its ambassadors in the most important capitals such as Paris, St Petersburg, or Constantinople, and elsewhere through hierarchical networks of ministers, consuls, political agents, or other lesser officials. At the centre of the stage, foreign secretaries dealt with an enormous range of responsibilities, which included not only the negotiation of treaties, war, and peace but also intelligence, commercial relations, slave trade diplomacy, and issues of extra-territorial rights and jurisdiction. The East India Company and, after 1858, the Government of India performed similar functions within their own geographical sphere. This included not only relations with many of India's princely states and British India's external neighbours (Afghanistan, Nepal), but the Persian Gulf and other territories around the Indian Ocean. A British agent, for instance, established at Zanzibar in 1841, came under the government of Bombay until 1873, as did ports such as Aden (1839); to the east, Calcutta controlled relations with the Straits Settlements (1826–67) and Burma.

The War Office and the Admiralty were responsible for strategic planning and the overall military and naval defence of Britain, together with its trade routes and possessions abroad. Expansion increased the need for troops and ships, and technological changes had to be absorbed if weapons were to be kept up to date and rivals were to be deterred or defeated. However, parliamentary concern to save money, inter-service disputes, and colonial expectations that Britain should pay, meant that defence policies were often less the product of long-term planning than the haphazard results of political conflict. London came to rely increasingly on the use of Indian troops abroad. Despite the reforms of Earl Grey and Edward Cardwell in the 1840s and 1860s, the coordination of Britain's armed forces and their integration into broader defensive structures or processes of imperial policy-making developed only slowly. Extensive modernization only came as a consequence of the disasters of the South African War (1899–1902), when a war which seemed quickly won turned into a teasing struggle of attrition, with farming families herded into 'concentration camps' and the imperial idea humiliated.

Until the 1840s Britain's pre-eminence was secured without undue difficulty by a fortuitous combination of her own diplomatic efforts and the limited power or internal distractions of her rivals. Her naval supremacy went unchallenged, signalled as it was by the major concentration of her warships in the home and Mediterranean stations, and until the mid-1830s spending on the navy and the army declined dramatically from the levels of 1815–20. At Queen Victoria's accession in 1837, nearly 90 000 troops, paid for out of British domestic taxes, were mostly dispersed around the empire in about 40 colonial garrisons; in India it was possible to maintain a further huge army of some 45 000 British troops and 230 000 Indian sepoys, by paying for it from local revenues.

The rise in levels of international tension which lasted intermittently from c.1840, linked to sporadic fears of invasion and the possibilities opened up by long distance steam shipping, prompted the complete overhaul of at least the military aspects of this system. Fundamental principles designed to meet the changed conditions were first set out in 1846 by the Whig secretary of state for the colonies,

Earl Grey, and were gradually refined and implemented with the aid of further reviews in 1859–61 and the determination of Edward Cardwell at the War Office in the Liberal government of 1868–74. With the exception of those retained in a small number of designated 'imperial bases' such as Halifax (Nova Scotia) and Malta, imperial troops were to be concentrated in Britain, available for dispatch to wherever they were required. It was expected that the white colonies, increasingly self-governing, would take on responsibility for their own internal defence, for the maintenance of defence installations, and even for a measure of external defence. As a consequence of the Mutiny in 1857, the Indian army was also completely remodelled, notably by a reduction in size to 180 000 and an increase in the proportion of British troops to sepoys to 1:2. The navy was not much involved in these changes. It was nevertheless to some extent modernized, expanded, and far more widely deployed, with fewer vessels in the Mediterranean, and many more in the North Atlantic and the Far East.

Despite some colonial protests, particularly from New Zealand and the Cape Colony involved in wars with their indigenous peoples, these adaptations brought about an apparent sharing of imperial defence burdens broadly acceptable even to those who, like Disraeli in the 1850s, had tended to see in colonial expenditure without proper control a complete waste of resources. Nevertheless, they were rapidly overtaken by events. French rearmament and renewed overseas expansion from the mid-1870s coincided with local wars in South Africa and the Second Afghan War between 1879 and 1881. Together with the still more serious Russian war scare arising out of the Turkish crisis of 1875–78, they prompted the establishment in 1879 of a royal commission under Lord Carnarvon to review 'the defence of British possessions and commerce abroad'.

Far more comprehensive in many respects than its predecessors, the commission's two secret reports in 1881–82 established the overriding importance of developing a tightly coordinated system of imperial and colonial defence, including all forces and a worldwide network of telegraphs, coaling stations, and bases. The navy was the most immediate beneficiary. Buoyed up by a major public agitation against 'Gladstonian' neglect of defence in 1884 as well as by professional lobbying, and adopting as the yardstick of adequate naval provision a British ability to match the combined forces of any two rival powers, both political parties proceeded to increase naval expenditure. Extensive building programmes were pushed ahead in 1889 and 1894.

The army's response to Carnarvon's agenda was more muted. Improved training, weaponry, and administration, pushed through by the 'Wolseley ring'—a new generation of ambitious officers associated with Lord Wolseley—were not in themselves sufficient to overcome two important limiting conditions: the widespread assumption that the army's role was restricted to little more than a succession of small colonial wars, and the relative ease with which the Indian army could be mobilized to cover any shortfall. Rather than corrupting British political life, as critics of Disraeli feared in the 1870s, the existence of Indian forces tended instead to inhibit clear thinking and reform of the British army at home. Late-century theatres in which Indian troops were used included China (1860, 1900), Abyssinia (1868), Perak (1875–76), Egypt (1882), Burma (1886), Nyasa (1893), Uganda (1896), the Sudan (1885, 1896–98), and even the South African War. Such reliance was only seriously questioned once the imperial government found itself obliged to contribute significantly to the costs of such expeditions after 1898. Reform was further hampered by the reactionary commander-in-chief from 1856 to 1895: the Duke of Cambridge who, as the queen's cousin, was held to be irremovable.

Carnarvon's plea for integration and the persistent imperial use of Indian troops were, however, also symptoms of a deeper problem than mere unimaginative leadership or institutional inflexibility. They pointed to the incontrovertible evidence that, after 1870, Britain's relative economic ascendancy was being eroded by the growth of her Great Power rivals, such as Germany and the United States; that the political economy of free trade which had served her so well now seemed less capable of sustaining her international competitiveness, especially as other industrializing states (even including her own self-governing colonies) steadily turned to economic protectionism; and that the imperial government's existing resources were less and less adequate to meet the swelling demands being made upon them both at home and abroad. Rather than finding herself in the vanguard of expansion, Britain was gradually being pushed onto the defensive in respect both of her empire and her position in the world.

The best example of this mounting defensiveness is provided by Britain's participation in the partition of Africa, something which came to seem increasingly necessary for the protection of what either were already significant national interests or might perhaps become so. The pressures on Britain to depart from her previously limited presence on the coasts came from several directions. Especially in north and west Africa, many societies were finding it increasingly difficult to contain the local social and economic changes and political demands generated by the growth of trade with Europe. Economic fluctuations and political instability, conflicts between local rulers, their merchants, and British commercial interests, all produced demands for imperial intervention. So, too, did the mounting interest of protectionist states like France and Portugal, whose concern with territory seemed designed to secure exclusive access for their own nationals to large areas of the continent. In the south, east, and north of the continent, while economic interests played parts of varying importance, Britain's wish to limit the incursions of European rivals, even at the expense of occupation or annexation, is ultimately only explicable if one recognizes her vital strategic concern with the safety of the Cape and Suez routes to India and the east. In Africa and elsewhere, however, such late-century annexations rarely if ever paid for themselves; normally they only exacerbated the general problems of security and expense, causing Gladstone, for instance, to lament 'the Plagues of Egypt'. Writing to the secretary of state for India in January 1885, he complained how the 'Egyptian flood comes upon us again and again like the sea on the host of Pharaoh, which had just as much business to pursue the Israelites as we have to meddle [there].'

It was to address these problems that many people turned after 1880 to the reordering of the empire as a whole. As a sign of the times, the Imperial Federation League was founded in 1884; with its goals of imperial political consolidation, imperial economic cooperation, and a fully integrated system of imperial defence, it posed a fundamental challenge to the free-trading, *laissez-faire* practices and often centrifugal tendencies of the previous half-century. At the heart of its vision of empire as the key to Britain's future in a world of ever larger states were the white settler colonies.

Support for these ideas came from many quarters—from front-rank politicians such as Lord Rosebery and Joseph Chamberlain, defence experts, administrators such as Sir Alfred Milner, and industrialists with an eye on imperial markets. There were also indications of colonial interest. The Australian Naval Agreement of 1887 showed colonial politicians willing to cooperate in pursuit of the security they felt they lacked. The Colonial Economic Conference in Ottawa in 1894 and Canadian economic policy thereafter held out the promise of a preferential system embracing the empire as a whole. Finally, the presence of more than 30 000 Canadians, Australians, and New Zealanders fighting on the imperial side in the South African War was widely interpreted as promising much for the future.

In the 1890s the extent to which Britain's future was to depend on the structure of her empire had emerged as one of the great questions of the age. The vigour with which British leaders defended imperial interests in South Africa, to the point of engaging with the Transvaal in the last, and by far the greatest, colonial war of the century, owed much to their concern to hold the country within the empire. That war exposed Britain's weaknesses—her military unpreparedness, her lack of dependable allies—to an unexpected and embarrassing degree, and resulted in a 'new course' for Britain's foreign policy, the search for security in Europe by association with France and Russia. Nevertheless, the commitment of almost half-a-million men and the unprecedented sum of £250 000 000 was perhaps not such a high price to pay for the conquest of the Afrikaner republics if it kept open the prospect of a united empire. Although the break-up of the Imperial Federation League itself in disputes over practical arrangements, and the lukewarm response of colonial prime ministers at the Colonial Conference in London in 1897, turned out to be more accurate omens of things to come, in 1901 the issue was still undecided and to many the prospect for the twentieth century seemed fair.

Plate 6
Windsor Castle in Modern Times. Edwin Landseer's painting (1840–45) shows Victoria, Albert and the Princess Royal (born 1840). Its domestic intimacy was new in royal portraiture. The Queen hung it in her sitting room and was well-satisfied: 'a very beautiful picture, and altogether very cheerful and pleasing'.

4

Gender, domesticity, and sexual politics

Janet Howarth

Relations between the sexes—issues of gender and sexuality—and the ideal of domesticity became, more than ever before, a preoccupation for the British in the nineteenth century. It was rooted in the political and economic upheavals of the first half of the century and the religious revival that accompanied them, sustained by later reform movements and encouraged by the unprecedented growth in powers to police and discipline the people. An insistent theme in public debate and policy became the links between sexual and social order. The patriarchal conjugal family, man and wife, each acting within their proper sphere, and the containment of sexuality within legal matrimony, became the keystones of social stability and moral progress. Post-Freudian and postmodernist perspectives have encouraged historians to ask how far we can take this repressive discourse at face value. How far did it reflect social practice? More so, perhaps, in relation to the control of sexuality than in the 'separate spheres' prescribed for men and women and, again, more so—in the long run at least—for the poorer than the more prosperous classes. If we can give only provisional answers to these questions it is at least becoming clearer how the domestic ideology of the nineteenth century and its associated sexual disciplines first gained their hold on the public mind, as perceptions of the French Revolution and the social consequences of industrialization sharpened, and sometimes changed, perspectives on the family and sexuality.

The origins of Victorian domestic ideology

Some elements in this domestic ideology were in fact inherited from earlier centuries. Patriarchal family values were embedded in English common law. Its courts did not recognize married women as legal persons. Unless she had the protection of a marriage settlement a wife could own no property; her debts were the responsibility of her husband and he had an absolute right to custody of their children. Nor was eighteenth-century society as lax in its sexual morality as the Victorians often supposed. Church courts had powers to discipline parishioners for fornication and adultery (they continued sporadically to do so in some parts of England and Scotland until the mid-nineteenth century). An attempt was made in 1754 to tighten control over marriage by Lord Hardwicke's Act, which gave the Anglican Church a monopoly (from which only Quakers and Jews were exempted) over the performance of legally recognized marriage ceremonies in England and Wales. The Anglican evangelical mission to reform the manners and morals of society that gained momentum after 1800 was launched by William Wilberforce, Hannah More, and the Clapham Sect in the 1780s. Driven by religious conviction, their belief that results would be achieved through the influence of women nevertheless owed much to the secular culture of the eighteenth century. The polite sociability of the gentry and urban elites, the concern of Enlightenment thinkers with education and child development and the Romantic sentimentalization of motherhood all encouraged a new sensitivity to women's domestic influence. This was to be a characteristic feature of nineteenth-century understandings of the moral economy of the family. Patriarchal in form, it nevertheless encompassed a sphere in which feminine influence was crucially important.

The French Revolution gave a new urgency to these evangelical concerns with morality and women's family roles. In the first place it politicized vice. Marie Antoinette was charged with adultery, lesbianism, and incest before she was sent to the guillotine. The Terror suggested the possible fate of decadent aristocracies. 'The awakening of the labouring classes after the first shocks of the French Revolution, made the upper classes tremble', commented Lady Shelley.

'Every man felt the necessity for putting his house in order' (cited by
C. Hall in R. Shoemaker and M. Vincent, *Gender and History in
Western Europe* (1998)). By the 1820s there was also a new sense of the
association between claims to citizenship and respectability, between
civic and sexual virtue, amongst plebeian Radicals such as the
artisans of Francis Place's circle. The Revolution also politicized gender. The French Constitution of 1791 did away with aristocratic privilege in the name of the 'Rights of Man', but it introduced a new
principle of order and hierarchy by denying women equal citizenship.
Mary Wollstonecraft, an Englishwoman who identified with the revo-
lutionaries of 1789, addressed her *Vindication of the Rights of Woman*
(1792) to Talleyrand, protesting against the exclusion of French-
women from citizen rights and arguing for the equality of the sexes.
Many voices were raised in opposition to this feminist manifesto but
none as influentially as Hannah More's. Her novel *Coelebs in Search
of Wife* (1808) went through 11 editions in nine months and 30 in her
lifetime. Women, More urged, were not equal to men but dependent
upon them and complementary in their feminine duties and virtues.
Both the well-being of society and personal salvation and
happiness—'the almost sacred joys of home' invoked in her poem
'Sensibility'—depended on recognition of the separate spheres of the
sexes.

Malthusianism and sexual morality

One contribution to the debates provoked by the Revolution
amounted to much more than a restatement of evangelical family
values. That was the response of a Cambridge academic, the Reverend
Thomas Robert Malthus, to the libertarian philosopher William
Godwin (to whom Wollstonecraft was briefly married before she died
in childbirth). Godwin's defence of revolution was based on his belief
in human perfectibility: it was society that corrupted human beings
and undermined their natural virtue. In the *Essay on the Principle of
Population* (1798) Malthus offered instead a political economist's
gloss on the Christian doctrine of original sin. The natural tendency
of population was to increase at an exponential rate, whereas the
production of food could increase only at a steady, arithmetical rate.

Left to itself, without social disciplines, the human race would breed to the point of universal misery, its numbers kept in check only by famine, disease, and war. This was a vision that seemed all too plausible in the years of high prices, rising poor rates, and intermittent famine in Ireland during and after Britain's wars with France. Malthus revived an association, more common in the Middle Ages than in the eighteenth century, between sin and procreation—with the expectation, unless sexuality was prudently regulated, of divinely ordained retribution.

Malthusianism became linked to domestic ideology in the public mind in two ways. On the one hand anxieties about procreation came to pervade the handbooks and medical literature that dealt with marital sex, encouraging an emphasis on self-restraint—and in some cases a belief, calculated to promote that virtue in husbands, that women took no pleasure in sex. Popular manuals such as *Aristotle's Master-Piece* (a seventeenth-century compilation that went through many editions in the following two centuries) now provided less explicit physical detail and dwelt on the sentimental rather than the erotic pleasures of marriage. But there was also a new emphasis on the special need for control over the reproductive habits of the poor. The only 'preventive' check on population growth sanctioned by Malthus was the traditional strategy of discouraging early marriage and intercourse outside marriage (artificial methods of birth control became associated with Malthusianism only in the last quarter of the century). Here there were implications for social policy. Population control was about the disciplines of family formation and required the poor to learn the habits of their betters. Reform of the Poor Laws became the means of instruction. The Scottish evangelical divine Thomas Chalmers tried unsuccessfully to persuade Parliament that public poor relief should simply be abolished. But the Poor Law Amendment Act of 1834 did away with the right to outdoor relief and underlined the husband's prime responsibility for supporting his family by requiring wives of destitute men to follow them into the workhouse. It also introduced a much harsher policy than had been customary towards unmarried mothers. Not only were they ineligible for outdoor relief but they also lost the right to sue the father for maintenance for their children. At the same time, by the Marriage Act of 1836, it was made easier for the poor to legalize their unions: Nonconformist ministers could now perform the marriage ceremony and the option of civil marriage became available.

Within the century these policies were remarkably successful in promoting a norm of married respectability in the plebeian classes, for whom in the past—and increasingly in the era of industrialization—common law marriage and (where work was plentiful for women) single mothers had been entirely acceptable. According to one modern estimate, in the early years of the century over a half of all first-born children were conceived, and almost a fifth were born, outside marriage. By the 1890s (although premarital pregnancy remained common in some parts of the country) recorded illegitimacy rates had fallen as low as 4% of live births in England and Wales and 7% in Scotland. At the same time this crackdown on illegitimacy at the expense of poor unmarried mothers led to a sharp increase in cases of infanticide—as late as 1895 231 dead babies were found in the course of the year in the streets of London—and, in the later years of the century, to a panic about increased rates of abortion.

Separate spheres and domesticity

As for the doctrine of 'separate spheres' for the sexes, that central tenet of Victorian domestic moralists, its social impact is less easily traced and yet there is no doubt that it became very widely diffused. Women and girls were the audience chiefly addressed in sermons and tracts, fiction, magazines, and advice books that prescribed womanly, submissive roles, while always dwelling on the importance of feminine qualities and the duties and the dignity of motherhood. This became a common theme in most religious traditions. 'The *great* and *weighty* business of life devolves on *men*, but important business belongs to *women* . . . Society does best when each sex performs the duties for which it is especially ordained': so ran the message of a Church of Ireland sermon delivered in Dublin in 1856, and cited by Maria Luddy in *Women in Ireland, 1800–1918* (1995). 'Mothers! arise in the greatness of your power, in the splendours of your strength, and be the regenerators of the world', wrote the Roman Catholic nun of Kenmare, Margaret Anna Cusack. Among English Nonconformists a leading early exponent of domestic ideology was the Birmingham

Independent minister John Angell James, whose prayer meetings for mothers foreshadowed the Anglican Mothers' Union (founded in 1876). Quakers and Unitarians, who stood aside from early nineteenth-century evangelicalism, retained their more sexually egalitarian values: women Friends continued to be recognized as ministers, while such Radical Unitarian journals as the *Monthly Repository* (1806–38) carried articles, often by women writers, exploring gender roles in the context of beliefs about human perfectibility. But the popular religious traditions that encouraged women preachers in the eighteenth century—early Methodism, the millenarian gospel of Joanna Southcott, who proclaimed that the Second Coming would overthrow the curse of Eve—died out or re-established gender boundaries. Wesleyan Methodists banned women from preaching to mixed congregations in 1803. It was not until the last quarter of the century that the role of the woman preacher was revived by the former Methodists William and Catherine Booth and the uniformed 'Hallelujah Lasses' of the Salvation Army.

Magazines for a domestic readership and suffused with the ethos of domesticity abounded. Well-known examples are Charles Dickens' *Household Words* (1850–59) and Charlotte M. Yonge's magazine for girls, *The Monthly Packet* (1851–91). The same message, in the idiom of chapel culture, was conveyed by the first Welsh magazines for women, *Y Gymraes* (started in 1850 to fend off allegations of immorality in Wales in the aftermath of the Rebecca riots) and the more successful *Y Frythones* (1879–89), edited by the temperance reformer and poet Sarah Jane Rees (also known by the bardic name Cranogwen). Among writers of secular advice literature none was more popular than Sarah Stickney Ellis, author of a series of books between 1838 and 1843 addressed to the women, daughters, wives, and mothers of England. Modern readers tend to notice particularly Mrs Ellis' realistic and cautionary tone: she reflects, sometimes pessimistically, on the woman's experience of the patriarchal family and gives advice on how to make the best of it. A more positive symbol of idealized womanliness was provided by the young Queen Victoria— moved to tears at her proclamation as queen, 'married as a woman, not as Queen' in a ceremony in which she vowed obedience to Albert, and depicted in Edwin Landseer's much reproduced painting of *Windsor Castle in Modern Times* (1841) in her family circle, with husband, baby, and dogs.

Hannah More had in mind chiefly the gentry when she wrote that 'the profession of ladies is that of daughters, wives, mothers and mistresses of families'. But domestic ideology appealed equally to the middle classes. For the successful tradesman, who began married life living over the shop, often with his wife's help in building up the business, the move to a house away from the workplace and the ability to support wife and family marked a gain in status. The home was charged with meaning as a refuge from the competitive, insecure, amoral world of the market. As the popular mid-Victorian maxim went, an Englishman's home was his castle. In John Ruskin's *Sesame and Lilies* (1865) it was 'the place of Peace, the shelter, not only from all injury, but from all terror, doubt and division'. Within the country houses of the gentry and the suburban houses of the upper middle classes, moreover, space was increasingly used to delineate separate spheres for members of the household. There were nurseries and schoolrooms for the children; servants' quarters—behind closed doors, in basements and in attics—and also gendered spaces: studies, libraries, smoking or billiards rooms for men, drawing rooms and boudoirs for the mistress of the house. Fashions in dress, meanwhile, exaggerated sexual difference. As men adopted the sober, functional uniform of dark trousers and jacket, women's dress passed through a series of fashions that accentuated their disabilities: tight-lacing (at its most extreme in the 1830s and 1870s), up to seven layers of petticoats in the 1840s, the crinoline from the 1850s, the bustle in the 1870s and 1880s. The coat, skirt, and blouse came into fashion as a practical day dress only in the 1890s.

Yet for business and professional families, as for the gentry, the role of women was always a matter of real consequence. They played their part both in the formation of the middle classes and in mediating class tensions. Much that lay within a wife's province affected the family's social standing, including transactions with neighbours and the local community and the practicalities of maintaining an appropriate lifestyle: the management of servants and the physical environment of the home, the deportment of children, keeping up appearances. Although the advice literature often exhorted middle-class women not to imitate the leisured lifestyle of the 'fine lady', conceptions of the woman's sphere were in some respects modelled on the roles of wives and daughters in the landed upper classes. Charitable and philanthropic work was always seen as falling within it. At one end of the social scale, there were wives of industrialists who played an active part in 'factory paternalism', such as the south Wales ironmasters' wives Lady Charlotte Guest and Rose Mary Crawshay, or Caroline Colman, wife of the Norwich mustard manufacturer. But charitable fund-raising and activities such as visiting the poor or Sunday school teaching became a normal feature of the lives of middle-class women. In 1893 it was estimated that about half a million women were working on a regular, quasi-professional basis as volunteers in philanthropic institutions.

The male-breadwinner family and women's employment

By that time the domestic ideal had made considerable inroads into the working classes too, although in some senses it merely threw into relief the contrast between the lifestyles of the poor and the better off. The 1891 census revealed that a third of Londoners and as many as two-thirds of the population of Glasgow were living in overcrowded conditions, two or more people to a room. Earlier in the century, however, the difference between classes had a well-recognized cultural as well as material dimension. For plebeian families the sexual division of labour had never entailed the expectation that men would be the only breadwinners. In cottage industry and many other occupations production was a family enterprise, while even the wives of artisans in trades that excluded women would normally have some paid work of their own. In agriculture women's harvest work declined as the heavy sickle replaced the scythe. But where work for women was in short supply this was recognized as a cause of hardship. The introduction of new machinery operated by women and children within cottage industry was seen as beneficial on social as well as economic grounds. Perspectives shifted with the coming of factory industry, which brought with it a crisis for the working-class family. Here workplace and home were separated—but textile factories employed a mainly female and juvenile workforce. A recent study of working-class domestic budgets shows that the contribution of wives and children to family income did, in fact, increase significantly between 1815 and 1835. 'By the action of Modern Industry all family ties among the proletarians are torn asunder'—the verdict of Marx and Engels's *Communist Manifesto* (1848) on the factory system was much the same as that of British evangelical observers, who found the economic independence it gave to women and children quite as appalling as the material conditions in which they worked. Meanwhile, the decline of cottage industry in southern England and in Ireland left families destitute. Domestic service, in other women's homes, became the main form of employment available to women in some parts of the country. It absorbed about a quarter of the paid female workforce in Britain in 1851, but over half in Wales between 1871 and 1901.

The view that the male-breadwinner family *ought* to be the norm for working people gradually gained support among male trades unionists, fighting to protect their jobs and wage rates. In some cases women were forced out of a trade by direct action—as in the London tailors' strike of 1834. There was backing, too, from workers for legislative restrictions on women's work, such as the limitation of their hours of work in Factory Acts from the 1830s, or the 1842 Mines Act which banned them from underground work in coalmines. In terms of the prevailing middle-class domestic ideology the marginalization of women's paid work was a step towards a new moral order in which the sexes would operate each within their proper sphere. How far did this regime become a reality—and was it imposed on working women against their own best interests? The evidence is far from straightforward. The censuses began to record women's occupations only in 1841 and they give an incomplete picture: historians differ as to their reliability as an index of women's full-time employment but there was certainly systematic under-recording of casual, part-time, and home-based work and much inconsistency from one decade to another in (for example) the ways in which women's contribution to family enterprises was recorded. For what they are worth, census data point to a gradual but steady fall in the proportion of women in employment from the 1860s on—but with much local variation. In England by 1911 one in ten married women were recorded as employed, but in Wales only one in twenty. As for Ireland, the number of employed females fell by nearly a half between 1861 and 1911 (from 845 000 to 430 000). Such variations are explained to some extent at least by economic rather than ideological factors.

There were industrial areas in which women continued to supply a large (and in some cases increasing) proportion of the manufacturing workforce: the textile towns of Lancashire and Yorkshire, for example; the Midlands potteries; and in Scotland, above all Dundee, centre of the jute industry. By contrast, the expansion of mining and heavy industry in south Wales, the Scottish Lowlands, and northern England created communities in which there was very little work for women. Nowhere in the UK was women's workforce participation lower than in the Rhondda, and the exceptionally high maternal mortality rate in that region suggests that this was not a regime that promoted women's welfare. It was everywhere taken for granted that a breadwinner was entitled to a privileged share of the family diet, especially protein foods and fats. But there is evidence, too, that as men's real wages rose, some women did choose to withdraw from the workforce and become full-time housewives. The average wage for women in Britain in the early twentieth century was less than half that earned by men. Once a husband earned enough to provide a basic subsistence, a wife might do more to improve the family's standard of life by her work within the home. A common saying among English countrywomen in the 1860s was, 'Between the woman that works and the woman that doesn't there is only 6d. to choose at the year's end, and she that stays at home has it.' On the other hand we know from Seebohm Rowntree's study of poverty in York at the turn of the century that the wages of an unskilled labourer were not sufficient to provide for the basic physical needs of a wife and three children. Working-class wives continued to make an essential contribution to the family income in hard times, especially when the children were young. Oral testimony from women of that generation suggests that most of them aspired to be full-time housewives even when this was not possible in practice. It seems clear, at any rate, that domestic ideology had the effect of devaluing women's paid work in the eyes of working women themselves.

In the middle classes, too, there were some single women and widows who had to earn their own living and a few married women who contributed to family income. Just over 30 000 women were recorded as occupied in education in 1841—among them not only family governesses who struggled to survive in an overcrowded market but also proprietors of private schools run on a commercial basis. Writing and the arts offered an expanding market for others. In 1841 some 900 women made a living as artists, musicians, or actresses; fifty years later there were over 17 000 in these occupations. One striking feature of this century was, moreover, the revival throughout Europe of female religious orders. In Catholic Ireland by 1900 a quarter of all women categorized as 'professional' workers were nuns. They had increased in numbers from about 120 at the beginning of the century to about 8000, the great majority in active orders engaged in educational and welfare work. In Britain, where convents had been suppressed in the Reformation, Roman Catholic female orders also found a new role, particularly in the education of Catholic girls: by 1900 there were 8–10 000 Catholic nuns in England alone. A further 2–3000 women belonged to the 54 Anglican sisterhoods that had sprung up since the 1840s and a rather smaller number to low church Protestant deaconesses' organizations. How far should we see these women, economically active or belonging to women's communities, as transgressing against the ethos of domestic ideology? By the end of the century many more were engaged in secular professional work—there was a fivefold increase, for instance, in the number of women in education, by then a thoroughly feminized occupation. Opinions differ, in fact, on the extent to which women were ever really confined to the 'private' sphere of the family or excluded from participation in 'public' life. If sermons and advice literature laboured this theme, might that have been because women were increasingly trespassing across customary gender boundaries?

Gender and politics

The politics of the first two decades of the century tend to support that view. The wars against revolutionary and Napoleonic France engaged women's patriotism. Georgiana, Duchess of Devonshire, who had been sharply criticized in 1784 for her flamboyant electioneering on behalf of Charles James Fox, now worked effectively behind the scenes to bring about the coalition that eventually resulted in the Ministry of All Talents (1806–07), confident that she was merely carrying out a patriotic duty. If war encouraged the cult of masculine heroism and glamourized the military man in uniform, women contributed to the war effort by donating money and clothing, and by making flags and banners for volunteer regiments and ceremonially presenting them with their colours. In post-war reform demonstrations there were echoes of these ritual occasions. At a meeting in Blackburn in June 1819, for example, an ornate cap of liberty, described as 'made of scarlet, silk or satin, lined with green, with a serpentined gold lace, terminating with a rich gold tassel', was presented to the speaker by the town's Female Reform Society. The presence of women at public political meetings of this kind took on a new significance the following month in the Peterloo Massacre, when the crowd was dispersed by a cavalry charge: that brutal assault on popular liberties was all the more effectively denounced because nearly a quarter of the 400 wounded and two of the nine people killed were women. The Queen Caroline affair of 1820 mobilized women of all classes in what Linda Colley sees as a 'woman's cause'. When the notoriously promiscuous George IV attempted to put his estranged wife on trial for adultery in the House of Lords, addresses supporting the queen were signed by tens of thousands of women—among them 17 600 'married ladies' of London and over 9000 women of Edinburgh. Sympathy for Caroline faded when, after plans for the trial were dropped, she claimed the right to be crowned alongside her husband. But this petitioning campaign was the first of its kind since the Civil War in which women took part in large numbers.

It seems that we should not take the metaphor of separate spheres too literally or suppose that women were ever wholly shut out from political processes. They had always (so it appears) been prevented by custom from casting a vote in elections, even when they possessed the necessary property qualifications. But there were some well-established customary political functions for women. In the aristocracy and gentry they played their part in the patronage networks on which the fortunes of families depended and in cultivating the support of electors in constituencies where there was a family interest. They continued to do so as long as the 'old corruption' survived. Few aristocratic women were as deeply involved in high politics as Georgiana Devonshire, but the personal influence of Victorian political hostesses such as Emily, Lady Palmerston, or Frances, Lady Waldegrave should not be underrated. Queen Victoria herself, despite the public image she cultivated as submissive wife or, later, reclusive widow, never ceased to work at her boxes or press her views on ministers. At the other end of the social spectrum, in Britain as in Europe, women—often accompanied by men in women's clothes—

took part in demonstrations, such as food riots, that were about the defence of family and community. This, too, was a tradition that continued into the nineteenth century, surviving longest in its classic form in agrarian protest in Scotland and Ireland. When tenants resisted the clearances on Scottish highland and island estates women were often placed in the front line. As late as 1881 at Tullamore six Irishwomen were imprisoned for violently beating a process server, taking the process from him and throwing it in the canal. The Rebecca riots of 1838–44 in south-west Wales involved chiefly male tenant farmers, dressed in women's clothes, or 'turncoats'—'Rebecca' was a scriptural image, suggested by a passage in the book of Genesis (24:60)—but women joined in the attack on the Carmarthen work-house that ended in a pitched battle with the army. In England, too, the Anti-Poor Law movement drew on the support of women. Tradi-tions of community protest in times of hardship fed into political demonstrations of a more programmatic kind, as in the agitation of the 1810s when high prices and unemployment were blamed on cor-ruption. 'The lazy Boroughmongering Eagles of destruction have nearly pecked bare the bones of those who labour'—so charged the Manchester Female Reformers in an address of 1819 (cited in R. and E. Frow, *Political Women 1800–1850*, p. 24).

For women of the middle and upper-middle classes a new form of involvement in public affairs came with the anti-slavery movement that began in the 1780s and resumed its campaign (which was sus-pended during the war years) when a new British Anti-Slavery Soci-ety was formed in 1823. This was a movement that evangelicals made their own, regarding slavery as a moral and religious rather than political issue. The help of women was essential in organizing boy-cotts of slave-grown sugar. It seemed fitting, too, that women should make their protest against the physical abuse of women slaves. 'Man-kind expects, that Women should sympathise with Women', wrote one supporter of the cause. Precedents were, however, set. Later polit-ical pressure groups, notably the Anti-Corn Law League, made use of women's control over household consumption to organize 'special dealing' campaigns against political opponents. The British Ladies' Society for Promoting the Reformation of Female Prisoners founded in 1821 by the Quaker Elizabeth Fry was an independent women's venture that took up the theme of women's compassion for women, but this time on behalf of their own countrywomen. By 1827 it had 34 branches in the UK. Within the anti-slavery movement itself women had by that stage begun to take initiatives. An early challenge to the cautious strategy of the Anti-Slavery Society, the pamphlet that demanded *Immediate, not Gradual Abolition* (1824), was published anonymously by the Leicester Quaker Elizabeth Heyrick. The following year the Female Society for Birmingham was formed, the first in a network of independent ladies' societies. By the 1830s a third of all UK anti-slavery societies were run by women. Precedents were set, too, by women's petitions to Parliament, breaching the convention that petitions to the legislature (as distinct from the Crown) should be signed by men only. There were over 400 000 female signatures to petitions for the abolition of slavery in 1833, amounting to nearly a third of the total number of signatures. After the ending of slavery in the British Empire, when men's interest in the issue declined, the ladies' societies forged links with the movement in the United States. Harriet Beecher Stowe's *Uncle Tom's Cabin* sold a million copies within a year of its publication in Britain in 1852; and Harriet Martineau and Elizabeth Barrett Browning were among the literary celebrities who wrote powerfully in support of the cause (on this, see C. Midgley, *Women Against Slavery*, 1992).

What significance can we attach to these female encroachments upon the 'public sphere'? The boundaries between male and female territory were unstable. They shifted gradually and not without resistance. William Wilberforce opposed the formation of ladies' societies, believing that women should be content to work under the leadership of men. John Angell James opposed women's canvassing or house-to-house visiting to collect money for good causes. One female supporter of the anti-slavery movement in Edinburgh complained in 1840 that 'a woman who holds really liberal opinions . . . is shunned as unfeminine and that [one] then is obliged constantly to converse on the most indifferent topics or else hold one's peace.' Public speaking by women to mixed audiences remained very rare. A pioneer in the 1840s was the temperance lecturer Clara Lucas Balfour, but the first anti-slavery speaker to break this taboo was the black American lecturer Sarah Parker Remond who toured the UK in 1859–61. At the London meeting of the World Anti-Slavery Convention in 1840 the men resolved to exclude women from the floor of the assembly, banishing them to their accustomed place at debates in the spectators' gallery—the incident that provoked the American feminists Lucretia Mott and Elizabeth Cady Stanton to launch the women's rights movement in the United States. By custom the public sphere did, after all, 'belong' to men, and they had the power to insist on their prerogatives. Elizabeth Fry and others who followed her example in seeking to reform conditions for women in public institutions—prisons, asylums, hospitals, workhouses—often ran into obstacles. Where the men in charge of these institutions felt their authority was under threat, it was a simple matter to exclude them.

In the working-class Radical movements of the 1830s and 1840s, too, gender became an issue, in the end with conservative results. There was a marked difference in ethos between the cooperative socialist movement inspired by the Lanarkshire cotton manufacturer Robert Owen and the Chartist agitation of 1838–48. The Owenites were thoroughgoing egalitarians who believed that the emancipation of mankind could not be achieved without the ending of sexual as well as class inequalities. The first socialist case for the emancipation of women was made by two Irish-born supporters of Owen, William Thompson and Anna Doyle Wheeler (though Thompson wrote it on behalf of them both), in the *Appeal of one Half of the Human Race, Women, Against the Pretensions of the other Half, Men, to Retain them in Political, and Thence in Civil and Domestic Slavery* (1825). The lodges for 'industrious females' in the Owenite Grand National Consolidated Trades Union of 1833–34 gave large numbers of women their first opportunity to join a trades union. But conflicts over their right of entry to male trades made solidarity between the sexes impossible. Owenites also attacked the institution of marriage, invoking traditional informal plebeian marriage customs as well as libertarian Enlightenment ideas, but they found little popular support—Owen himself was denounced as an advocate of 'farmyard morality'. A more conventional line was taken by the Chartists, who set out to win sympathy for the respectable working man as a head of household with dependants to support. The Charter demanded manhood suffrage and one Chartist slogan, in response to unemployment, was 'no women's labour, except in the home and the schoolroom'. Tens of thousands of working women were active in this movement—there were about 150 female Chartist associations, one for every 9 male associations (although some of these also admitted women)—but few Chartists were prepared to argue for female suffrage.

In the second half of the nineteenth century women of the upper and middle classes became better integrated into party and pressure group politics, whereas in the labour movement women were increasingly marginalized. Where women's industrial employment fell, female friendly societies declined in numbers and membership. Female trades unions, though represented at the Trades Union Congress from 1875, had only 150 000 members in 1899 (about 3% of the female workforce). They depended heavily, moreover, on the leadership of middle-class well-wishers—Emma Paterson, Emilia Dilke, Annie Besant—as did the success of the Women's Cooperative Guild (founded in 1883) on the Cambridge-educated woman who became its secretary, Margaret Llewelyn Davies. The mens' trades unions, now the dominant voice in labour politics, although their membership amounted at the turn of the century to less than 17% of the male workforce, had roots in a distinctively working-class masculine associational culture. Very rarely were women admitted to working-men's clubs nor did many working women have the time or money to frequent football matches. When a terrace collapsed at Glasgow's Ibrox Park stadium in 1902, injuring or killing over 500 spectators, only one woman was among the casualties. At the end of the century the socialist societies and the Independent Labour Party drew in many women members. Yet before the foundation of the Women's Labour League (1906) there was no labour equivalent for the party political organizations which, in the 1880s and after, mobilized mass support from women—the Conservative Party's Primrose League (which recruited members of both sexes across the class spectrum), the Women's Liberal Federation, the Women's Liberal Unionist Association, even the short-lived Irish Nationalist Ladies' Land League led by Anna Parnell in 1881–82.

The woman question and the origins of the women's movement

A development that turned out to be beneficial chiefly for middle-class women was the emergence of what was known in the early years of Victoria's reign as the 'woman question'. Perennial debates about the relations between the sexes now began to impinge on national political issues—reform of the legal system, the 'Condition of

England' question, public health, educational, and parliamentary reform—drawing attention to the rights and wrongs of women and winning influential male allies. Lord Brougham and fellow legal reformers, who were concerned about conflicts of principle between common law and the law of equity, helped Caroline Sheridan Norton in 1839 to recover her three small sons, abducted by a jealous husband, by promoting an Act that allowed a mother (provided she was not guilty of adultery) to petition for custody of children under the age of seven. In 1848 Queen's College, Harley Street was founded by the Governesses' Benevolent Institution and the professors of King's College, London, led by F. D. Maurice, to provide an education for impoverished governesses. For Maurice this was as much part of his integrative Christian Socialist project as the London Working Men's College which he founded six years later. But Queen's was soon followed by other educational ventures in which women took the lead: Bedford College, London, founded by the Unitarian widow Elizabeth Jesser Reid (1849); the two schools that became a model for the girls' public day and boarding schools of later years, Frances Mary Buss's North London Collegiate School (1850), and Dorothea Beale's Cheltenham Ladies' College (which was, in effect, refounded when she became its principal in 1858); and Alexandra College, Dublin (1864), modelled on Queen's and founded by Anne Jellicoe with help from Dublin's Archbishop Richard Chenevix Trench.

In the 1850s the focus shifted onto broader questions concerning middle-class women's work. The 1851 census, the first to record marital status, provoked debate on the problem of 'surplus women' who had no husband to support them. Over 16% of the female population in England and Wales aged 35–44 were single and a further 8% were widows. Meanwhile the work of Florence Nightingale as a pioneer of women's military nursing in the disease-ridden hospitals of the Crimea made her a war heroine, honoured by the gift of a publicly subscribed Nightingale Fund for the training of nurses and presented with a brooch by the queen—the first such decoration bestowed upon a woman by royalty for public services. 'Must we lose another army by mismanagement ere we shall acknowledge the administrative skill of women?', asked the writer Caroline Cornwallis (cited in L. Holcombe, *Wives and Property*, 1983). The place of women's issues on the agenda of social reform, and the part that women themselves would play in resolving them, were recognized by the Social Science

Association, founded in 1857. Unlike the British Association for the Advancement of Science, which excluded women from its early business and section meetings in the 1830s, the SSA gave them a platform from the start. This was the background to the formation of Britain's first women's movement.

The movement began with the committee to promote reform of the law on married women's property organized in 1855 by the painter and philanthropist Barbara Leigh Smith (shortly to marry and become Madame Bodichon), and the foundation of the *English Woman's Journal* (1858–64) by her friend Bessie Rayner Parkes. A rented house at 19 Langham Place provided offices for the journal, a women's reading room, and a focus for various other projects. These included the Society for Promoting the Employment of Women, founded by Jessie Boucherett; Emily Faithfull's Victoria Press, which employed only women as compositors; Maria Rye's Female Middle Class Emigration Society; and the campaign to open university examinations and the medical profession to women, launched by Emily Davies and her friend Elizabeth Garrett (later Garrett Anderson), who became the first woman to qualify as a doctor in the UK. Significantly, although women of the Langham Place set came largely from upper middle-class families, their religious and political backgrounds varied widely. Bodichon, for example, was the illegitimate daughter of a Radical Unitarian MP, Davies the daughter of a Conservative Anglican clergyman. Here was a broad-based alliance for the advancement of women that transcended sectarian and political loyalties. It was after a debate at an essay society to which Bodichon and Davies belonged, the Kensington Society, that the decision was taken to organize a petition for women's suffrage. The petition, signed by 1459 women from many parts of the country, was presented to parliament in 1866 by John Stuart Mill. But the vote continued to be just one of a range of issues associated with the 'woman question' in the later-Victorian era—nor did all those involved in reform campaigns on behalf of women have 'advanced' views on the subject of gender. 'I, for one (I, with millions more), believe in the natural superiority of man as I do in the existence of God', declared Caroline Norton. The appeal to male chivalry for relief of women's hardships and grievances was a strategy that was frequently used.

Family law

The reform of family law lent itself particularly to that approach, given its manifest injustices. 'Marriage is the only actual bondage known to our law', wrote Mill in his *Essay on the Subjection of Women* (1869). 'There remain no legal slaves except the mistress of every house.' Changes in the law brought it into closer harmony with modern sensibilities without purging it of patriarchal bias. The most important of these were the Married Women's Property Acts of 1870 and 1882, by which wives gained recognition for their 'separate property' in capital, possessions, and earnings. The law on child custody was also liberalized. From 1873 the Court of Chancery could award custody of children up to the age of 16 to a mother, even if she was not 'innocent' of adultery, while the Guardianship of Infants Act of 1886 widened the court's discretion to make custody orders in the interests of the children. A third set of reforms concerned divorce and separation. Scottish law already allowed both husbands and wives to sue for divorce on grounds of adultery, and nearly a half (47% between 1771 and 1830) of the petitioners for divorce in Scotland were women. A peculiarity of English law before 1857 was, by contrast, that divorce was available only to the wealthy minority who could afford to pay for a private Act of Parliament; and Parliament operated a double standard, allowing a husband to divorce his wife for a single act of adultery—since a man must be sure of the legitimacy of his heirs—whilst a wife had to show that her husband's adultery was aggravated by cruelty, desertion, or some other offence. There were, of course, Christian objections to divorce on principle but secular considerations prevailed in the Act of 1857, which set up a new Court of Divorce and Matrimonial Causes. It retained the old double standard in divorce cases but also recognized women's right to release from abusive marriages. 'Wife-beating' was a term that entered the language in the 1850s and marital violence—generally assumed, on dubious grounds, to be confined to the working classes—was a particular concern for reformers. The Divorce Court had powers to award judicial separations in cases of cruelty, and in 1878 it became possible to sue for separation in a magistrate's court. An Aggravated Assaults Act of 1853 allowed magistrates to sentence violent husbands to six months' imprisonment. Frances Power Cobbe may have done more good, however, by her campaign in the 1870s to get the courts to enforce adequate maintenance orders on behalf of separated wives.

Education

A more controversial issue was the education of middle and upper middle-class women. Here the 'separate spheres' of the sexes had been underlined by processes of professionalization and educational reform—especially in England, where there was no equivalent to the Scottish tradition of mixed secondary education in burgh schools and academies. Single-sex public or grammar schools prepared English boys for a career: from the 1850s many schoolboys sat public examinations administered by the universities—the precursors of GCSE and A levels—and some (though fewer in England than in Scotland) went on to study at university. The 'accomplishments' taught to their sisters, on the other hand, mostly by unsystematic home education with a brief period at a private school to 'finish', in effect prepared them for marriage. Yet they were in fact much less likely to marry than working-class girls. The suggestion that women, too, should be equipped to earn a living was, however, alarming. Universities were centres of male sociability and professional vested interest. And if girls were educated on the same lines as boys, would this not poison relations between the sexes and put women off marriage? Alfred Tennyson, though personally sympathetic to the case for reform, conjured up in his medley *The Princess* (1847) the vision of a university for women with the motto, 'Let no man enter in on pain of death.' The most persuasive argument against alarmists turned on the distinctive characteristic of the education provided for 'gentlemen' in English public schools and universities: the 'liberal', non-vocational education which, it was claimed, gave a mental and moral training that equipped men for all walks of life. Why should this education be less suitable for ladies? It would make them better wives and mothers as well as providing for those who needed to prepare themselves for employment.

Cambridge took the lead in opening its school examinations to girls in 1863 but the real breakthrough came with the Schools Inquiry

Commission of 1864–67. Appointed to survey middle-class education, it was persuaded to include girls' schools within its remit and
became the first royal commission to take evidence in person from
women witnesses. Its survey of the inadequacies of provision for girls'
education made the case for mobilizing resources for reform. The
state did not yet fund secondary education in Britain, but the
Endowed Schools Act of 1869 provided for the redeployment of educational endowments to found grammar schools for girls as well as
boys. Equally important were voluntary initiatives, stimulated by the
commission and supported by men as well as women, which led to
the foundation of schools and the creation of lecture schemes for
ladies, often paving the way for the admission of women to universities. A book published by Alice Zimmern in 1898 (the jubilee of
Queen's College) could reasonably take as its title *The Renaissance of
Girls' Education*. Over 90 girls' grammar or 'high' schools had by then
been founded under the Endowed Schools Act and more than 30 by
the Girls' Public Day Schools Company (which began as a commercial venture but became a trust early in the twentieth century). St
Leonard's St Andrews (1874), Roedean School (1885), and Wycombe
Abbey (1896) offered a female equivalent to the boys' public boarding
school, with an emphasis on the character-building value of sport.
The girls' private schools to which more conservative families still
preferred to send their daughters were also more likely now to provide a decent academic education. University colleges for women had
been founded at Cambridge, Oxford, London, and Glasgow—the first
of them Girton College, Cambridge, Emily Davies' foundation
(1869)—while Bedford College and Alexandra College, Dublin now
prepared women for degrees. From 1878 the University of London
allowed women to graduate and University College London became
coeducational. The newer universities and university colleges, including the federal University of Wales, were mostly coeducational from
the start. The ancient Scottish universities, where hackles were raised
in the 1870s by Sophia Jex-Blake's battles for access to medical education in Edinburgh, opened their degrees to women in the 1890s, as did
Trinity College, Dublin in 1904. By 1914 women amounted to more
than one in five of all full-time students in British universities, and
only Oxford and Cambridge held out against giving them degrees.

The professionalization of women's work was one important
consequence, above all in the education sector, which now offered a

structured career in girls' schools and women's colleges to university-educated women. Here, at last, was paid work that a 'lady' could do without loss of status—even, if she became a headmistress, with the prospect of a comfortable income and public influence. As for the opening of the male professions, a start had been made in medicine. In 1900 there were about 200 women doctors in Great Britain, 60 of them practising in Scotland. Patchy—and often hotly contested—advances were made in other fields, from the opening of the Royal Academy's art schools (though not the life-classes that worked with nude models) and the admission of women to the professions of pharmacy (1879) and architecture (1898) to the appointment by H. H. Asquith in 1893 of the first two women factory inspectors.

For working-class girls, in this era of class-specific education, there were much more modest improvements in educational opportunities. In one sense they were less disadvantaged by comparison with their brothers. Both the voluntary schools which had provided elementary education since the early years of the century and the Board schools created in England and Wales under the 1870 Elementary Education Act were mixed. Before the introduction of compulsory schooling (1872 in Scotland, 1880 in England and Wales) girls were on the whole less likely to be regular attenders, however, and there was a gender gap in literacy. In 1855 41% of brides in England and Wales and 23% in Scotland were unable to sign the marriage register: the corresponding figures for men were 30% and 11%. By the end of the century this most basic form of illiteracy had all but disappeared. The teaching offered to girls in elementary schools had always been chiefly intended to fit them for domestic roles: the three Rs and religious instruction plus sewing, which was commonly taught while the boys did extra arithmetic, history, or geography. Cookery and other domestic subjects were later added to the curriculum, subsidized from 1882 by a separate state grant. But the expansion of elementary schooling generated an increased demand for schoolteachers and opportunities for training, with scholarships—by the 1890s in day training colleges attached to universities, as well as in residential teacher training colleges for women (of which Whitelands College in Chelsea, founded in 1842, was the first). Nursing, shop, or (by the end of the century) clerical work were other occupations that could provide some elementary schoolgirls with an escape route from domestic or manual work. Of 4.5 million (out of 13 million women) in work in Britain in 1891, 2 million were in domestic service, 1.5 million in textiles and clothing, 264 000 in the professions, and 80 000 in agriculture.

Prostitution

A further dimension of the 'woman question', often referred to as the 'social evil' but discussed in increasingly plain terms as the years went by, was prostitution. Here intervention by voluntary and state agencies was often well meant but ultimately punitive. A tradition of philanthropic concern for prostitutes went back to the eighteenth century, when the first Lock Hospital was opened to treat venereal diseases (on the site of a medieval loke or leper house in Southwark) and the first magdalen asylums were founded in London, Edinburgh, and Dublin. By 1900 there were over 70 institutions of this kind in the UK, at least 20 of them in Scotland and at least 23 in Ireland. We have no means of knowing whether the numbers of prostitutes increased—there were said to be around 50 000 in late eighteenth-century London—or whether it was rather that the Victorians were particularly drawn to the mission of rescue work, encouraged by the common stereotype of these 'fallen women' as victims of male (often upper-class male) vice. Modern studies make it clear that the typical mid-Victorian prostitute was not, in fact, the maidservant seduced and ruined by her master but the young working-class woman eking out a living in hard times, commonly with the expectation of marriage later in life. Most of her clients were from the same social class. Police records show, predictably, very large numbers of arrests in the impoverished 1840s; and the steep decline by the end of the century was doubtless in part the result of rising working-class incomes. But it also reflected the success of repressive policies, adopted as prostitution was identified as a public health hazard and a disorderly element in city life. Police harassment shamed and stigmatized the prostitute, distancing her from respectable working people. No longer could a woman resort to prostitution as a temporary expedient without foreclosing her chances of a respectable future.

Repression took one of two forms. In Scotland a straightforwardly punitive approach was adopted, heralded by the 1866 Glasgow Police

Act which gave increased powers to imprison and fine prostitutes and brothel-keepers, together with powers of entry and search. More controversial was the system of regulated prostitution introduced in England and Ireland in the hope of reducing the incidence of venereal disease in the armed forces. The Contagious Diseases Acts of 1864, 1866, and 1869, enforced in 18 garrison towns and ports and surrounding areas (within a 15-mile radius), required women identified as prostitutes by the police to submit to internal examination by a doctor and, if infected, to detention and treatment. Some Continental countries took regulated prostitution for granted, but men and women who opposed the Acts made much of the un-English character of a system that both gave an official sanction to vice and breached civil liberties, exposing working-class women to instrumental rape at the discretion of the police. There was a strong libertarian current in the movement for the abolition of the Contagious Diseases Acts. Josephine Butler, leader of the Ladies' National Association, spoke for those who connected the 'new abolitionism' with the anti-slavery cause—once again women were protesting against the violation of women's bodies. The Contagious Diseases Acts were suspended in 1883 and repealed in 1886.

Butler herself, though a clergyman's wife and deeply religious, thought it 'fatuous' to believe 'that you can oblige human beings to be moral by *force*' (cited in L. Bland, *Banishing the Beast*, 1995, p. 100). Yet she was passionately committed to raising the age of consent for girls and it was the efforts of her ally, the journalist W. T. Stead, to mobilize opinion against child prostitution that ultimately led to the adoption of more draconian policies. In a series of sensational articles in the *Pall Mall Gazette* in 1885, 'The maiden tribute of modern Babylon', Stead described how he had bought a 13-year old girl, 'Lily', from her mother, paying the going rate of 'Five pounds for a virgin warranted pure'. Legislation followed immediately. The Criminal Law Amendment Act of 1885 raised the age of consent to 16, and also tightened the law against brothel-keeping. A moral panic set in, heightened by melodramatic press-reporting of the Jack the Ripper murders in London's East End in 1888. A newly formed National Vigilance Association (1885) encouraged repressive action against prostitutes by police and vigilante groups, while Ellice Hopkins's White Cross Army, with branches throughout the UK, worked to recruit men to the cause of purity. For the women's movement 'vice'

raised more complex issues than slavery, exposing, above all, differences in class perspectives on sexuality. But feminists could agree in
attacking the double standard of sexual morality that routinely visited punishment on prostitutes but not their clients. Both the campaign against the Contagious Diseases Acts and the moral panic of
the 1880s had the effect of making it easier to 'speak out' on such
subjects, which became an important theme in the women's suffrage
movement.

Women's suffrage

That movement came into being in 1867, after the failure of Mill's
attempt to secure an amendment to extend the franchise to women in
the second Reform Bill. Permanent suffrage committees were at once
formed in London, Manchester, and Edinburgh; Birmingham and
Bristol followed suit in 1868. The mood was optimistic. Some held
that women were already entitled to vote. The 1832 Reform Act and
the Municipal Corporations Act of 1835 had restricted the vote to
male persons; but Brougham's Act of 1850 decreed that legislation
that referred to men should be understood to apply to women, too,
unless Parliament explicitly stated the contrary. In the general election of 1868 a number of women were mistakenly placed on the
register. In Manchester eight of them actually cast a vote and it was
only later that year that the courts ruled definitively against women's
right to qualify as voters in parliamentary elections. Parliament's willingness to grant new civil rights to women was, however, shown by
the passage of the private member's Bill introduced by Jacob Bright
in 1869 that enabled female ratepayers to vote in municipal elections.
The Education Acts of 1870 and 1872 gave them the right both to vote
and to stand as candidates in school board elections (an American
observer of the London School Board elections of 1874 wrote to the
Victoria Magazine of her excitement at the spectacle of ladies voting,
as yet unknown in the United States). It was not until 1907 that
women were allowed to stand for election to borough councils, or for
the new county councils that were created in 1888. Yet when a woman
stood for election as a Poor Law Guardian in 1875, no challenge was
attempted. By 1900 there were nearly a thousand women Guardians

in England and Wales. In Ireland the right of election to boards of Guardians and district councils was conceded rather later, by Acts of 1896 and 1898, but 89 women had been elected to these bodies by 1899. From 1880 women in the Isle of Man even voted in elections for the island's legislature, the House of Keys.

Millicent Garrett Fawcett, who emerged as the movement's leader at the end of the century when a new umbrella organization, the National Union of Women's Suffrage Societies was formed (1897), firmly believed that it would succeed as the inevitable corollary of incremental gains in women's citizenship and the social changes that accompanied them. The surprisingly large majority (228 votes to 157) in the House of Commons for the second reading of the Women's Suffrage Bill introduced in 1897 by a Conservative backbencher, Faithfull Begg, suggested that she might be right—although there could be no prospect of getting a measure of such importance onto the statute book until it had backing from the government of the day.

How widespread was support for women's suffrage in reality before 1900? In geographical terms, at least, this was a national movement. Outside London its strongholds were in Scotland (where over 2 million signatures were collected for suffrage petitions between 1867 and 1876), south-west and north-west England. The *Women's Suffrage Journal* (1870–90) was throughout its existence edited from Manchester by Lydia Becker. In Ireland early suffragists were largely Protestant, the leadership coming from upper middle-class women who were active in other forms of public work. A representative Belfast figure was Isabella Tod, founder of the Northern Ireland Society for Women's Suffrage (1871), temperance reformer and leading lobbyist for the education of Irish women and girls: a Dublin counterpart was Anna Maria Haslam, whose husband Thomas Haslam was also a keen suffrage propagandist. Support was weakest in Wales where there were no comparable urban elites, although Rose Mary Crawshay (herself an Englishwoman) and missionaries from the English suffrage societies attempted to drum up support at public meetings. It was in the Victorian suffrage agitation that it became for the first time common for women speakers to address large mixed audiences. One popular speaker was the Scottish working woman, Jessie Craigen, and in 1900–01 nearly 30 000 signatures in support of a suffrage petition were collected from women workers in the Lancashire cotton mills. But at this stage working-class suffrage activists were rare. As for the aristocracy, there were a few sympathizers in high places, Lord Salisbury among them, but the only prominent activist before 1900 was Lady Frances Balfour, daughter of the Duke of Argyll.

Patriarchy reaffirmed?—biology and empire

It was in a private letter of 1870 that the queen denounced 'this mad, wicked folly of "Women's Rights", with all its attendant horrors', but her views were well known and widely shared in the upper classes. Unlike women's work in the voluntary and local bodies which dealt with education, poverty, and questions of 'social housekeeping', the claim to a vote in national elections offered a direct challenge to public patriarchy. A women's 'Appeal against Female Suffrage', prompted by fears that Lord Salisbury might give it official backing, was published in the *Nineteenth Century* in 1889. About 2000 women signed it, over 200 of them with titles or names well known to the public. The novelist and philanthropist Mrs Humphry Ward, who drafted the appeal, argued that equality of status for women in national politics was 'made impossible either by the disabilities of sex, or by strong formations of custom and habit resting ultimately upon physical difference, against which it is useless to contend'. In late-Victorian political culture age-old beliefs about women's physical and mental inferiority were reinforced by the ascendancy of evolutionary biology and also by the ideology of imperialism, to which biologists contributed. As religious perspectives on the separate spheres of the sexes faded, their place was taken by science and the cult of empire.

Evolutionists offered an account of the inequality of the sexes that was, like the hierarchy of races, based on processes of natural selection. Craniologists, interested in comparing brain size in different races, showed also in the 1860s that women had smaller brains than men. Charles Darwin argued in *The Descent of Man* (1870) that women of 'advanced' races developed an increasingly specialized reproductive function, their nervous system remaining less developed. The medical profession debated the implications for female pathology. Was intellectual effort damaging to the health and reproductive capacities of women? Did a woman who rejected her biological destiny of motherhood run the risk of insanity? In practice women outnumbered men in lunatic asylums in the second half of the century. In 1873 William Gull identified a hysterical condition peculiar to females, anorexia nervosa: treatment took the form of an enforced 'rest cure' and forcible feeding, sometimes administered through the nose or rectum (foreshadowing the tortures suffered by hunger-striking suffragettes in prison in 1909–14).

For those who believed in a biologically determined hierarchy of race and gender it did not necessarily follow that the law should privilege white males. The liberal biologist T. H. Huxley, for example, supported women's higher education and the enfranchisement of both women and 'black' races. Patrick Geddes and J. Arthur Thomson, in *The Evolution of Sex* (1889), even produced a biologists' version of the doctrine that woman was not inferior but complementary to man, endowed by her metabolic processes with greater altruism, intuition, and common sense. But were these the qualities that would sustain the British Empire? Or was imperialism, literally, the 'white man's burden'? Individuals who took that view, like Gertrude Bell and Lord Curzon, became prominent in the Edwardian anti-suffrage movement. Patriotic feminists, on the other hand, took pride in the part that women did, in practice, play in the colonies as missionaries and advocates of women's education and welfare, nor did their contribution go unrecognized. When conditions in the concentration camps where Boer women and children were interned by the British army were denounced in 1901 by Emily Hobhouse, the government's response was to send out a women's commission of inquiry, led by Mrs Fawcett. But the racist and chauvinistic rhetoric of feminist imperialism divided the women's movement and embittered relations between patriots and pacifists in both the South African War and First World War.

Masculinity and late-Victorian sexual politics

Some historians have suggested persuasively that one important feature of the sexual politics of the *fin-de-siècle* was a crisis of masculinity, brought about partly by women's encroachment on male territory in public life but also by unresolved tensions in the private sphere of the family and sexuality. The trend towards smaller families that affected all social classes to a greater or lesser extent from the 1870s was doubtless an unmixed blessing for wives—but how did this affect men who had grown up with the stereotype of the paterfamilias whose virility was affirmed by the abundance of his offspring? And how was the fall in marital fertility achieved? The evidence suggests that, despite the availability of contraceptive devices, it came about chiefly through abstinence from intercourse, still for many the only culturally acceptable method of birth control. Meanwhile, private patriarchy became increasingly circumscribed by laws that undermined male authority within the family. New agencies—school attendance officers, the National Society for Prevention of Cruelty to Children (founded in 1889)—came into existence to enforce them. In divorce cases, reported in lurid detail in the press, the court became increasingly willing to accept wives' charges of 'cruelty', previously defined in law as applying only to cases of severe and unprovoked physical assault. Even in less dysfunctional marriages, perhaps, patterns of domestic life had evolved that gave men little satisfaction. The disputes over household spending, control of servants, and children that were aired in suits for divorce suggest chronic difficulties in agreeing on the division of authority in middle and upper middle-class families. More men in these classes were choosing to remain bachelors. In London the expansion of gentlemen's clubs provided a refuge from domesticity and an alternative focus for social life, more in harmony with the masculine values of the boys' public boarding schools where increasing numbers of them, married or single, had been educated.

Domesticity in the working classes was no less fraught with problems, although the variety of cultures and conditions makes generalization perilous. Some historians endorse the view of contemporary social workers that good housewifery encouraged husbands to be sober and considerate. Others suspect that in a low-wage economy the model of the male-breadwinner family was more likely to create conflict than the regime that continued in northern textile towns, where both partners were wage-earners and husbands might take a share in childcare and housework. Domestic violence, often unreported, remained a common experience for women—seven out of ten wives in one London survey—and even a cultural norm, a point of reference for audiences at the music-hall or Punch and Judy show. The working-class home was, on the other hand, typically the woman's sphere in a more absolute sense than in better-off families. The mother's control of domestic spending made her a powerful figure in the eyes of children. The father, even if he had his special chair and place at the head of the table at Sunday dinner, had no domestic space to which he could retreat. Families ate and lived in the kitchen; where there was a parlour or 'front room' it was kept for special occasions and visitors. Even in harmonious marriages the husband's role in home and family might remain marginal.

The policing of sexuality, lastly, did nothing to promote personal happiness in late-Victorian Britain. Nor did the part played by women in repressive purity movements endear them to the male public. And yet sexual puritanism manifested itself in many ways that owed little to female influence. Malthusian fears of a population crisis had vanished by the 1860s, but the sense that sexuality was above all else dangerous lingered on. Doctors reinforced the eighteenth-century belief that masturbation was sinful with warnings that it endangered physical and mental health—this was the main form of 'impurity' that public schoolmasters monitored in their pupils. Both the medical profession and the state opposed the dissemination of contraceptive information. The sixpenny edition of Charles Knowlton's *Fruits of Philosophy*, published by Charles Bradlaugh and Annie Besant in 1877, and Dr H. A. Allbutt's *The Wife's Handbook* (1886) were the subject of criminal prosecutions, and Allbutt was struck off the medical register. Medical men were also behind the criminalization of abortion before the 'quickening' of the foetus in a series of Acts, the first passed in 1803. Male homosexual relationships between consenting adults in private were criminalized, and a socially stigmatized identity (like that of the prostitute) imposed on those who engaged in them, by an amendment to the 1885 Criminal Law Amendment Act proposed by the Liberal backbencher, Henry Labouchere. Although homophobia was no new phenomenon, this amendment—a by-product of the moral panic of the 1880s—and the new penalties for male soliciting introduced in the 1898 Vagrancy Act meant that homosexuals were at greater risk of prosecution in the UK than in any other European country. Oscar Wilde's trial under the 1885 Act took place ten years later and he died, destroyed by his two years of imprisonment in Pentonville, Wandsworth, and Reading gaols, in Paris in 1900. Lesbians escaped the attentions of the law chiefly because, except for a tiny minority of women who had begun to find reference points in classical literature, homosexual relations between women were not culturally defined until modern, secular, non-pathological understandings of sexuality gained ground. Early moves in that direction were made in the 'Men's and Women's Club', convened by the eugenist Karl Pearson in London in the 1880s, and in the publications of Edward Carpenter, especially his influential *Love's Coming of Age* (1896). But Havelock Ellis' *Sexual Inversion* (1897) was targeted in further police prosecutions as a 'lewd, wicked, bawdy, scandalous libel'.

'It has been a fighting century in the women's world, and we are but beginning to enjoy the fruits of victory', wrote the Countess of Aberdeen, reflecting on the International Congress of Women that was held in London in 1899. It cannot be denied that the second half of the century brought new freedoms to women of the upper and middle classes. But a less optimistic view of relations between the sexes emerged in the controversial 'New Woman' fiction of the 1890s—and equally in the 'modern masculine novel' of the period, preoccupied (in John Tosh's phrase) with fantasies of 'quest and danger, a world without petticoats'. No new consensus challenged the regime of domesticity and sexual puritanism that had seemed to offer solutions to the problems of the early nineteenth century. Tensions within that regime found expression instead in the language of 'sex war' associated with the Edwardian suffrage agitation.

The Handiest,
Lightest,
most Portable, and
most Convenient
LANTERN
in the Market.

Invaluable to
Science Lecturers,
Mission Workers,
Schoolmasters, and
for Evening
Entertainments.

Plate 7 *The Triumph of Light*, advertisement from *The Optical Magic Lantern Journal and Photographic Enlarger* for 1895.

5

Religious and intellectual life

Jane Garnett

The image opposite is an advertisement for a magic lantern: 'The Triumph of Light', which promises to banish the demons of Prejudice, Incredulity, Ignorance, Obscurity, and Error. The lantern is 'Invaluable to Science Lecturers, Mission Workers, Schoolmasters, and for Evening Entertainments.' It serves as an appropriate frontispiece of this chapter for the multiple resonances which it carries, for it symbolizes the flexibility of intellectual boundaries in Victorian Britain. Such slide projectors reached their peak of popularity in the second half of the nineteenth century, when technical improvements had succeeded in producing 'wonderful effects . . . far out of proportion to the apparatus from which they spring'. The rhetoric used to promote them played on metaphorical associations with the Christian mission to bring light into darkness. Churchmen were quick to see their potential as an exciting new way to propagate religious ideas, both at home and abroad: David Livingstone took a magic lantern to Africa in the 1850s. The rhetoric also celebrated the illusion of magic—the use of science to produce wonder, and to stimulate the imagination beyond a mere appreciation of the technical process. Science, religion, education, and entertainment were linked as beneficiaries of the medium. The advertising image reminds us of the continued interrelationship of these contexts at the end of the century; it also hints at the lack of social or geographical limitations to their activity. These are the themes of this chapter.

Interpretative approaches

A distinguished medieval historian remarked that everybody should study the nineteenth century, because it is a period so remote from our own. He was suggesting that whereas the need for such a recognition of difference was obvious when confronting the Middle Ages, it was all too easily forgotten in relation to the last century. This is particularly true when we try to understand the centrality of religion in Victorian life and thought. Historians have all too often adopted an implicitly modernist and secularist approach to the Victorian period, framing their questions in terms of a preoccupation with the roots of modern developments: secularization, professionalization, rationalization, and specialization of spheres of knowledge. These social and intellectual processes were in train in the nineteenth century, when they were already the subject of sophisticated debate. But instead of singling them out, we should see them in their wider cultural context. Distortions of perspective have been partly a product of twentieth-century academic specialization. Moreover, distinctions drawn by the Victorians themselves for particular rhetorical effect have too often been taken as static and normative. The true range and complexity of Victorian views and values are only now being recognized. Intellectual and religious life were not contained— or even necessarily directed—by universities and churches, or by the state. We are beginning to get a much richer sense of a culture which even at the end of the century was not dominated by professionals, and in which intellectual debate was not abstract, but was bound up with day-to-day life.

Because the different strands of Victorian intellectual life were so interconnected, metaphors were constantly transferred from one to another. Yet critics were also sensitive to the danger which followed when the language of one sphere was adopted in others. A case in point was the wider dissemination and application of metaphors first elaborated in the sphere of economic theory. The case illustrates both the complex layering of resonances of a particular analytical motif, and the centrality of the religious context—both to the construction of intellectual argument and to the practical living through of an economic role. As economic competition intensified, the model of 'economic man'—someone dedicated to the self-interested pursuit of wealth—derived selectively from Adam Smith's famous *Wealth of Nations* (1776) threatened to become detached from an effective moral framework. This problem was not dealt with, indeed it was actually exacerbated by the early nineteenth-century idea that natural theology and classical political economy were mutually reinforcing. The notion that God's laws and economic laws went hand in hand (particularly convenient at the time of the campaign to repeal the Corn Laws and to free trade more generally) was, some felt, corrupting to a sense of individual responsibility. Leslie Stephen was later to comment that around 1850 it was all too common to believe complacently that 'the philosopher was to march from one triumph to another with the *Wealth of Nations* in his right hand and the Sermon on the Mount in his left'.

Against this elision of economic and religious imagery there developed in the mid-Victorian period an ethical critique. This questioned the appropriate philosophical parameters of the developing discipline of economic thought. The critique came partly from Catholics (in England and Ireland) who condemned the damaging social effects of what was generally agreed to be an essential relationship between Britain's capitalist progress and her Protestantism. In Ireland from the 1850s a rhetoric developed which associated the feminine, the Catholic, and the Celtic in opposition to what were characterized as the English, Protestant, 'male' assumptions of political economy. Female critics challenged an economic model which was based solely on exchanges in the market, and which neglected the household. Criticism also came from Protestants who, indeed, contested the smugness of a triumphalist Protestant ethic—especially from evangelicals in urban business communities who found themselves so often identified with the values (and perceived immoralities) of commercial society. It came, too, from cultural critics such as Thomas Carlyle and John Ruskin, who were both formed by and challenged Protestant culture. Their rhetoric, which resonated with the cadences of the Bible, employed the language of history and art criticism, invoking the values of the Middle Ages as a point of critical reference for the present. It reached a working-class as well as a middle-class audience, especially in the large commercial and industrial towns. Issues of scope and of ethical context were also addressed by the utilitarian philosopher, John Stuart Mill, who argued for the establishment of clearer lines of analytical demarcation, but who was also sensitive to the degree to which particular hypothetical models could overpower the imagination: people could come to believe that the pursuit of wealth was an end in itself.

This debate was to develop throughout the century, reinforced by Continental historical approaches, which suggested that the British model was far from universal, and also by increased awareness of the uneven benefits of capitalism (an awareness sharpened by the widening franchise and developing trade union movement). The eventual restatement of classical economics (principally by Alfred Marshall) in the late nineteenth century took some account of these criticisms. However, the boldest appeals to consider the quality of life as a fundamental matter of economic theory (rather than as a consequential social concern) were to seem quixotic and 'unscientific' to mainstream twentieth-century economics, which began to develop on much narrower professional lines. The complexities of the nineteenth-century debate and the range of its participants were thus forgotten. Only very recently, as economists have begun to engage more fruitfully with moral philosophers, and Western capitalist models have been challenged by non-Western perspectives, have historians started to rethink some of these questions in their Victorian context.

This extended example makes several points which will be elaborated in this chapter. It underlines the plurality of vantage points which existed within a common discursive framework; political economy was one of many contested territories of debate in Victorian Britain. Changing political and social conditions both helped to shape ideas and to create conditions favourable to their development. The example also indicates how religious positions were bound up with questions of national identity.

This suggests a further issue of perspective: that of nation and of locality. It is equally important to avoid generalizing from the vantage point of London, and to avoid complete disaggregation. There were cross-fertilizations between centre and periphery, even as there were misunderstandings and distinctions of viewpoint. The impact of a canonical critic like Matthew Arnold, who casts such a long shadow over the early twentieth century, has led to an often unconscious absorption of his particular cultural prejudices. There is a strong metropolitan bias evident in his much-quoted dichotomy in *Culture and Anarchy* (1869) between Hebraism and Hellenism, and his disdain for provincial (especially Nonconformist and evangelical) culture. Protestant evangelical culture in cities like Manchester or Newcastle was far from intellectually restricted, and indeed situated itself proudly in a national and imperial context. In 1852 the exiled art historian Gottfried Kinkel lectured to the Manchester Athenaeum in German, and the local press carried full résumés. It is also important to interconnect the voices of Scotland, Wales, and Ireland, which were neither so removed from English intellectual experience as some nationalist critics would suggest, nor as susceptible to seamless incorporation into a greater English culture as Matthew Arnold hoped. Here, too, the development of empire is significant: for Scotland, Wales, and Ulster, a sense of national self-consciousness was reinforced within the framework of British imperialism. Distinctive Protestant (especially Calvinist) traditions, denigrated as narrow by metropolitan critics (and by some modernizing locals) then and since, provided the drive for missionary enterprise and other forms of imperial service.

Victorians faced the challenge of the proliferation of perspectives, and recognized the difficulty of establishing a coherent point of view. Hence, indeed, Arnold's attempt to construct an over-arching model of culture, which could build on the Anglican tradition in which he had grown up and bind a pluralist nation together. His rhetoric made obeisance to the variety of contributions which could be made by Protestantism or by Celtic spirituality, but these were to be stripped of the cultural roots which kept them alive: dogmatic faith and native language, respectively. The Roman Catholic critic George Tyrrell pointed up the irony: what Arnold seemed to hope for 'was, roughly speaking, the preservation of the ancient and beautiful husk after the kernel had been withered up and discarded'. The tension between pluralism and integration was one which was confronted in all areas of intellectual enquiry, and in which the shaping force of different religious perspectives was to be particularly strongly felt.

Religious and intellectual contexts

The thinking public

Intellectual vitality in Victorian Britain was more widely diffused, both socially and conceptually, than at any other period before or since. Moreover, such diffusion was not passive, but dynamic and engaged. Intellectual activity was seen as a way of shaping one's own world and establishing a position morally, socially, and politically. This was as true for industrialists as it was for artisans.

Periodical literature proliferated to an astonishing degree. It has been estimated that about 25 000 journals of all kinds, including newspapers, were published in the Victorian period. These were often (and increasingly) aimed at specific readerships—whether defined by economic or professional interest (*The Sussex Agricultural Press*; *The Edinburgh Medical and Surgical Journal*; *Ironworkers' Journal*); by denomination (*Baptist Magazine*; *Primitive Methodist Magazine*; *British Quarterly Review*); by political identity or pressure group status (the Chartist *Northern Star* or the *Suffragette*); by area of knowledge (*Art Journal*; *Nature*); or by gender (*The Englishwoman's Domestic Magazine*; *The Queen*; *Boys' Own Paper* and *Girls' Own Paper*). In the second half of the century Scottish, Welsh, and Irish journals were established to cater for a local market, appealing to particular language, political, and Celtic interest groups. But the general interest periodical retained its hold on the articulate classes (which were not simply the middle classes). In such volumes many formative Victorian works were first published: John Ruskin's *Unto this Last* and Matthew Arnold's *Culture and Anarchy*, for example. And it is clear that knowledge of many scientific ideas—conspicuously Charles Darwin's *On the Origin of Species* (1859)—came through reviews in non-specialist periodicals. In such periodicals—especially the quarterlies and monthlies (many of which had originated in Scotland and had been aimed at a Scottish–English audience)—a reader could still at the end of the century move easily from an article on history to one on the solar system, to one on philosophical logic, to one on theology, to one on recent French or American literature, to one on aesthetics. The survival of a common culture should not, of course, be taken to imply uniformity of approach; general interest periodicals had distinct political and social identities. But the important point to emphasize is that the range of intellectual themes for debate remained wide.

Such variety encouraged the drawing of analogies between areas of knowledge—a practice which was not just relevant to the presentation of ideas, but was constitutive of their development. The physicist James Clerk Maxwell substituted the metaphor of a magazine for the traditional image of the 'book of nature' in order to characterize the new models of reality in which, instead of a coherent progressive sequence, there were gaps, discontinuities and unexpected connections. In the case of a magazine, of course, such connections were made by the individual reader, and Maxwell, who himself made creative analogies across existing conceptual boundaries, was committed to stressing the role of mind in scientific endeavour. John Ruskin saw clearly the potential of the periodical press to target particular readers and to challenge conventional expectations. By publishing the essays which became *Unto this Last* in the ultra-respectable, middle-of-the-road *Cornhill Magazine* (in 1860), Ruskin knew exactly how provocative he was being. The series was stopped after four issues, amidst howls of protest that he was using inappropriately emotional language to discuss the scientific subject of political economy. He had made his point. Moreover, it would be a mistake to imagine that the extensive denominational press was narrowly sectarian. A wide range of literature was reviewed, and opinion was far from monolithic. The names of Proudhon, Marx, Darwin, Mill, and George Eliot would jostle with those of the authors of recently published sermons, and the level of critical discussion was high.

Such literature was available for subscription or for consultation in an increasing number of cultural contexts, where it sat alongside scholarly monographs, novels, sermons, and tracts in abundance: debating societies, mechanics' institutes, literary and philosophical clubs, and (after 1850) public libraries. Metropolitan and regionally based societies devoted to the study of natural history, geology, archaeology, statistics, meteorology, and antiquarianism published their own transactions. Self-educated artisans formed botanical and geological societies alongside these predominantly middle-class groupings. From the 1840s the Young Men's Christian Association provided reading rooms, published their own material, and organized interdenominational lecture series on an eclectic range of subjects including history, geography, and geology, as well as theology. From the 1860s the Young Women's Christian Association did the same, fulfilling an even more important role in providing a context outside the home in which lower middle-class working women could associate. On the shelves of the library of a working-class Protestant Operatives' Association in Lancashire in the 1840s Dante sat next to Bunyan. Gladstone's gift of a library of classical books to the workers on the Forth Bridge was not seen as strange.

A survey published in the first volume of *Nature* (1869–70) attempted to calculate the number of people devoted to 'science' in the sense of the membership of learned societies. The calculation was 45 000 men, and the comment that the 'upper ten thousand of the aristocracy of learning [was] thus three times as many as the aristocracy of wealth'. The terms of comparison used are striking. The number estimated is impressive; it would be even more so if it had not (by definition) excluded a large number of other contexts in which 'science' was pursued. Even at the level of the broadly middle-class intellectual aristocracy addressed, many intellectual contexts were necessarily less formally constituted. In deploring the limitations on women's pursuit of scientific work, Lydia Becker in 1869 pointed to the contrast between the Irish Royal College of Science, which from the 1850s had given women access to lectures and laboratory work, and the exclusion of women from scientific societies in England. For women especially, private scholarly projects as well as wider subjects of debate were more characteristically discussed over the family dinner table. Until higher educational opportunities began to expand later in the century, it was much more difficult for women to find formal contexts in which to develop intellectual pursuits. But middle-class women who were members of prominent intellectual families—the Arnolds, the Wedgwoods, the Macaulays, the Stephens, the Bradleys—gained intellectual confidence within the family circle; and the same could be true in less famous families. In some cases specific intellectual fields were colonized by women by astute extension of traditional female accomplishments: for example in the mid-century women were particularly called upon to prepare translations of art-historical texts from Italian or German.

Other informal contexts of debate were important. Mary Smith (born in 1822), the daughter of an Oxfordshire shoemaker, who later became a schoolmistress, became interested in ideas through hearing theological discussions in her father's workshop when she was five or six. Artisan botanists in Lancashire resisted the pull of the Manchester Mechanics' Institute and continued to meet in pubs, where they were in control of the social situation. In many cases facing threats to their work skills, these artisans retained a sense of status by developing their botanical skills, collecting specimens, and learning Linnaean names for plants orally even though they knew no Latin. The intimate relationship between oral, literate, and indeed visual culture is worth recalling. The imagery of the Bible was in most cases acquired orally in childhood. In the 1830s and 1840s developments in engraving processes permitted the expansion of illustrated books and graphic journalism: the *Penny Magazine* was founded in 1833 with an estimated initial readership of one million; *Punch* in 1841 and the *Illustrated London News* in 1842. Although William Wordsworth was to regard the proliferation of cheap engravings as a symptom of intellectual decline, the technology helped to expand the available range of debate, and the relationship of the visual and the textual, especially in the understanding of the natural world, was carefully discussed. Those who attended popular lectures or scientific demonstrations participated in a carefully choreographed theatrical experience, designed to inspire interest by means of dramatic impressions. In one of his lectures, John Tyndall created an 'artificial sky' by passing a beam of light through a dish of sulfurous acid: the gas was invisible at first, then became an intense sky-blue, followed by white, and finally a cloudy white. He was concerned to stimulate ideas through creating a sense of wonder, just as did those who lectured or conducted services using magic lanterns.

Religious groups

The London Post Office Directory for 1882 listed 1251 places of worship in London alone, belonging to about 30 distinct churches and sects (a figure which did not include those religious organizations that held meetings in public rooms, or services in parks or under railway viaducts). Equivalent figures for Paris at the same date gave 169 places of worship, including congregations in private buildings: that is, one place of worship for about 17 000 inhabitants, where London had one per 2000. Whitaker's *Almanack* for 1885 cited more than 180 different sects for the country as a whole, many of which were evidently subdivisions of each major branch of Protestantism. Sub-groups of the Salvation Army alone, formally constituted in 1877, included the Army of the King's Own, the Christian Army, the Gospel Temperance Blue Ribbon Army, the Holiness Army, the Hosannah Army, the Royal Gospel Army, and the Salvation Navy. Industrialization, urbanization, and social fragmentation were accompanied by the proliferation and pluralization of religious groups. The nineteenth century was one of religious vitality in response to potentially secularizing social and intellectual challenges.

The ecclesiastical structures of the churches in the four nations of Great Britain were in important respects distinct. In Scotland the established church was Presbyterian, and in 1843 the majority of Church of Scotland evangelicals seceded to form the Free Church. The Church of Scotland lost 38% of its ministers and about 40% of its adherents. Hardly any part of Scotland was unaffected. The competition created by this 'Disruption' led to increased activity in all the Presbyterian churches. In 1847 the two main churches which had seceded in the eighteenth century joined to form the United Presbyterian Church, which became a strong, predominantly urban, middle-class denomination, with particular influence in Glasgow and Edinburgh. It cooperated with the Free Church, but maintained a distinct identity until falling church attendances in the 1890s moved the United Presbyterians and the Free Church towards amalgamation in 1900. In the mid-Victorian period the Presbyterian dissenters dominated religious life, although from as early as 1860 the established church began to show a faster growth rate. The increasingly Catholic Scottish Episcopal Church, with its strength in the Highlands and amongst rural landowners, remained small, as did other Protestant denominations. Roman Catholics showed a faster growth rate in the second half of the century, especially in cities like Glasgow.

The Anglican episcopal Church of Ireland was disestablished in 1869 in acknowledgement of the provocative nature of its claim to represent the religious nation. In 1834 it was estimated that 81% of the population of Ireland was Catholic, Protestant episcopalians only making up 11% and Presbyterians 8%. In England and Wales the Anglican establishment held firm, although it was coming under increasing pressure in Wales, where Protestant Nonconformity (chiefly Baptists, Calvinistic Methodists, and Congregationalists) increasingly dominated the Welsh-speaking areas. The Liberal government put forward a Welsh disestablishment Bill in 1894, but it was defeated in the Lords, and disestablishment was only enacted in 1914 and put into effect in 1920. Yet theological traditions and organizational ethos could cross national boundaries: Scottish Calvinism and Presbyterianism had strong links with their English and Welsh counterparts, and with Ulster. Welsh Calvinistic Methodists translated works of evangelical popular science by the Scottish secessionist Thomas Dick for circulation amongst Welsh workers. Anglican High Churchmen referred—sometimes enviously—to the relative autonomy of non-established Scottish episcopalianism. The balance within and between different religious groups was never static, and there was little scope for complacency.

In the wake of the French Revolution and the Napoleonic wars, the privileged relationship between the Church of England and the state came under renewed attack, culminating in the repeal of the Test and Corporation Acts in 1828 and Catholic emancipation in 1829. In the wake of these changes, all sorts of questions were raised about the nature of Anglican authority. Anglicans were forced into a sharper degree of definition, which in turn led to the tightening of boundaries between competing parties within the Church, each of which developed an extreme wing. The Oxford Movement grew up in the 1830s to rally the Catholic forces within Anglicanism; extreme and moderate evangelicalism battled for primacy; and both High and Low Church identified liberal tendencies as the greatest danger. The period of most intense internal conflict was between the 1830s and the 1850s. At the same time the Church of England was faced with radical criticism of the way in which it was run, and also with competition from Nonconformity. All these pressures stimulated heightened Anglican activity to promote a revival of commitment. From the 1840s there was a massive church-building campaign, an expansion in the number of clergy (in part boosted by the recruitment of non-graduates), and the organization of lay people as visitors and mission workers. Protestant Nonconformist strength in England increased especially in the first half of the century, the Methodists expanding particularly rapidly up to 1840. They were concentrated in the north, the west and north Midlands, and Devon and Cornwall. The major older dissenting denominations—the Baptists and the Congregationalists—predominated in the south and east.

The Unitarians were much smaller in number, but maintained a strong liberal and radical intellectual tradition. Evangelical Nonconformity in general was more successful than non-evangelical groups, some of which (such as the Quakers) acquired evangelical characteristics in this period. The fragmentation of denominations—the periodic process of revival and breaking away to form an allegedly purer and more authentic version of a religious community—acted as both a symptom and a reinforcement of growth in religious activity. Such breakaway groups often appealed to particular regional or class communities, whose identification with them helped to keep them strong. Within Methodism, for example, the Bible Christians were concentrated in Devon and Cornwall, and took a very independent localist view of their own religious development; the Primitive Methodists were formed because they felt that the Wesleyans had become too respectable and that there was a need for a Methodist body specifically appealing to the working classes.

By the mid-century there was also a lively and broadly based interdenominational evangelicalism, which transcended the Anglican–Nonconformist divide in cooperative debate about social and pastoral theology, even though there were still strong political divisions over issues like church rates and education. This evangelical culture was particularly evident in urban industrial and commercial contexts—in Scotland and Ulster as well as in England—and key figures in the various regions debated on common platforms. Such a culture could offset secularizing developments such as the professionalization of philanthropy in the latter part of the century. In Glasgow, although middle-class involvement in district visiting under the auspices of religious mission declined in the 1890s, the active involvement of Christian businessmen in moral pressure groups and municipal government lent the city a distinctive image. Glasgow as a whole gained a reputation as the model of a Christian city in action—as a city which instituted social reform within a respected Protestant evangelical framework. An awareness of Glasgow's challenge of accommodating both Jewish and Roman Catholic immigrants was to resonate no less with municipal reformers faced with social and religious pluralism in late nineteenth-century Bombay.

In the cases of both the Jews and the Roman Catholics, a very small indigenous community was reinforced by immigration in the nineteenth century. In both cases, the result was vitality, despite some internal frictions, but also tension with the dominant Protestant culture, which erupted at moments of particular social or political stress. The Jewish community in Britain grew by immigration from the Continent in the last quarter of the century. Numbers remained small, but the communities were concentrated, especially in London, Manchester, Leeds, and Glasgow. The new arrivals from Russia and Eastern Europe brought with them a devotional intensity and a desire to keep alive their traditions which were met through the establishment of extra-synagogal *chevroth*. The popularity and uncontainability of these meetings—for education and debate as well as worship—created tensions within the established Anglo-Jewish community. Yet ultimately Orthodox Judaism was the more vital for these divisions. Roman Catholicism flourished and created new forms of social organization. Irish immigration to England (especially Lancashire and London) and to west central Scotland boosted Catholic membership levels dramatically between 1840 and the 1860s. Many of these immigrants were not in fact practising Catholics when they arrived. There is debate as to the degree to which levels of churchgoing and membership of confraternities were swelled in part by the post-famine change in cultural context—in Ireland as well as in Scotland and England—and also by a devotional revival which was in many respects akin to contemporary Protestant evangelical revivalism. Eighteenth-century English devotional literature and practices survived and were revived in Ireland and in England to an extent which both nationalist and liberal historians have neglected in their concern to stress the impact of Continental ultramontanism.

How can we assess the vitality of these religious groups? By comparing figures of church attendance? By looking at statistics of church or chapel building or numbers of clergy or ministers? These are certainly suggestive, and were regarded as important indices at the time. But they do not give the whole picture. On 30 March 1851 there was a religious census of church and Sunday school attendance in England, Wales, and Scotland, which had a considerable impact, because it estimated that nearly half the population had not attended any place of worship on that particular Sunday. Anglicans were particularly concerned, because it also showed that nearly half of those who had attended were Nonconformists. Horace Mann, the author of the Report, published in 1854, pointed also to the low levels of working-class attendance in towns. This finding in particular fed contemporary anxieties about the challenge of urbanization to religious life, and was taken by twentieth-century commentators as proof of the inevitable march of secularization. Yet in almost every way this snapshot can be misleading, not least because it was the only official religious census in the century, so for contemporaries this was the first time that they were presented with apparently authoritative figures for the country as a whole. Recent work has drawn on other sources of statistical comparison—visitation records, denominations' own published figures, church records, censuses conducted by local newspapers from the 1880s—and has also looked at the original census returns for each individual district, which give a more helpful impression of the local situation.

The picture which has resulted is much more vivid and more complicated. Any glib association between industrialization, urbanization, and secularization is challenged by pointing to a town like Merthyr Tydfil, which in 1851 had higher attendance than almost any other large town of England or Wales. Here Nonconformity defined Welsh working-class identity in relation to their English Anglican employers. In fact analysis of the 1851 returns shows no clear correlation between the size of towns and the percentage of the population attending church. On this analysis later nineteenth-century suburbanization (affecting middle-class attendance and commitment to church-based organizations) may have been more of a threat to churches than urbanization. Working-class attendance in Glasgow, in industrial Lancashire, and in Bradford was much more significant than had been realized. There was often a correlation between churchgoing habits in urban areas and their rural hinterland. Perhaps surprisingly, urban Protestant churchgoing started to decline as Sunday school attendance was growing. In England and Wales Sunday school attendance grew to a peak in 1901, and remained relatively high until the 1920s. (In Scotland the peak was in 1890.) Oral history confirms that many working-class families who did not go to church regularly felt it to be important to send their children to Sunday school. Such interviews, with working-class people born at the end of the century, have indicated the substantial diffused influence of Christianity on those who did not go to church every Sunday: they observed the rites of passage; went to watchnight services at the new year; made sure that mothers were churched after childbirth;

attended weekday religious meetings; went to magic lantern shows and said prayers with their children.

One of the ironic effects of the 1851 census may have been to intensify the drive to church and chapel building. Indeed such building was advocated by Horace Mann, even though his own figures showed that in many areas lack of seating was not the fundamental problem. A spokesman at the Anglican Church Congress in 1888 reported that between 1860 and 1885 over £80.5 million had been spent on building and restoring churches, missions, charities, and education. This represented a terrific surge of energy, which helped to extend the impact of Anglicanism, even if the proportion of that money spent on church building may not have resulted in fuller churches. The Protestant Nonconformist churches also built vigorously in the second half of the century. In Barrow-in-Furness, where the population mushroomed between 1851 and 1881, Nonconformist success led the Anglicans to commission four identical new churches in the 1870s, none of which attracted congregations. Nor, however, were the Nonconformist churches full. In the diocese of St Asaph in Wales the population barely grew between 1831 and 1906, yet the number of churches and mission halls more than doubled. In Llanelli, where in 1851 there was seating for 85% of the population, by 1881 the population had doubled, yet church and chapel seating was said to have exceeded it, and churches were less full in 1881 than in 1851. The same pattern is evident in Scotland, the Protestant dissenting churches in this case over-expanding more than the Church of Scotland, and ending up in the wrong place as population shifted. The Roman Catholic Church in all areas never provided seating for more than half of their average attendance, and churches remained full. This was good for morale, and also reduced the likelihood of debt and church closures.

The energy which sustained this building programme, however, had incidentally creative results, and kept the profile of Protestant Christianity high in the latter part of the nineteenth century. Nor should one forget the symbolic significance of churches and chapels in the landscape. Even occasional church attenders expressed loyalty to particular local churches, regarding them as lucky, or seeing them as emblematic of civic pride, and such sentiments have always been part of the social and imaginative experience of religion. The resources devoted to missions, to street preaching, to visiting, were significant. Indeed some clergy and ministers in 1851 had already observed, when making their returns, that statistics of church attendance gave a very limited view of religious life—that many more people were in contact with the churches than were counted on census Sunday. Every Sunday afternoon in the parks of cities like London, Liverpool, and Glasgow there were popular set-piece debates, like boxing matches, between the champions of Protestantism and Catholicism, or of Christianity and secularism.

A Belgian commentator on English religious thought in the 1880s remarked on the fact that, whereas every contemporary nation contained a body of secularist opinion, only in England had there been any attempt to make a religion of secularism. There were indeed secularist societies which asserted that secularism was not to be confounded with the utter negation of religion, and which provided themselves with rituals which imitated the forms of orthodox Christianity. Moreover, secularism did best where religious life was also lively. Both groups thought that theology and religious practices still mattered enough to be argued about. The most potent enemy of both was apathy, which was to begin to threaten the position of all participatory voluntary societies in the early years of the twentieth century. To point to this analogy between patterns of participation in religious and other types of organization is also to suggest that an adequate account of the role of religion in the development of systems of meaning cannot proceed solely from a focus on the practices of religious institutions. At both elite and popular levels identities were created by reference to a range of overlapping cultural resources. Religious belief could be interpreted as part of a variety of narratives—including nationality, class, folk memory, and magic. It is of crucial importance to identify the lens through which certain lines of enquiry are viewed. The focus is often distorted for us by the difficulty of building an imaginative engagement with Victorian allusions—steeped as they were in familiarity with the Bible and a rich range of religious metaphor.

Education

Education was a central arena for debate about the cultural values which shaped society, and late twentieth-century interpretations of Victorian education have made bold claims about the implications both of continued religious influence on it and of the maintenance of liberal, non-vocational educational ideals. To what extent did resistance to specialization, particularly in scientific and technical subjects, militate against the development of a successful modern industrial culture? Here again, modernist paradigms reinforce assumptions about the inherent worth of professionalization, and also conflate different educational contexts (and time periods) in a distorting way. A comparative framework is helpful here in avoiding an anachronistic approach to these debates.

A belief in the cultivation of quality of mind and the role of education in the broad development of character was universal in this period, although there were different definitions of how this was to be achieved, and of how far there were to be distinctions between what was appropriate for different social classes. The radical promotion of 'useful knowledge' in the 1820s, 1830s, and 1840s was rooted in the reformist thrust of associationist psychology and in a belief in such knowledge as a weapon against obedience to custom. The cultivation of rationality carried a strong moral charge. Cultivating a very different moral ethos, denominational Sunday schools remained a very significant educational influence until well into the twentieth century. Over 70% of those in Keighley aged between 5 and 20 were affiliated to a Sunday school in 1881. In Wales at the turn of the century there were eight Sunday school teachers operating in Welsh for every one day school teacher. These schools—whether or not they issued in adult church membership— were immensely powerful in shaping assumptions and in developing a confidence which could then be maintained in mutual improvement societies or many other social, intellectual, and political contexts. Development of day schooling at the elementary level in England remained voluntary and denominational until 1870 and beyond, and full-time education did not become the norm until 1918. Although a supposedly non-sectarian national school system was introduced in Ireland in 1831, Catholics and Presbyterians turned it to their own denominational purposes. In doing so they defied the liberal ideal of Thomas Arnold (which was to prove such an influence on his son Matthew) of a broad-based religious education which could rest on those areas of belief which were uncontested and would thus serve to unite the nation. A pluralist model, predicated on the belief that moral strength could only be derived from dogmatic conviction, was ultimately more powerful, even after 1870.

The attitude of the state towards the goals and content of this education was to develop markedly with the extension of the franchise, so that by the 1880s it was emphasized that education for citizenship required not just the three Rs, but the cultivation of a critical and flexible intellect. The liberal ideal, previously the preserve of the debate over secondary and higher education, had by this stage begun to penetrate (at least at the level of rhetoric) to the lowest educational rung. The Scottish model was very different: the responsibility for provision rested with the parish. The curriculum was broader, including Latin, mathematics, and sometimes Greek. Universities retained a generalist thrust, and access to them—direct from the parish schools—was much wider than in England and Wales. In England a continued emphasis on the classics guaranteed the exclusiveness of Oxford and Cambridge, exacerbated by the fact that from the 1850s and 1860s many of the smaller grammar schools pulled out of the teaching of Latin and Greek. Moreover, it was not until 1871, when the tests of subscription to the Anglican Thirty-Nine Articles were abolished, that Oxford and Cambridge ceased to be exclusively Anglican. This Anglican domination provoked accusations of obscurantism from self-conscious modernizing outsiders like Thomas Huxley. At the same time, debates about the expansion of higher educational opportunities for women raised questions of which disciplines were appropriate, and for which girls could be prepared at school. Should women have access to a classical education on the same basis as men? Could liberal principles be extended to include the study of modern languages and literature, or did this risk the feminization and hence reduction of status of these disciplines? The different approaches taken by Girton and Newnham Colleges in Cambridge worked through this dichotomy. At the behest of the scientists themselves, science was institutionalized at Oxford and Cambridge as part of a liberal education, rather than as a training for the scientific professions (unlike the German model). The prior study of Latin and Greek continued to be defended. It is too easy, however, to see this as a simple case of short-sighted cultural conservatism or social insecurity. It was rather an affirmation of an ideal of moral integration through a shared cultural basis—an ideal which was socially, but not necessarily educationally, restrictive (as the Scottish comparison shows).

In this context it is also important to stress the expansion of educational provision at the higher and technical level in the industrial cities of England: Owens College in Manchester and Mason's College in Birmingham were to become the Universities of Manchester and Birmingham, respectively. Both catered to a broader range of students and also offered subjects and approaches which reinforced their status as industrial and commercial centres (Schools of Mines and Brewing, for example). At the same time, as they became universities they affirmed their commitment to a liberal ideal. This was a mark not of a cultural inferiority complex, but of confidence. The decoration of Birmingham University's Great Hall (1901–08) underlined the projected transformation of what had been the narrower conception of Mason's as a technical, vocational institution into a more expansive vision of instruction. The friezes below the domes depict the science and technology of the Midlands as an image of the close relationship between the University and the region. At the same time the links were made more universal: over the main doorway were placed Midland worthies: Faraday, Darwin, and Watt, alongside Shakespeare (also a local boy), Plato, Newton, Michelangelo, Virgil, and Beethoven.

An analogous point about cultural confidence and the context in which it might be undermined is raised by looking at the status of the engineer in Victorian society (especially by contrast with our own). Engineering was in many ways the archetypal practical subject—not given much place in higher education, learnt predominantly through apprenticeship, yet requiring, according to Sir John Rennie (the engineer who completed London Bridge) in 1867, the previous study of the following subjects: arithmetic, algebra, geometry, natural philosophy, geography, geology, astronomy, chemistry, surveying . . . and also grammar, English composition, history, French, German, and Latin. Apart from mechanical engineers (who always remained more self-consciously practical), the new telegraph and electrical engineers took pride in requiring a broad theoretical as well as practical background. They could thus the more readily fit Samuel Smiles's lyrical description of engineers as the makers of modern civilization. There was no social prejudice about engineering. It was encouraged at some of the public schools, and was a popular profession for the upper middle classes. Cable technology, a field dominated by British engineers, and, by the 1870s, supported increasingly by laboratories in

British universities, in turn gave an important commercial impetus to the development of electrical physics, calling for a higher degree of accuracy in measurement. The physicist William Thomson (Lord Kelvin) was knighted in 1867 and ennobled in 1891 for his work on cables and services to imperial communications. In the pursuit of this work, there was no fundamental tension between 'commercial' and 'pure' values. Arguably, it was only the overtaking of British engineering by German and American electrical engineers at the very end of the century which began to undermine confidence, and then to lead to that separation of practical skills and philosophical ideals which helped to conduce to modern anxieties about the relationship between means and ends.

Religious and intellectual paradigms

Reason and faith: doubt and hypothesis

It is a commonplace to say that the Victorian age was one of increasing religious doubt. How does this square with the emphasis already laid on religious vitality? In part the answer lies in plurality of perspective: different constituencies were subject to different influences. More fundamentally, it lies in the development of a critical and agnostic spirit in different intellectual fields which cross-fertilized each other. Scientific certainty was not the counterpart of religious doubt. New approaches to questions of authority arose in various spheres. Even as the new evolutionary geology and biology of Charles Lyell and Darwin challenged traditional understandings of the Bible, so some of the religious responses intersected with growing intellectual dissatisfactions elsewhere. The universalist and materialist claims of early nineteenth-century utilitarianism came increasingly under question, and the pursuit of systematic certainty came to seem a chimera. As Walter Pater commented, on reading Darwin in 1866: 'To the modern spirit nothing is, or can rightly be known, except relatively and under conditions.' In such circumstances there could be scope for the incorporation of doubt into new understandings of faith based on different criteria of certitude.

The century began with an emphasis on the systematic collection, classification, and dissemination of knowledge. This impulse was in part rooted in late eighteenth-century encyclopaedism and in Scottish common sense philosophy; in part in the increasing requirements of the state for accurate information; in part in the concerns of radicals and reformers about establishing a secure basis for future progress. In the 1830s statistical societies sprang up (as they did in Europe and the United States), self-consciously dedicated to the acquisition of neutral facts. In the same way the British Association for the Advancement of Science, which met annually in different cities from 1831, tried to secure the respectability of science by presenting it as non-controversial. In fact, of course, it was to become clear that facts could never be neutral. Initially, the Belgian theorist Lambert Adolphe Jacques Quetelet's concept of statistical aggregates was welcomed as a means of establishing wide-ranging social laws which could transcend individual particularity, and this seemed to be in tune with other scientific developments of the period: phrenology and physiognomy proposed deterministic views of human character which were to be very influential (Darwin was nearly rejected by the captain of the *Beagle* for having a nose which signified insufficient energy); Hermann von Helmholtz's theory of the conservation of energy was invoked to support arguments for determinism; Jeremy Bentham's utilitarianism rested on the theory of associationist psychology which saw the individual psyche as a passive recipient of environmental impressions.

Such challenges to free will and personal responsibility were to become troubling, even as their scientific basis came under question. John Stuart Mill, identified in the 1840s and 1850s as the high priest of utilitarianism, had to exercise considerable ingenuity in trying to reconcile a deterministic science of society with an individual's consciousness of his own freedom, without which, he felt, there could be no impetus to reform. But he retained a commitment to associationist psychology, the inadequacy of which was demonstrated by later nineteenth-century developments in physiology which showed the individual subject as an active and contingent force. Moreover, in arguing that knowledge of the natural world was statistical, the religious physicist James Clerk Maxwell was making the paradoxical point that such knowledge was very imperfect. Far from implying the possibility of certainty, as had been confidently asserted, statistics actually suggested the incompleteness of knowledge.

The early nineteenth century saw the transformation of many areas of scientific inquiry—in chemistry, in physiology, in geology, in biology, and in physics. New discoveries and hypotheses suggested new analogies, and issues of control became highly significant. Precisely because such inquiry was in the public arena, ways of understanding it related very closely to other preoccupations. Shifts of emphasis related not just to internal intellectual developments, but also to changes in the contemporary social, political, and religious context. Different intellectual positions acquired different connotations in new circumstances. Thus Anglican High churchmen like Adam Sedgwick or William Whewell in Cambridge could have the (justified) reputation of being open to new scientific ideas and of being key opponents of Biblical literalism up to c.1832–33. But in the context of fundamental debates about political reform and Anglican authority in the early 1830s, the perspective shifted, and they could begin to appear reactionary. At a point when rationalism, empiricism, and naturalism seemed in the ascendant, and to present a challenge to established traditions, a new division opened up between those churchmen who felt that the way forward was to reassert yet more confidently a belief in natural theology (that the design of the universe proved the existence of a Creator) and those (like Whewell and Sedgwick) who saw the explanatory flaws in such a synthesis.

One of the emblematic moments of this shift came in 1844 with the anonymous publication of the Edinburgh publisher Robert Chambers's *Vestiges of the Natural History of Creation*, which incorporated geology and biology into an argument for progressive transmutation by natural laws ultimately instituted by God. The book went through four editions in seven months, and was into its tenth edition by 1853. It aroused fury on the grounds of its bad science, as well as provoking criticism for its religious and social analogies—regarded as the more serious because of the book's popular audience. Evangelicals disliked its triumphalist progressivism; Sedgwick saw that such a naturalistic explanation of the development of life, instead of reinforcing a sense of God's presence in the world, could in fact support materialism and the undermining of religious belief. Whewell saw the dangerous potential connections between Chambers's work and the positivism of Auguste Comte. There were those, however, like the mathematician Baden Powell in Oxford, who felt that his own work had prefigured Chambers's, and who continued to try to develop an analogous synthesis. It is important to recognize that all these critics were concerned to retain a harmony between new scientific ideas and both natural and revealed religion. The question was whether natural theology was not becoming too flexible and pluralistic to carry conviction.

The reception of *Vestiges*, which was published in the same year in which Darwin produced the first pencilled draft of his evolutionary hypothesis, formed part of the background to Darwin's reluctance to publish his own ideas. The delay, until he was pushed into publication in 1859 to avoid being upstaged by Alfred Russel Wallace, was partly induced by his congenital nervousness; more fundamentally, by anxieties about the materialistic implications of his theory, and by a concern to reinforce the scientific basis of his argument. His notebooks show that he was worried that the idea of natural selection would prove culturally and socially subversive. When Darwin published *On the Origin of Species by means of Natural Selection, or, the Preservation of favoured races in the struggle for life* in 1859, he played down the links with human development, and indeed his style of argument emphasized the tentativeness and speculativeness of his hypothesis—the difficulty of adducing hard and fast evidence for such a theory. The metaphors chosen permitted the retention of a superintending divinity. These were not simply rhetorical devices. He believed that the habit of scientific research made a man cautious in admitting evidence. Thomas Huxley, who was to act as chief promoter of Darwin, was at this stage much more positivistic in his scientific method, and much more confident in the scope for achieving scientific certainty. Two apparently paradoxical developments occurred. One was that Darwinian support for evolution was to a surprising extent absorbed into earlier cultural and biological views of progressive adaptation (although the more radical and disturbing aspects of his ideas had a powerful effect on the imagination of some); the other was that his scientific method, where the weight of individual cases carries cumulative conviction even though no single one would, seemed to offer helpful analogies to the way in which religious apologetic was moving.

The Unitarian James Martineau was to point to the curious affinity between 'a Religion which exaggerates and overstrains the validity of an external authority, and a Science which deals only with objective facts, perceived or imagined'. This was very apparent in Henry

Longueville Mansel's Bampton Lectures delivered in Oxford in 1858 and published as *The Limits of Religious Thought* (1859). Solicited by the High Church party, increasingly suspicious of ideas of evolution and development in the wake of John Henry Newman's conversion to Roman Catholicism in 1845, Mansel's lectures were intended to provide an Anglican answer to the various challenges of Biblical criticism, positivism, and rationalist empiricism. He offered a philosophically sophisticated argument (drawn from a very particular reading of Kant, the Scottish philosopher William Hamilton, and the English eighteenth-century philosopher Joseph Butler) for the unknowability of God. By arguing—in Hamilton's terms—that a God understood was no God at all, Mansel laid renewed stress on scriptural authority. One perplexed don in his audience said that 'he never expected to hear atheism preached in the pulpit of the university church', and it was indeed one of the ironies of Mansel's argument that it was philosophically very attractive to Huxley, Herbert Spencer, and other incipient agnostics. Martineau's own response was to reiterate that speculative, metaphysical thought was fundamental to both science and theology. In Scotland, Henry Calderwood argued that developments in scientific method were bringing the logic respectively of science and religion closer together on the common basis of probability. John Henry Newman commented that to assert 'that nothing is known because nothing is known luminously and exactly, seems to me saying that we do not see the stars because we cannot tell the number, size, or distance from each other.' The Anglican Christian Socialist F. D. Maurice and the Congregationalist R. W. Dale, from different doctrinal positions, protested against the sterility of Mansel's position and the narrowness of his definition of reason and of knowledge. Liberals who had been pressing for expansion of the syllabus in Oxford were given the impetus to produce the controversial *Essays and Reviews* in 1860: an attempt to demonstrate the compatibility of Christianity with contemporary critical methods—whether philosophical, scientific, or historical. Since the critical method made the quest for certainty impossible, it did not need to conflict with the well-established probabilistic inheritance within Anglicanism, but this was less readily perceived at a time when Anglican authority seemed under threat, within Oxford and without. However, within 20 years the contentions of the essayists seemed generally unremarkable.

Newman, the acknowledged leader of the Tractarian movement in Oxford until his conversion to Roman Catholicism in 1845, was preoccupied both as an Anglican and as a Catholic with the necessary place of intellect and the power of reason in relation to feeling as a basis of religious faith. In response to the constitutional crisis of church and state of 1828–33, as well as to the growing strength of utilitarianism, Newman came to attack what he termed liberal thinking—that is, the sort of deductive reasoning which consists in looking at all conclusions as strong only in proportion to the degrees of evidence supporting them. He came to define faith as not being opposed to reason, but as a particular kind of reasoning upon 'presumptions rather than evidences'. He made the point often in his writings that the order of development of argument in strict logic and the chronological order do not necessarily concur. Intellectual conviction may be the culmination of a process which has begun with an imaginative or moral insight or presumption. Faith was an intellectual act done in a certain moral disposition, and this basis of awareness of conscience was a fundamental assumption. This conception was drawn in part from Bishop Joseph Butler's theory of probability: that evidence for Christianity could only provide probable answers, but by a preliminary act of assent the mind could turn an accumulation of probabilities into a necessary certitude—the sort of moral certitude which is necessary for action. In part Newman drew also on romantic writers, particularly on S. T. Coleridge, who stressed the importance of a religion of inward conviction, rather than outward proof, and who argued against the mechanical Lockean tradition, as well as against the tradition of natural theology associated with William Paley. Both Butler's and Coleridge's influence were in fact felt much more widely—on a wide spectrum of Victorian religious thinkers.

Newman stressed the need to develop a sharper sense of what was evidentially *appropriate* to God's working in the world. Here liberal theism and varieties of natural theology seemed particularly dangerous. Just as Darwin did, Newman rejected the external arguments from design as being problematic to anyone who did not already possess faith: 'The truth is that the system of Nature is just as much connected with Religion, where minds are not religious, as a watch or a steam carriage. The material world indeed, is infinitely more wonderful than any human contrivance; but wonder is not religion, or we should all be worshipping our railroads.' Here Newman addressed indirectly the potent moral challenge of the existence of suffering in the world, and provided one defence against a critique of Christianity on these grounds. For him, the ground for the outward defence of Christian belief lay in the authority of the visible church and the community of tradition. It was his belief that the Anglican Church had broken with the continuity of this tradition that drew him to Rome. Ironically, the theory of development which was to underpin his conversion intellectually was in itself liberal and relativist in its basis of argument. Its conception of vitality and variety as criteria of reality could only be focused by reference to a centre of consciousness (which the Anglican Church lacked) to resolve which were true developments and which corruptions. By this centre Newman did not mean the dogmatic power of the papacy as such; for an idea to become an active principle it had to be actively, not passively accepted within the living structure of the church as a historical and poetic entity.

Newman was perceptive in recognizing that it was the moral challenge to Christian orthodoxy which was most fundamental. There was in fact a general shift in the emphasis of apologetic from the later 1860s and 1870s in response to the demand for a firmer basis in moral theology. This was inherently related to the philosophical reaction against materialism and the predominant utilitarian ethics. Robert Flint, successively professor of moral philosophy at St Andrew's and of divinity at Edinburgh, stressed the cumulative force of arguments in his pursuit of a secure apologetic which would refute positivism. The revival of idealist moral philosophy, associated with T. H. Green in Oxford, with the Scottish philosopher Edward Caird, and with J. H. Bernard at Trinity College, Dublin, was fundamental to the strengthening of confidence in Christian doctrine and social purpose. At the same time the idea of hell and the central doctrine of the atonement were re-examined, in order to attempt to confront the moral challenges which they presented, without losing a sense of the necessary creative tension between sin and grace. It was reaffirmed that the fundamental principle of faith was a personal and experienced knowledge of Christ. What the Gospels contained was not philosophy but the recognizable reality of Christ's life. This conviction was to inform the approach of those Anglicans and Nonconformists who in the last quarter of the century developed an incarnationalist social and political philosophy—a revived Christian socialism. This was defined both in opposition to the perceived narrownesses of the Tractarian and hyper-Calvinist traditions, and also to the liberal stance characterized in Benjamin Jowett's remark that it was impossible to feel a personal attachment to Christ, 'a person scarcely known to us, who lived 1800 years ago'.

Moreover, the scepticism inherent in scientific naturalism was challenged by new theories of psychology which stressed the richness of mental experience and demonstrated that conscious reasoning is never pure reasoning. Again, there was scope here, as James Ward's *Naturalism and Agnosticism* (1899) underlined, for acts of faith to be revalidated as necessary first steps towards intellectual conviction in all fields of knowledge. The turn of the century saw the analogous reformulation of vitalism as a scientific principle—a plea for the understanding of organisms as a whole, and for the rejection of the analysis of life as a mere series of physical and chemical processes. Prominent agnostics like the philosopher Henry Sidgwick, Frederick Myers, and Alfred Russel Wallace turned to psychical research, or spiritualism as it was popularly known (not at this point seen as a marginal or cranky activity), in an attempt to find scientific evidence for life beyond the grave. Naturalism for them, as for James Ward, seemed to present too many limitations. Even Thomas Huxley, who had coined the term agnosticism, although his own initial rejection of Christian belief had in fact been aggressively certain, became less dogmatic. His *Evolution and Ethics* (1893) exposed and could not resolve the teleological questions still raised by the evolutionary process: the relationship between cosmic evolution and ethical progress. Oliver Lodge, the devout physicist (and member of the Psychical Research Society) who became the first principal of Birmingham University, looked back in 1901 over scientific developments in the previous century. There was some plausibility in his claim that scientists had become not less, but more essentially religious, 'employing the term in a broad sense without reference to churches or sects'. By this he meant that they were more able to recognize that 'all our boasted progress is, after all, only a beginning . . . that the human mind is only beginning to realize its power of exploring.'

Past, present, and future

John Stuart Mill was to remark in 1831 that the idea of comparing one's age with former ages, or with our notion of those which are yet to come, had occurred to philosophers, but was never before the dominant idea of an age. All ages are ages of transition, but Mill was right that the perception of change and the need to make sense of it by reference both to the past and to the future was omnipresent in Victorian Britain. This sense of temporality was related to many things: the impact of the French Revolution; the rapidity of social and economic transformations; the development of nationalist ideas on the Continent and within Britain; faster and more complex means of communicating between different localities on a national and inter-national scale. The new sciences—uniformitarian geology, nebular astronomy, and evolutionary biology—were rooted in a temporal methodology, as was evolutionary social science. Archaeological dis-coveries were proving the much greater antiquity of man than had hitherto been suspected, and raising the issue of the prehistoric. Anthropology was increasing awareness of the particularities of non-European cultures. Preoccupation with points of historical comparison was all-pervasive, and highly pluralistic, in ways which references to 'Whig history' do not begin to capture. Victorians looked back for points of reference; they also looked forward. T. B. Macaulay noted the apparent paradox: that looking forward 'with eager speed' ran in tandem with looking back. He saw both tenden-cies springing from an impatience with the present. The author of the famous image of the New Zealander of the future sitting on the broken arch of London Bridge sketching the ruins of St Paul's, he commented that 'we too shall, in our turn, be outstripped, and in our turn be envied'. Less measured prospects were envisaged. The ancient myth of the death of the sun was reworked in the early nineteenth century in romantic nightmares of the blotting out of literal and metaphorical light by the black hell of industrialization and the Gradgrindian utilitarian language which drove out poetry. This was to be given specificity by the second law of thermodynam-ics, which announced the ultimate exhaustion of useful energy and the threatening of all organic life. H. G. Wells's *The Time Machine* (1895) drew on this vision of degeneration to undercut contem-porary faith in progressivist evolution. Thomas Carlyle's often apocalyptic vision of history was translated into the world of science fiction.

Awareness of relativity could be disturbing. At a time of rising nationalism and political turmoil on the Continent, of Union with Ireland, and of imperial expansion, there was a particular need to define a convincing narrative of Anglo-British development. There was a prevailing confidence in English historical continuities and stability, although different aspects of it were emphasized by different constituencies—Anglican, Nonconformist, Whig, Tory, Radical. The dominant theme and variations were to remain Protestant and constitutionalist. At the broadest level, competing Scottish and Welsh histories were contained under this umbrella. But the vitality of the variations was crucial to the success of the theme. The incorporation of Catholicism into the English narrative was imperfect. English schoolboys continued to stick pins into the eyes of Mary I in their history books. The notion of Catholics as unreliable because of their allegiance to the pope, fed by ignorance and hence suspicion of Catholic religious culture, never entirely disappeared. It is significant that the most respected Catholic history of England, written by John Lingard between 1819 and 1830 and extensively republished, recognized the need to stress the positive contribution of Catholics to the maintenance of English liberties. He emphasized the Catholicism of the Anglo-Saxon Church as the basis for English civilization and constitutional development.

Choices of historical focus within English history were informed by political and religious allegiances; whether in choosing different defining moments within the seventeenth century, where different Whig, Nonconformist, and Radical traditions could be very closely addressed; or in celebrating Magna Carta as the foundation of English nationality; or, like Joshua Toulmin Smith, in choosing to look back before the Norman Conquest to discover the roots of a vital tradition of local government which the growth of parliament was threatening to undermine; or, like the liberal Anglican John Seeley, in invoking England's expansion in the eighteenth century, which had particular relevance for her development as an imperial nation in the later nineteenth century. In Scotland around 1843 competition within Presbyterianism led to a proliferation of historical writing vindicating in different ways Scotland's status as a Protestant nation, and a sense of burgeoning national self-consciousness was reinforced by debate in the new historical societies founded in the 1880s. This (hybrid) sense of identity was created by reference especially to Scotland's traditional links with Europe, and also to her role in the British Empire, which formed an important new context for Scottish activity. National heroes like Robert the Bruce and William Wallace were commemorated in public monuments in Scotland, although in some respects they came to be more readily appropriated by Scots abroad. Wallace was cited as justification for the black revolt in Nyasaland in 1915 (where the native church leaders had been educated in Church of Scotland schools). Meanwhile in Scotland, when chairs of history were established in universities in the last quarter of the century, they were overwhelmingly filled by English historians. For the Welsh, too, national identity was defined within an imperial and European context. When the University of Wales at Aberystwyth was established, its links with European culture were initially emphasized rather than its Welshness. The nineteenth-century revival of the eisteddfod and of the study of Welsh antiquities was initially encouraged by Anglican clergy and gentry. However, by the 1850s, when there were many more Welsh-speaking Welsh than in 1800, and Nonconformity was increasingly confident, the eisteddfod came to be seen as the symbol of the national soul, and struggles for control of it intensified. But ambitious Nonconformists straddled the Welsh and English cultures, and emphasized also their intellectual links with Europe and America.

In Ireland in the early to mid-nineteenth century history became a critical context for debates between Irish Catholics and Presbyterians, Anglo-Irish and English over how Irishness was to be defined, and how Ireland was to relate to England. In the 1830s and 1840s Irish Anglicans struggled to root their church in early Irish Christianity (rather than Tudor imposition). Early Irish texts were published and a series of histories to boost a sense of Irish culture. In the wake of the famine and the rise of Fenianism the stakes were raised. History became a much more fundamental field of battle, and there seemed less ground for the reconciliation of different perspectives. Physiognomic caricatures of the Irish as apes, and ethnographic accounts of the Celts as a degenerate race, were reinforced by debates on biological evolution. The Irish fought back: in 1867 A. M. Sullivan published a popular history of Ireland which dwelt on a catalogue of English betrayals and prejudices. Matthew Arnold's attempt to shift the ground by presenting an Englishness which happily combined the Teuton, the Latin, and the Celt, and thus argued a case for the benevolent assimilation of the Irish (as of the Welsh and Scots), added a powerful stereotype to the mixture: the Celt as spiritual and imaginative, but impractical. In the 1870s and 1880s the English were caught between the poles of James Anthony Froude's work on Ireland in the eighteenth century, which reinforced the view of the Irish as incapable, and the Anglo-Irish William Lecky's, which tried to redeem a viable rational unionism. In the context of intense debates about Home Rule, contested readings and misreadings of Irish history fed directly into political rhetoric. In Ireland, as elsewhere, constructions of the past continued to have a crucial ideological significance in both supporting and contesting political and religious values.

From the second quarter of the nineteenth century there was a rapid expansion in the editing and publishing of texts, and in the third quarter history started to become established as a discipline within the curriculum, in schools and universities. However, to see this as a straightforward process of professionalization, and thus to see a broad transition from history as *belles lettres* to 'scientific' history, is misleading. There was certainly a contemporary rhetoric of professionalization—an appropriation of authority on a new basis. This could be wielded to privilege certain types of history or to exclude certain types of historian, as witnessed by the criticism in 1851 of Agnes Strickland's *Lives of the Queens of Scotland* (1850–59) on the grounds that she did not aspire to profundity or to 'the scientific accuracy of a professed antiquarian'. Women historians were undeterred and made a virtue of colonizing the biography of women, social and cultural history, and the writing of books for children—all genres in which considerable influence could be exercised. E. A. Freeman's virulent attacks on J. A. Froude for inadequacy in using archives are similarly to be recognized as rhetoric. Whilst Freeman expressed hatred of 'literary' history of the sort which Froude practised, his own history of the Norman Conquest had features of a romantic epic, and he was concerned to write for a non-professional audience—of 'girls and curates'—as well as satisfying his peers. Freeman himself was found wanting by F. W. Maitland and S. R. Gardiner, who adopted a much more rigorous approach to manuscripts (and a much drier style). On the other hand, Froude had pioneered the use of Spanish archives, as well as working extensively on English and Scottish material, and the inaccuracies and distortions were certainly not of the order which Freeman suggested. Froude was critical of the ways in which history had been used by both Protestants and Catholics to justify their positions, and his study of the Reformation was far from triumphalist. In focusing on this sixteenth century as a period of transition, he was pointing the comparison with the nineteenth century, and seeking to insert critical points for his readers' attention. The greater stridency of his work on Ireland, and on the West Indies in the 1880s, relates both to assumptions of racial superiority and to growing anxiety about the maintenance of imperial control. But it was also an extension of his fears about the weakening of English Protestant moral integrity, which he felt that attention to the sixteenth century could address. At the same time Froude kept alive the tradition of Carlyle, and set out to write in a way which would convey both the drama and the contingency of history. It is a nice irony that it was the literary and imperialist Froude who articulated most clearly the need for students to study primary sources in order to be able to appreciate imaginatively the relationship between people in the past and those of the present: 'We see them in pictures; in the pages of Chaucer and Shakespeare, so like ourselves and yet so unlike; but we have never measured the points of difference or attempted to penetrate into their hearts.'

This chapter has tried to suggest ways in which we can set about measuring the points of difference between ourselves and the Victorians. It has argued that if we can recapture something of the complexity of juxtapositions which they confronted, we will come closer to penetrating into their hearts and understanding how they thought. Froude's style of writing on the sixteenth century was compared to a series of slides in a magic lantern, vivid and suggestive, but not adding up to an entirely coherent narrative. The Victorians continued to have faith in such narratives, of which Protestantism and empire were two of the most important. But they also became aware that these were not linear, but prismatic: there was an increasing number of ways in which light could be refracted through them. The spectacular use of multiple magic lanterns to heighten the intensity of a single image, or to dissolve several images into each other, provides a powerful metaphor for Victorian ways of thinking. The habit of constantly relating new questions raised in one context to the process of thinking in another was testimony to a continued feeling that affinities of intellectual *approach* were even more crucial to the maintenance of values than identity of conclusion.

Plate 8 Daniel Maclise's portrait (1839) shows the young Charles Dickens at the height of his early success. Here only 27, he had, astonishingly, already completed *Pickwick Papers*, *Oliver Twist* and *Nicholas Nickleby*, and was working on what would become *The Old Curiosity Shop*.

Literature, music, and the theatre

Kate Flint

Looking back from the end of the nineteenth century, contemporary commentators were in no doubt about the variety and quality of cultural artefacts that it had brought into being. They linked achievement in the arts to the status Britain had achieved as a world power, emphasized how the technological developments on which the country's industrial strength rested had aided the spread of print culture, pointed to the changing, broadening audiences with time and money to spend on leisure pursuits. In terms of literature, they were keen to establish a break, roughly coterminous with Victoria's succession in 1837 (and it is no accident that many of these self-congratulatory retrospective surveys coincided with her golden or diamond jubilees), between writers of the Romantic period, influenced by the ideals and aftermath of the French Revolution, and those who developed a new voice, inflected with economic, urban advancement. Simultaneously, the importance of Alfred Tennyson's 1842 volume of poems was habitually noted as interventionist and innovative, providing a lyrical escapism in which contemporary debates were addressed only obliquely, a counterweight to the pressures of modernity. Yet the stress on imaginative creativity tended to take second place to other forms of literary achievement. Chief among these were the biographical—and here Thomas Carlyle's work was regarded as of particular importance—the historical (with Thomas Babington Macaulay singled out), and the scientific. This last category ranged from the writings of Charles Darwin to the psycho-physiological researches of Alexander Bain, with John

Ruskin's eclectic blend of art criticism, social analysis, geology, and general speculation forming a free-floating but unavoidable presence. 'That alliance of imagination with practical aims'—as Richard Garnett, writing on literature in Thomas Humphry Ward's *The Reign of Queen Victoria* (2 vols, 1887) termed the period's most valuable trait—could be traced onwards into poetry and novels, but there was no doubt that substantial works of history, philosophy, and science were regarded as providing the period's quintessential literary contributions.

Literature: contexts, narratives, and issues of identity

Such retrospective accounts offer a useful starting point for surveying the cultural productions of the nineteenth century. They offer pointers towards taste; they demonstrate the terms in which literary values and aspirations were expressed; they illustrate something of the process of canon formation, that anxious classification and evaluation of texts deemed to hold particular and lasting value. Codification of quality went hand in hand with the proliferation of print culture attendant on the growing numbers who formed a literate readership, cheapening costs of paper and production, the abolition of newspaper taxes and advertising duty (which had amounted to taxes on knowledge), and the multiplication and increased efficiency of channels of distribution. More newspapers and periodicals and more column inches within them generated more reviews, more opinions, more advertisements: these operated to infuse literary production with an urgency, to turn literary consumption into a question of fashionability, a marker of status, and of class differentiation. Within the literature of literature, genres jostled against each other. Take, for example, the contexts in which two major works were greeted. Charles Darwin's controversial, timely, interventionist *On the Origin of Species* (1859) was reviewed in the weekly, middle-of-the-road *Athenaeum* alongside a study of Schiller, a treatise on *Ancient and Modern Wild-Fowling*, a history of the British and Foreign Bible Society, three novels, and a long poem in the style of a Spanish gypsy ballad. George Eliot's *Daniel Deronda* (1876) was later juxtapositioned in the same periodical with editions of the complete poems of Sir John Davies and the fourteenth-century Northumbrian poem, *Cursor Mundi*, a work on Persian art, another novel (Maria Grant's *The Sun-Maid*) and several children's books, including a reprint of some twopenny reward books by Charlotte M. Yonge.

For us, looking backwards, the dominant literary form of the nineteenth century appears undoubtedly to have been the novel. To pause on *Daniel Deronda* is to consider some of the reasons why this might be so. Its complex plot demonstrates both the novel's capacious potential for inclusiveness, and the problematics of organizing experience. Its emphasis on branching connections, on questions of cause and effect—symptoms which it shares with Darwin's more ostensibly scientific inquiry into the operations of the natural world—are intensified by the manner of its telling. It discards a conventional chronology for a disrupted time scheme which demands that the reader consider the importance of individual and racial histories in relation to the conditions of the present time. Although there is a controlling, commenting narrative voice, it resembles, say, Emily Brontë's *Wuthering Heights* (1847), Charles Dickens' *Bleak House* (1854), or Wilkie Collins's *The Moonstone* (1861), with their duality or multiplicity of narrating positions, in the way it refuses the reader a steady focus on the point of view of any one character. It hence emphasizes the subjectivity inherent to all narratives, and indeed—as contemporary non-fictional prose writers were pointing out—to all histories. Yet, in the way it enters intimately into the vacillations of individual consciousnesses, it shows the novel's capacity for dealing with the workings of the mind, the same subtle, changeable, contradictory, self-interrogatory, self-deceiving states which were impelling studies in physiology and what came, by the end of the century, to be termed psychology.

This focus on the inner and outer lives of the individual, and the acknowledged discrepancies which could exist between them; this concern with the formation of identity; the constant negotiations between a person's desire for self-determination and their social existence; the ways in which they could be represented as coming to terms with questions of morality, purpose, and duty in a period in which religious certainty was a thing of the past, informed fictional characterization. This was not to say that religious novels were outmoded: from Charlotte M. Yonge's family sagas aimed at young women, informed by High Church sentiments, to Samuel Butler's account of an evangelically oppressed upbringing in *The Way of All Flesh* (1903); from John Henry Newman's celebration of Catholicism in *Loss and Gain* (1848) to Mrs Humphry Ward's investigation of religious doubt in *Robert Elsmere* (1888), the substantial sales of works with religious themes testified to their popularity, just as devotional writing more generally retained a wide readership. But all these fictions gained their strength through the depiction of the impact of theological debate on individual minds and lives, rather than through a more abstract consideration of doctrinal issues. The same might be said to be true of religious poetry, whether one considers the intensity of Christina Rossetti's inward-turning mysticism, her figuration of Christ as bridegroom; or Tennyson's slow working-through, in *In Memoriam* (1850), of the blank despair into which he was plunged after the death of his friend Arthur Hallam, or Gerard Manley Hopkins' attempt to find a language adequate to express both his celebration of the created world, and, later, his struggle to feel contact with his God.

The strong voices of Victorian poetry are not, however, all autobiographical. Robert Browning's verse monologues are articulated by artists, by corrupt Renaissance dukes and popes, by murderers, musical composers, and Caliban, all demonstrating their individuality through broken speech rhythms or glib fluency, through exclamations, cursing, spluttering, and hesitation. Related, in their self-inclusiveness and their frequent use of historic settings, to Romantic verse tales, such as Lord Byron's 'The Corsair' or 'Lara', their origin also lies in dramatic verse: classical modes adapted to suit modern preoccupations, as P. B. Shelley addresses questions of creativity, power, and the liberation of the human spirit in *Prometheus Unbound* (1820). As well as using this way of writing to suggest the workings of the mind, poets frequently employed this mode to give voice to the dispossessed. Elizabeth Barrett Browning's 'The cry of the children' was stimulated by reading in *Blackwood's Edinburgh Magazine* of the conditions suffered by children employed in mines and factories. Like Thomas Hood's 'The song of the shirt', protesting against the exploitation of seamstresses, or Elizabeth Barrett Browning's own anti-slavery 'The runaway slave at pilgrim's point', or, later, Augusta Webster's 'The castaway', speaking out concerning the circumstances that might drive a woman to prostitution, such ventriloquization of social cruelty proved a highly effective, emotive form of reformist campaigning. Elsewhere, laments were put into the mouths of Native Americans and Aborigines, deprived of their traditional lands, or brutally widowed, or holding dead children; Indian women comment on the wrongs of child brides and of sati. Speaking through another voice gave geographical as well as social mobility to poets—something especially notable in the productions of women writers, whose actual lives were frequently more circumscribed than those of their male counterparts. Freed, in lyric utterances, from the demands of plot, and from producing the happy fictional resolutions which publishers so frequently insisted upon, poetry could be a more striking means of comment on the modern world than the novel.

Yet many poets chose narrative forms, emphasizing the period's fascination with motivation and outcome, with the interaction of individual and social forces. George Crabbe's *Tales, 1812*, are a series of vignettes of rural society, less overtly didactic than the moral prose tales of Hannah More or Maria Edgeworth, or the economic lessons imparted by Harriet Martineau in her short fictions, but related to them, in the sense that a self-contained story is also required to act in an exemplary way, providing the source for generalizations. But other writers were more experimental, even if they adapted existing genres. William Wordsworth wrote his autobiography, *The Prelude* (1850), as an epic, appropriating a style associated with public, historical themes to something as subjective as the growth of a poet's mind. George Meredith's *Modern Love* (1862) is a sonnet sequence, but whereas other writers—Dante Gabriel Rossetti, Elizabeth Barrett Browning—employed their sonnets to capture epiphanic moments of sexual and emotional rapture, this traces the slow and painful breakdown of a marriage. Tennyson's *Maud* (1855) is simultaneously the study of an obsessive mind, fixated on an unobtainable woman; a critique of the damaging effects of social structures stratified by economic exploitation and social status; and—the unstable first-person voice rendering the reading interpretively open—a study of how purging individual difficulties through fighting for one's country may be seen either as restoratively anti-individualist, or sublimating escapism. Arthur Hugh Clough's *Amours de Voyage* (1858) is an epistolary novella in verse, its chief male protagonist hamstrung by inertia and cynicism, unable to commit to the present, but, even in Rome, bored by 'this rubbish of ages departed'. In its refusal to be moved by ruins, with their messages of the inevitability of decay, the folly of individual grandeur, and the sublimity of the desolate, Clough's poem is an emphatic mid-century repudiation of some central Romantic ways of viewing the past.

In *Middlemarch* (1872), Eliot's heroine, Dorothea, also visits Rome, and is jolted into a consciousness of the limitations of the provincial English society from which she has come—as well as, more troublingly, into a kind of understanding of her own sexuality and of the scope of human passions. Like many of Eliot's novels, *Middlemarch* is set back in time (together with *Felix Holt* (1866) it treats the time of the 1832 Reform Bill; *Adam Bede* (1859) and *The Mill on the Floss* (1860) are located in turn-of-the-century rural England; *Romola*, (1863), furthest back of all, in Renaissance Florence). They hence raise questions of historical, political, and social process and progress, as well as prompting more personalized issues of memory. *Daniel Deronda*, by contrast, is set only a few years previous to its composition. Its topicality is very evident. Through one of its central figures, Gwendolen Harleth, Eliot presents that topic of 'a certain young woman affronting her destiny'—as Henry James phrased it in the Preface to *The Portrait of a Lady* (1881). This theme formed the central pivot of novels that balance the need for occupation with the demands of romance, from Jane Austen and Mary Brunton's writing, through Charlotte Brontë's *Jane Eyre* (1847), *Villette* (1851), and *Shirley* (1854), through to the works of James himself, and of the so-called New Woman writers of the 1890s (like Sarah Grand, Mona Caird, and Ella Hepworth Dixon), facing head-on polemical issues about woman's place in a patriarchally dominated society. As a woman writer herself and one who commented about gendered attitudes towards fiction in such early articles as 'Silly novels by lady novelists' (1856) and in her private correspondence, Eliot was well aware of the demands placed upon those women who shared her profession, and of the tendency of reviewers to place particular expectations on their productions. The public issues with which she deals in *Daniel Deronda* are a firm repudiation of the expectation that women preoccupy themselves with the domestic sphere. The treatment of race, as well as gender, helps determine *Daniel Deronda's* radical engagement with the present day. By revealing the Jewish ancestry of Daniel himself and having him both learn about Jewish tradition and take up a role within a postulated Jewish future, Eliot addresses forms of racial politics and discrimination within Britain—within a society which, in turn, is shown to lack direction and to be overly concerned with class position and with materialism. Published at a time when the British Empire was becoming consolidated and supported by confident expansionist rhetoric, Eliot, in this novel, is far from sanguine about British attitudes towards overseas and towards racial others. National identity, in other words, was not only constituted through cultural works, but critiqued by them.

As we see in the case of *Daniel Deronda*, throughout the nineteenth century British cultural relations may be characterized by the continual dialogue between centre and peripheries in which they engage, and which they incessantly dramatize. This dialogue takes many forms. It is one, as has already been indicated, which occurs at the level of the mode of literary production: the claims of a dominant high culture—the supposedly enduring qualities of 'the best that is known and thought in the world', to use Matthew Arnold's formulation in 'The function of criticism at the present time' (1865) were set against a whole range of popular demons. These ranged from Newgate novels (the crime fiction of the 1830s) and the 'sensation novels' by writers such as Wilkie Collins, Mary Braddon, and Ellen Wood in the 1860s, through to the penny weeklies (like *Tit-Bits, Home Chat*, or *Ally Sloper's Half-Holiday*) that emerged, aimed at a mass market, in the later decades of the century. A similar diversity may be found in the theatre, with Shakespeare occupying one end of the spectrum (at least in the middle and later decades), and burlettas, melodramas, and pantomime the other—although elaborate spectacle and tricks of illusion worked to blur clear distinctions in the field of staged entertainment. A far more precise demarcation was maintained in the musical world, between the 'classical' works performed by orchestral, chamber music, and choral organizations on the one hand, and music-hall songs, drawing-room ballads, and popular waltzes and polkas on the other. Class differentiation, a source of both anxiety and comedy which permeated the period, lies at the bottom of the need to force such distinctions: this is intimately bound in with gender relations, and with the doctrine of separate spheres which—despite the compromises that both the practices of living demanded, and which literary works often exploited—underpinned bourgeois ideology. But the dialogue is also one between the metropolis and the rural, between London and the provinces, England as differentiated from Scotland, Wales, and Ireland, England as different from, and dominant over, its colonies.

At the opening of Elizabeth Gaskell's industrial novel, *Mary Barton* (1848), Manchester millworkers walk out in the fields on the edge of the city and observe 'the country business of hay-making, ploughing, etc., which are such pleasant mysteries for townspeople to watch'. Whilst the roots of the antithesis of country and city are embedded in classical writing, the nineteenth century's treatment of this topic may be used to trace certain shifts in dominant aesthetic forms. For the first generation of Romantic writers, notably Wordsworth and Samuel Taylor Coleridge, the countryside had been not only the source of personal restoration and regeneration, but also the repository of a literary genre, the ballad, which could be reappropriated and reworked for a metropolitan audience. Not only did the ballad, the lay, the verse narrative which recounted an apparently archetypal theme remain a useful tool, particularly for commenting on social issues, but the rural past continued to be plundered for the ideals of simplicity, pastoral purity, and coherent social ordering which were projected onto it. At the same time, wilder nature, its representation informed by notions of the sublime, provided both a source of awe in itself and, informed by Kantian philosophy, awe at the mind that could respond to it. Nature becomes internalized, according to human needs. 'I love all waste/And solitary places;' claims the narrator of Percy Shelley's 'Julian and Maddalo' (1818), 'where we taste/The pleasure of believing what we see/Is boundless, as we wish our souls to be.' Such solitary places may, however, be the landscapes of fear, as well as of possibility, over which stalk Mary Shelley's Frankenstein-created monster; or the faithless 'vast edges drear', of Matthew Arnold's 'Dover Beach' (1851); or the 'waste sand by the waste sea' on which Arthur's last battle is fought in Tennyson's 'The passing of Arthur' (1869), symptomatic of the drear wasteland into which his kingdom, and by extension all of civilization, will fall. 'What would the world be, once bereft/Of wet and of wildness?', asks Hopkins in 'Inversnaid' (1881). But in this question, we may trace a crucial transition. For Hopkins is not so much invoking the metaphysical potential of nature, and its capacity to typify states of mind, as he is making a conservationist plea. His landscape is not the infinite vista created by the mind, but the specific and limited location threatened by urban sprawl or intensive farming methods. This tension, between the demands of agricultural capitalism and the abstract qualities of the wild, may be found in John Clare's eloquent laments against the rural wreckage caused by enclosure, and traced through to the writings of Thomas Hardy and Richard Jefferies, among others.

But Hardy recognized the perils of rustic nostalgia, and the urban arrogance which prompted it—'it is too much', he writes in 1883, to expect farm labourers 'to remain stagnant and old-fashioned for the pleasure of romantic spectators'. Nearly 30 years earlier, Gaskell, in *North and South* (1855) had similarly acknowledged that 'if the world stood still, it would retrograde and become corrupt', and, moreover, debunked that urban perception that agricultural work comprises a 'pleasant mystery'. Rather, in the countryside, men and women 'labour on, from day to day, in the great solitude of steaming fields— never speaking or lifting up their poor, bent, downcast heads'. This combination, of physical exactitude with the rhetoric of compassion is characteristic of that writing which formed the converse to Romantic metaphysics and its French-inflected cognate of the latter decades of the century, symbolist writing. It is not that poverty is absent from Romantic poetry, as the depiction of the 'ruined cottage' in Book One of Wordsworth's *Excursion* (1814) shows: lacking the sublimity of classical decay, it, and its occupants, are victims of the aftermath of the Napoleonic wars. Nor is it the case that the later Victorian writing which deals with social issues refuses to engage with abstracts. Dickens' novels, for example, are as notable for the ways in which they find symbolic form for forces of greed and materialism and corrupt selfishness, for states of imprisonment, paralysis of the will, and self-delusion, as they are for their depictions of urban decay. But this concentration on the urban world—whether represented by the Manchester back streets in Gaskell's fiction, or by the seething tenement blocks of Dickens' *Bleak House*, the collapsing edifices of *Little Dorrit* (1855), or the gritty, dusty London of *Our Mutual Friend* (1865); by the poverty and violence of the slums in George Gissing's *The Nether World* (1889) or Arthur Morrison's *A Child of the Jago* (1896), or even the anxious lower middle-class suburban respectability, the continual life of compromises articulated in Gissing's *In the Year of Jubilee* (1894) or the Grossmiths' *The Diary of a Nobody* (1894)—this urban topography is both setting and theme of much powerful Victorian writing.

Whether it is seen as a location in which exploited labour and fashionable life is juxtaposed, as in Elizabeth Barrett Browning's epic of contemporary social life and gender politics, *Aurora Leigh* (1856), or its combination of fashionable society, snobbery, and financial greed is satirized, as in William Makepeace Thackeray's *Vanity Fair* (1848) or Anthony Trollope's *The Way We Live Now* (1875), or its environment is transformed into a kaleidoscope of gas-lamps, echoing pavements, bar-tenders, pushing crowds, and blood-red sunsets in the lyrics of such nineties writers as W. E. Henley, John Davidson, Arthur Symons, and Amy Levy, London's symbolic centrality exercised a mesmeric pull. It represented power and danger: promised success or could swallow one up into anonymity. In *Dombey and Son*, Dickens presents the city as a voracious beast. Travellers seemed 'impelled by a desperate fascination' as they move towards it: 'Food for the hospitals, the churchyards, the prisons, the river, fever, madness, vice, and death,—they passed on to the monster, roaring in the distance, and were lost.'

Yet the force which London exerted was centrifugal as well as centripetal. Joseph Conrad's *Heart of Darkness* (1899) begins and concludes on the Thames, that 'tranquil waterway leading to the uttermost ends of the earth'. 'The dreams of men, the seed of commonwealths, the germs of empires' have sailed away down that river. However, tidal waters flow in two directions, for as the sun sets—over the heart of Britain rather than over the British Empire—'the place of the monstrous town was still marked ominously on the sky, a brooding gloom in sunshine, a lurid glare under the stars.' As in *Dombey and Son*, where the central themes of money and value are articulated through commercial relations with the empire as well as within a domestic environment; as in a text so apparently England-oriented as Austen's *Mansfield Park* (1814), in which Sir Thomas Bertram's management of his family is not unrelated to the management of his West Indian estates, Conrad's fiction lays bare the interdependence of British cultural identity and the overseas 'others' against which this identity could be measured and constituted.

Welsh, Scottish, and Irish writing

British cultural identity, or English cultural identity? For if British-ness could increasingly be located in relation not just to the prevalent eighteenth-century points of reference—Europe, the Orient, America—but to India, Africa, the Antipodes, so its own internal coherence, in cultural as well as political terms, came increasingly under question. Matthew Arnold expressed the contradictory pulls of centralization in the name of British unity, versus the strengths of specific national cultures, when he lectured on 'The study of Celtic literature' in 1866. 'The fusion of all the inhabitants of these islands into one homogenous, English-speaking whole,' he wrote, 'the break-ing down of barriers between us, the swallowing up of separate pro-vincial nationalities, is a consummation to which the natural course of things irresistibly tends; it is a necessity of what is called modern civilization.' On the other hand, he was extremely keen to encourage the study of Celtic language and literature, including not just Welsh, but Irish and Gaelic. To do this will add, he believes, to the powers of the Englishman, with his 'strong sense and sturdy morality': the 'greater delicacy and spirituality of the Celtic people' is a force to be co-opted against philistinism.

In some ways, Arnold's homogenizing desires were already being fulfilled, although he would hardly have approved of the mercantile forces that were bringing them about. Wales' links were, by the early nineteenth century, closer to England than were those of Scotland or Ireland. It had supported the Royalist cause during the Civil War, and no major nationalist movement had disrupted subsequent political relations; its industrial resources, particularly in the south-east, tied its economy closely to English factories' needs for coal and iron. The opportunity for work led to considerable immigration, at the expense of indigenous culture: whilst the population of the principality almost quadrupled during the century, by the end of it the propor-tion with a working knowledge of the Welsh language declined to around 50%. But the issue of language formed a focus for national identity which was to be built on by twentieth-century political movements, and awareness of a distinct national culture was strengthened by the revival of the eisteddfod in 1819 (complete with some dubiously authentic druidic pageantry). When Arnold wrote about the importance of studying Celtic literature, he was staying in Llandudno, witnessing the National Eisteddfod at first hand. The century saw an increase in the number of newspapers, books, and periodicals published in Welsh, and a growing interest in earlier literature and folklore, as demonstrated, say, by Lady Charlotte Guest's translation of the legends of *The Mabinogion* (1838–49), or George Borrow's quirky travelogue, *Wild Wales* (1862), a melange of local traditions, anthropological detail, and idiosyncratic linguistic theories.

By contrast to Wales, nineteenth-century Scotland possessed a strong and separate cultural life, having been a notable philosophic, literary, and scientific centre during the eighteenth century: a position consolidated by the founding of the *Edinburgh Review* in 1802, and by the fiction of Sir Walter Scott. The strongly plotted narratives of such novels as *Rob Roy* (1818) and *The Heart of Midlothian* (1818), pivoting around feuds and violence, sexual tension and illegitimacy, intrigue and romance, and the sharp contrasts Scott draws between urban and rural settings and manners, provide elements that were to be reappropriated, in more contemporary contexts, by later sensationalist writers. In his own writing, these components give dramatic power to his carefully researched Scottish history. The sense of national identity is transmitted not just through the resuscitation of the past, but through inserted snatches of the ballads which Scott also collected, and, above all, by an energetic use of dialect. His importance, however, was not merely in helping to establish the value of Scotland's distinctive national literature. The emphasis he placed on the medieval period as the source not just of colourful, dramatic historical incidents, but as containing elements worthy of consideration by historiographers and novelists alike was to feed into the work of, among others, Carlyle, Ruskin, and Edward Bulwer Lytton. More broadly, the fact that both Carlyle and Macaulay praised his fiction not only alerts one to the uncertain boundaries between the narratives of a novel and the writing of history, but also points to his influence over the latter genre: Scott, wrote Carlyle, 'taught all men this truth, which . . . was as good as unknown to writers of history and others, till so taught: that the bygone ages of the world were actually filled by living men, not by protocols, state-papers, controversies and abstractions of men.' Moreover, of all British writers active during the early years of the century, not even Byron was to have a greater influence on the literary, dramatic, and artistic culture of Continental Europe.

Yet after Scott, who died in 1832, writers from north of the border—with some notable exceptions who continued to collect stories and folklore—frequently moved away from their geographical origins, even if they continued to refer to Scottish tradition and culture in some of their writings. This is true of the fantasy writer George MacDonald; of James Thomson, whose long poem 'The city of dreadful night' (1874) presents the wasteland of urban scenery and consciousness with hallucinatory vividness; and of James Barrie, who combined a career writing sentimental fiction and drama, and nostalgic whimsy, with some mawkish portrayals of Scottish rural life, starting with *Auld Licht Idylls* (1888). Rather than antiquarian revivalism, these can be seen as a commercial exploitation of Celtic difference. The same could not be said to be true, however, of Robert Louis Stevenson. Whilst he certainly exploited the genre of the adventure story in *Kidnapped* (1886) and *Catriona* (1893), both explore historically rooted conflicts between Highland and Lowland Scots, and revisit Jacobite/Whig tensions. In his other fiction, he similarly harks back to Scottish and Scottian writing from earlier in the century. *Dr Jekyll and Mr Hyde* (1886) is, like James Hogg's *The Private Memoirs and Confessions of a Justified Sinner* (1824), an intricately constructed story of a divided self. But Stevenson was not British-bound. His poor health led him to live abroad: settling in the South Pacific, *The Beach of Falesá* (1892) functions both as a record of displacement, of the problems inherent in failing to read a different culture, and as a new form of fiction of empire, intimating the possibility of settling in a new place, and of transformation, becoming changed by it, and by its people, to the extent that return is a complete impossibility.

In this novella, we see something of the anxiety that the status of Britain, in relation to the empire in general, and racial otherness in particular, was producing in the later decades of the century. This may be contrasted with earlier confidence, whether specifically in the power of English language and literature, which gave 'access to all the vast intellectual wealth, which all the wisest nations of the earth have created and hoarded in the course of ninety generations', as Macaulay put it in his 1835 'Minute on Indian education', or in the expansion of, first, trade, then administrative rule. These sentiments can be found in their enthusiastic crudeness in adventure fiction, which celebrated not just fantasies of contemporary heroism, but exploits in the national past. Charles Kingsley, for example, presents Amyas Leigh, the Elizabethan protagonist of his *Westward Ho!* (1855)—written at the time of the Crimean War—as a 'symbol . . . of brave young England longing to wing its way out of its island prison, to discover and to traffic, to colonise and to civilise, until no wind can sweep the earth which does not bear the echoes of an English voice'. They can be traced from Captain Marryat's seafaring stories of the 1840s, through R. M. Ballantyne's narratives of Canadian trapping and trading, and spirited survival in the face of cannibalistic savages in *The Coral Island* (1857), to H. Rider Haggard's romances of African exploration and conquest, such as *King Solomon's Mines* (1886), *Allan Quatermain* (1887), and *She* (1887). In their turn, the determined masculinity celebrated in these works, the sense of accomplishment against both human and environmental odds, was inseparable from the triumphalism of much male-authored travel writing, such as H. M. Stanley's best-selling *Through the Dark Continent* (1878) and *In Darkest Africa* (1890). Notably, women travellers, whether Mary Kingsley (*Travels in West Africa*, 1897) or Isabella Bird, tended to be far more self-deprecating about their exploits. Whereas this could be read as a self-defensive capitulation to gender norms, it simultaneously ensures an openness to experience, and a good-humoured acceptance of the absurd, which often brings them closer in sympathy to members of other races than their male counterparts. They remind one, too, about the dangers of generalizing about the literature of empire from some of the more notoriously jingoistic examples which it undoubtedly generated.

Racial tension was particularly evident in the writing which followed the so-called Indian Mutiny of 1857. The memoirs of survivors, the flurry of patriotic verse, and the subsequent appearance of novels which took the uprisings as their theme all tended to work towards emphasizing the need for strong British control to be asserted over the subcontinent. But even novels like Meadow Taylor's *Seeta* (1872), which derive a good deal of their dramatic dynamics from the violence of this period, suggest that the political issues are not cut and dried; that British administration needed, and needs, to pay more attention to local concerns, and not assume automatic superiority. Rudyard Kipling's writing exhibits especially well a paradoxical blend of condemnation of colonialist insensitive obtuseness, real love of India's cultural complexity and multiplicity (as he shows in *Kim*, 1901), and yet belief in the ultimate rightness of enlightened British rule. These contradictory pulls—acknowledging not just the attraction but also the autonomy of the localized and national Other, while simultaneously being unable to shed an Anglocentric approach—increasingly marked the fiction and poetry which dealt with the conditions and tensions of empire.

New allegiances came to be forged which bypassed the metropolitan centre. In 1912, William Butler Yeats published his introduction to *Gitanjali*, the translations of Bengali poems published by Rabindranath Tagore. 'A whole people, a whole civilization, immeasurably strange to us,' he wrote, 'seems to have been taken up into this imagination; and yet we are not moved because of its strangeness, but because we have met our own image.' In part, Yeats was attracted by Tagore's mysticism, and by the musicality of his writings. The same kind of characteristics also appealed to him in the writings of Dante Gabriel Rossetti, which, like the poems of the French symbolists, he praised for their ability to evoke imprecise but powerful thoughts and emotions, 'spray flung up from hidden tides that follow a moon no eye can see', as he put it in 1898. Yet it is also worth considering that Yeats, dedicated to the founding of an Irish literary movement, saw Tagore as another colonial subject, coming from a culture which, like that of Ireland, acknowledged the importance of the ecstatic and the visionary, and which was also in a troubled relation to the imperial centre.

Ireland's formal political position in relation to England had been established by the Act of Union in 1800. Subsequently, many of the wealthier and more powerful families moved to England, and writers, like Maria Edgeworth, both used elements from their Irish pasts, and looked towards an English market. The country's poverty was greatly worsened by the famine of the 1840s: 20% of the population either emigrated, or died from disease and starvation during this time, which resulted in a rapid decline of Gaelic, both as a spoken language, and in terms of literary tradition. William Carleton, in such works as *Traits and Stories of the Irish Peasantry* (1830), gave an uncomfortably double-edged—part affectionate, part condescending—view of this vanishing culture: he addressed the effects of the famine directly in some longer novels, including *The Emigrants of Ahadarra* (1848).

Emigration served, in part, to weaken social and cultural ties with England. Although many people crossed the Irish Sea to work in industrial centres, others crossed the Atlantic. Subsequently, American tours became as mandatory for literary figures as for revolutionary political leaders, and American writing, especially Walt Whitman's poetry, fed into Ireland's sense of what constituted literary modernity.

But overseas influences were far from being the only ones at work in establishing Ireland's growing acknowledgment of its intrinsic cultural differences. The Young Ireland movement was launched in the early 1840s, with its newspapers circulating poetry, ballads, and essays as well as commenting on contemporary politics, particularly land reform. Thomas Davis and James Mangan, among others, used the ballad form, and appropriated Gaelic usage of rhymes and accents, to nationalistic ends. The revival of earlier literary forms continued with Samuel Ferguson's attempts to elevate the Irish epic, and his prose retelling, in his *History of Ireland: The Heroic Period* (1878), of myth and heroic legend, introducing to English-speaking readers such figures as Deirdre and Cuchulainn. These traditional stories and fabular personages were at the centre of Yeats's *The Wanderings of Oisin and Other Poems* (1889) and his subsequent writings—in poetry, prose, and drama—of the 1890s, which signalled the terms of the so-called Irish renaissance, increasingly blending traditional folklore and mythology with a more explicitly political nationalism.

Theatre: melodrama and modernity

However, by the end of the century, as is indicated by the role played by America, the debate about Irish national identity was not clear-cut. Was Ireland, and Irish literary culture, to cherish a romantic notion of its own self-referential integrity, or did its cultural future lie in a more expansive embrace of modernity, of other, cosmopolitan influences? Such influences were not by any means necessarily figured as being English ones, although Irish writers had continued to adapt Irish themes and settings to the tastes of an English market. The neo-Gothic fiction of Sheridan LeFanu, for example—in particular *Uncle Silas* (1864)—both looks back to the psychological horror of Charles

Maturin's *Melmoth the Wanderer* (1820) and exploits the form of the contemporary sensation novel. Bram Stoker's *Dracula* (1897) blends the legendary figure of the vampire (given nineteenth-century literary form by John Polidori, popularized by the Scotsman James Malcolm Rymer in *Varney, the Vampire* (1847), and kept in lively circulation by LeFanu, among others) with the technology of modernity, including the typewriter and phonograph. Dion Boucicault, the most prolific of all Victorian dramatists and adaptors for the stage, explored, albeit through a mixture of comedy and melodrama, Anglo-Irish relations in such plays as *The Colleen Bawn* (1860) and *Arrah-na-Pogue* (1864). Others, however, looked to Europe. George Moore was heavily influenced by French naturalism, whether in novels, like *A Drama in Muslin* (1886) which were set in Irish society, or in those which, like *Esther Waters* (1894), took an uncompromising look at English class relations and the living conditions of the poor. Oscar Wilde, too, was strongly affected by French writing: symbolist poetry and art, from Charles Baudelaire to Gustave Moreau, lies behind his early poetry, whilst Parisian farce inspired the pace and plotting of his dramatic satires. Wilde's plays represented a much-needed interjection of energy into British theatre. *A Woman of No Importance* (1893), *The Importance of Being Earnest* (1895), and other works not only satirized contemporary society, but threw the audience's attention onto dialogue, onto stage business. Language and acting came to the fore in his plays, rather than the spectacle which had dominated so much nineteenth-century theatre, whether in increasingly elaborate productions of Shakespeare, with Cleopatra's barge being pulled onto stage accompanied by balletic Egyptians, or *Macbeth* being set against a painstakingly accurate backcloth representing Iona, or Byron's *Sardanapalus* being produced—as was the case in 1852—in a 'Hall of Nimrod' based on Layard's Assyrian excavations. At the beginning of the period, the theatre was very sharply divided between the two theatres licensed under the terms of the monopolies established at the Restoration to perform 'legitimate' drama, Covent Garden and Drury Lane (which reopened their doors in 1809 and 1812, respectively, after both suffering fires), and the rest. Whilst there was a good deal of theatre-building in the 1830s, the majority of performances were of melodrama, farce, and pantomime, whilst more 'serious' drama, like Shakespeare, was largely left to the old established locations, even after theatrical free trade was established in 1843. This act, incidentally, simultaneously confirmed the lord chamberlain's right of censorship. Melodrama, however, unquestioningly possessed much more appeal than productions of Shakespeare and the remnants of Romantic drama, in which rhetoric was delivered in a laboured way designed (whether the play was tragedy or comedy) to emphasize its seriousness. It took the efforts of Samuel Phelps at Sadler's Wells, between 1843 and 1862, to start to rid Shakespeare of its eighteenth-century 'improvements', to introduce a more fluid style of acting, and to re-introduce a number of other Renaissance and Restoration dramatists. The actor and theatre manager Henry Irving, despite, or perhaps because of his love of lavish spectacle, consolidated not just the revival of earlier drama, but the growing social respectability of the theatre, the actor, and, increasingly, what had been the somewhat suspect occupation of the actress.

Irving's fame was created not just by his Shakespearean performances, but by his appearances in melodrama, notably in *The Bells* (1871). The distinction between 'respectable' and other forms of theatre was becoming increasingly blurred. The plots of melodramas were unquestioningly improbable, the genre depending not just on extremes of virtue and villainy, but on deception, conspiracy, coincidence, unmasking, and revenge, frequently coupled with violence and strong romantic passions. It thrived on cliché. But it was often, also, a form which foregrounded contemporary issues—whether British naval domination (and shipboard corruption) in Douglas Jerrold's *Black-Eyed Susan* (1829), or industrial exploitation, in John Walker's *Factory Lad* (1832), or urban crime (Tom Taylor's *Ticket of Leave Man*, 1863).

Moreover, it deliberately made use of the modern in its stage business. Thus the hero in Boucicault's *After Dark* (1868) is tied to the rails of the London Underground as a train bears down upon him; in *The Octoroon* (1859), Boucicault not only centres on the topical theme of abolition, but employs photography to solve a crime. Later playwrights, Wilde included, continued to use the theatre as a vehicle for social satire and comment, addressing an increasingly middle-class audience, and coming to rely less on the completely improbable. Thomas Robertson's work, like *Caste* (1867), looked at the class stratification of society. Arthur Wing Pinero's plays, including *The Second Mrs. Tanqueray* (1893) and *Notorious Mrs. Ebbsmith* (1895), dealt with women's sexuality, building on the space which had been created for the public airing of such issues not just by the late-century efforts of the women's movement to speak out about prostitution, venereal disease, sex education, double standards, and hypocrisy, but, more specifically within the theatre, by Henrik Ibsen. William Archer translated and produced a number of his plays, beginning with *A Doll's House* (1889) and *Ghosts* (1891). Archer collaborated with George Bernard Shaw—yet another Irishman pursuing his career in London—on *Widowers' Houses* (1892), about slum landlords, and other early works by Shaw, particularly *Mrs. Warren's Profession* (1893) and *The Philanderer* (1893), also pivoted around the question of sexual practices and morals, albeit whilst displaying something of Shaw's own equivocation about women's power. In Ireland itself, Yeats, and Lady Augusta Gregory ensured that the nationalistic literary revival included drama, attacking, in their 1898 'Prospectus for the Irish literary theatre' the commercial theatre's fondness for the buffoon 'stage Irish' and for linking Irishness with sentimentality, and promoting, instead, the heroic, the mythic, and the traditional. Yeats's *The Countess Cathleen* was put on in 1899, and in 1901 Douglas Hyde's *Casadh an tSugain*, the first play ever performed in Irish.

Music and nationhood

Ireland was by no means the only part of the British Isles to witness a revival of concern for local tradition in the latter years of the century. There was considerable interest in folk music, rural customs, superstitions, dialects, proverbs and ballads, consolidated by the formation of the Folk-Lore Society in 1878. Its key members, including Andrew Lang, George Gomme, and Edwin Harland, pursued an anthropological approach—very much in the school of E. B. Tylor, and in contradistinction to Max Müller's comparativism—which stressed the specificity of different local beliefs. If within Britain the accumulation of example was tinged with nostalgia, with a desire to preserve vanishing forms in the face of modernized urbanization, in the broader context of empire the collection of folklore also served to bolster evolutionary theory, allowing enthusiasts to express the superiority of their civilization. Folk music afficionados initially favoured music associated with local rituals, such as Morris dancing and May celebrations, and religious music, particularly carols; to this were added work songs, like sea-shanties and plough songs. Urban music, especially ballads, tended to merge with other growing popular forms, like parlour songs and music-hall numbers, themselves witness to an increasing acknowledgement of the place of the musical within nineteenth-century life.

For when commentators in the late century looked back, they were far readier to trace achievement and progress in the area of music than in the more complicated history of literature, and were keen to present the earlier years of the century, in particular, as an unmelodious wasteland. This was due to two major factors: the unarguable failure of any native composer with a status equivalent to the major Continental names to emerge (hence the tendency to claim Mendelssohn as a British composer), and—a legacy of Puritanism—a lack of church music. Music in a domestic sphere was associated with the feminine, and hence undervalued (and even then, it was often thought 'unfeminine' for women to play the larger string instruments, or wind instruments); moreover, there were few opportunities for musical training. Much of this was to change. From 1843, music was included in the curriculum of teacher-training colleges, and with the introduction of the sol-fa system of teaching singing around 1850, singing in schools—supported by government grants from 1874— became far more common. Two years earlier, grants for teaching music in elementary schools were introduced for the first time. At a more professional level, the Royal Academy for Music was supplemented in 1873 by a National Training School: when attempts to merge the two failed, the Prince of Wales—a great musical supporter—inaugurated a scheme to found the Royal College of Music. This opened, under the directorship of George Grove, in 1883. The Guildhall School of Music was launched in 1880 with 62 pupils; by 1886, it taught two and a half thousand people. Concerts aimed at the general public were successfully staged, such as the Crystal Palace Saturday Concerts, firmly established in 1855 (many works by Schubert and Schumann received their British premieres there), and Arthur Chappell's Monday Popular Concerts of Chamber Music, started in 1859. There was an enormous growth in church music. Whilst hymn singing had for a long time formed part of Nonconformist worship, it was, in the early decades, at best only tolerated within Anglican services. High Church enthusiasm, in particular, provided an impetus for inaugurating not just much more use of hymns—especially following the publication of *Hymns Ancient and Modern* in 1861—but introduced a sung Te Deum and canticles, then versicles, responses, and on some occasions psalms. In 1856, the first meeting of Associated Church Choirs was held in Lichfield Cathedral, symptomatic not just of the growth in active musical life within the church, but of the wider growing popularity of choral festivals, from the long-established Three Choirs Festival to the Crystal Palace's Handel Festival, first held on a large scale in 1859, with a band of 460, and a chorus of 2700. Meanwhile, the Salvation Army, founded in 1865, was foremost among revivalist movements in taking hymns onto the streets, accompanied by brass bands: there were 10 000 Salvation Army band musicians by 1900. Military band music itself, heard in concerts and parades as well as processions, and boosted by the founding of the Royal Military School of Music in 1857, played an important role in the spread of the brass band movement. Initially a product of northern England, encouraged by industrialists and landowners, the London brass band festival of 1860 marked the expansion of this music into the south: by 1900, more than 20 000 amateur brass band players were participating in organized gatherings. The status of such music is ambiguous since, although its practitioners and audiences tended to be working class, and it could be said to represent pride in one's workplace, it was fostered by a paternalistic outlook: its tunes (whether military marches or quicksteps, adaptations of dance music, or orchestral and operatic favourites) allowing for none of the irreverence or subversion to be found in other types of working-class music.

Other factors were important in the consolidation of a musical culture, from the growing availability of cheap music, in which the publishing house of Novello took the lead, through the growth of music criticism in the general press and the development of specialist publications like the *Musical World* (1836–91), the *Musical Times* (1844–) and the *Tonic Sol-Fa Reporter* (1851–1920), to the increased range of instruments found in drawing rooms, and the improvement in their quality. In particular, the piano was increased in compass and strengthened in construction, its possession, a mark of status in the artisan parlour, provided a general stimulus to amateur music-making. But although Victorian commentators tried to make out a strong case for a number of indigenous composers, from Sterndale

Bennett, active in a range of genres from symphonies through concertos to cantatas and chamber music, to the operatic works of Michael Balfe and Edward Loder, it remained true that the most popular works were written by non-natives. Handel and Beethoven were highly favoured throughout the century (the *Messiah* an almost obligatory number at choral festivals); Bach grew in popularity, whereas enthusiasm for Mendelssohn waned, and that for Spohr dropped even further. Schubert and Schumann were widely performed; Brahms tended to be considered as rather too abstruse and learned for the general public, whereas Wagner completely divided the musical community. Arthur Sullivan, whilst now remembered for his collaboration on the Savoy operas with William Gilbert, for the tunes to 'Onward Christian soldiers' and for the very popular mawkish ballad, 'The lost chord', was generally thought to have frittered his talents. The 'regret' of Walter Parratt, writing in *The Reign of Queen Victoria*, was that 'such good workmanship should be bestowed [by Sullivan]upon trivial themes of ephemeral interest'.

Such works as Gilbert and Sullivan's *Patience* (1881) and *Princess Ida* (1884), attacking the aesthetic movement and the women's movement, are as valuable as *Punch* for the satirical record of contemporary preoccupations that they provide. But this was hardly the trajectory envisaged by Carl Engel, when, in 1866, he called for a 'national music'. Although folk music could be said, from one perspective, to supply this (at the same time that it highlighted differences between metropolis and provinces), the call was more publicly answered by three late-century composers: Hubert Parry—the composer of 'Jerusalem'—who in addition to orchestral, choral, and organ music produced 12 volumes of *English Lyrics*; Edward Elgar, who followed the *Enigma Variations* (1899) and *The Dream of Gerontius* (1900) with the piece which has come to stand for unquestioning patriotism, the first *Pomp and Circumstance* march (1901), and Charles Stanford. But if Stanford also has come to be associated with a harmonious version of empire, through such works as *The Revenge* (1886) and *Songs of the Sea* (1904), he may also be seen as part of the Irish revival movement: born in Dublin, he composed six Irish rhapsodies, and arranged a number of Irish songs. Like Parry, he was also a writer on music. Notably, the growth in serious musical activity in the latter half of the nineteenth century was accompanied by theorization of its effects. Notions put forward in Hermann von Helmholtz's *The Sensations of Tone* (1863) were popularized by John Tyndall, among others; Herbert Spencer considered music in relation to mind. Its status as a 'pure' art, non-referential, capable of producing pleasure through its own internal characteristics, gave it a particular status within the aesthetic movement, a status encapsulated in Walter Pater's phrase from *The Renaissance* (1873): 'All art constantly aspires toward the condition of music.'

Subjectivity, multiplicity, and the *fin-de-siècle*

Pater's volume was remarkable for more than this celebration of the effects of music. In his preface and conclusion, he expressed what was to become the defining principle of the British aesthetic movement: the fact that what matters in one's effort to know the object of one's aesthetic perception 'as it really is, is to know one's impression as it really is'. If the cultural manifestations of the nineteenth century may be characterized by their movement between centre and periphery in social and national terms, so one may also trace the development of a new form of centre: the perceiving self. Pater wrote:

Experience, already reduced to a swarm of impressions, is ringed round for each one of us by that thick wall of personality through which no real voice has ever pierced on its way to us, or from us to that which we can only conjecture to be without. Every one of those impressions is the impression of the individual in his isolation, each mind keeping as a solitary prisoner its own dreams of a world.

The movement between the isolated being and the society in which she or he finds themself, the lacunae between subjective impression and views which are held socially in common, are related to two further nineteenth-century phenomena. The first of these—something which is inseparable from that interest in character which has already been noted—is the development of theories of the unconscious: the growth of what came to be termed psychology. Its effects can be traced most obviously through the differing ways in which dreams, visions, and, more broadly, the effects of the supernatural are incorporated in the writing of the century, from

Lockwood experiencing the power of Catherine outside his bed-chamber window in *Wuthering Heights* or Jane Eyre's dreams of children, to the ghost stories of Amelia Edwards or Margaret Oliphant. Henry James's *The Turn of the Screw* (1898) shows the uncertain boundaries between the fiction of the supernatural and that which dramatizes the workings of the inner mind. The apparitions in this tale may be ghosts, or they may be interpreted as projections of the unstable unconscious of the governess who witnesses them. In his longer fictions, James is the most notable of all late-Victorian novelists in his attempts to show the workings of the inner life, representing, in works like *The Wings of the Dove* (1902) and *The Ambassadors* (1903), the mind's dialogue with itself as well as the narrator's dialogue with the motivations of the characters.

In these, as well as in earlier novels—*The Portrait of a Lady* (1881), or *What Maisie Knew* (1897)—James resists a neat conclusion, leaving the reader with unresolved questions. His deliberate refusal to pin down meaning is related to the second important phenomenon which places the perceiver at the centre of cultural interpretation: the growing acknowledgement and exploration of the limitations of language. Wordsworth, in *The Prelude*, looks back to the 'spots of time' which encapsulate, epiphany-like, crucial moments in the formation of his poetic self, trying to recapture them, 'so far as words may give' an image of the past. Tennyson, in *In Memoriam*, attempting to put his grief into language, writes how 'words, like Nature, half reveal/ And half conceal the Soul within': a revealing turn of phrase since, in its turn, it suggests that the visible world is only part of the 'truth' of the world. *The Ring and the Book* (1868–69), Robert Browning's long poem, was written under the influence of nineteenth-century historiography. It dramatizes, through telling the same story a number of times through different voices, how any narrative is open to multiple interpretations, according to the range of vested interests which are brought to both its telling and its comprehension: 'Art' is perhaps a privileged means of expression, since it 'may tell a truth/Obliquely, do the thing shall breed the thought'—suggest, in other words, rather than dictate: 'write the book shall mean, beyond the facts'. But perhaps there is no truth, no centre at all, only different angles of vision. This is the notion put forward near the opening of Conrad's *Heart of Darkness*, where the unnamed voice who introduces Marlow's narrative notes that 'to him the meaning of an episode was not inside like a kernel but outside, enveloping the tale which brought it out only as a glow brings out a haze'.

By the end of the century, the notion of what constituted a 'centre', what a periphery, could no longer be voiced with unquestioned confidence. In the case of many literary works, the mode of narration, or the effects of sound or imagery, were self-consciously rendered as important as the events or the content which simultaneously formed the focus of a piece. More broadly, the idea of what counted as central was destabilized in cultural politics just as it was in internal issues of nationalism, or when considering the relations of Britain and its overseas empire. If powerful social groupings attempted to invest certain types of writing, music, or theatrical entertainment with particular values, they were doing so in the light of expanding literacy, and a multiplicity of new voices expressing themselves in print. And the borderline between 'serious' culture and more popular forms was, in any case, increasingly unclear. *Heart of Darkness* itself, for example, was first published, like many tales of adventure, in *Blackwood's Edinburgh Magazine*. This cultural diversity was seen with pride by those immediate commentators who looked back on Victoria's reign and on the century as a whole: they put it forwards as a sign of Britain's greatness. Yet this very diversity, experimentation, and multiplicity of voices was to provide the site for the many challenges to this presumed greatness in the century which followed.

Plate 9 An Iron Style University Museum, Oxford. For this important building, in which Ruskin took an intense interest, a competition was held in 1853. Benjamin Woodward's design won, out of 32 plans submitted. For all its Gothic forms, it was an intensely modern building, its medieval detail disguising up-to-the-minute planning and services, and the main hall using 'railway materials'—iron and glass—throughout.

Cities, architecture, and art

Andrew Saint

Cities

Cities offer what the visual arts require: skilled labour, access to special equipment and materials, an alertness to fashion, contact with clients, and chances for stimulus, rivalry, and collaboration. So if, as is often said, the nineteenth century was an age of cities, that meant no great change in the way the fine and applied arts in Britain were created. The novelty was that they were now not just originated in cities but directed overwhelmingly towards them as well.

The onset of Britain's nineteenth-century urbanization was sharp indeed. In 1800 there were no cities outside London with a population over 100 000; at the time of Victoria's accession in 1837 there were 5; in 1891, 23. Birmingham, Bradford, Leeds, Liverpool, Manchester, and Sheffield all grew by more than 40% between 1821 and 1831. Thereafter, urban growth was remorseless but not quite so rapid. Yet some cities were more or less products of the second half of the century, among them Belfast, Cardiff, and Middlesbrough. We tend to think of such growth as due to industry, yet resort towns grew just as rapidly; Brighton, for instance, increased from 7 000 in 1801 to 123 000 in 1901. By then, 80% of English and Welsh people lived in cities.

As for London, over a million people lived within ten miles of Westminster in 1800; at the mid-point of the century, the figure was 2.6 million, and by 1900, 6.5 million, amounting to 20% of the population of England and Wales. The cultural dominance of the capital diminished a little in the middle decades of the century as the industrial cities matured, but then rose again after 1880 with the tide of imperialism, the boom of the service sector, and the rise of the commuter suburb.

As the role of urban populations in the production of wealth and art alike was so strong, most of the surplus available for culture was also spent in cities. Along with this went a shift from the individualism of Georgian patronage towards a collective sense of civic culture—towards the belief that cities should foster good art and design. That creed, long familiar among the communities of Continental Europe, spread gradually across nineteenth-century Britain, in tandem with the pursuit of better local government and healthier cities. The grandest gestures were attempted in the capitals of London, Edinburgh, and (to a lesser extent) Dublin, the established centres for making and trading all kinds of art, and the venues for the national institutions of culture that sprang up during the century. But the movement for expressing local pride through the arts and sciences was almost more striking in Britain's merchant cities. The Liverpool banker and art-collector William Roscoe was only a trifle ahead of his time when he compared his city's energy and aspirations to Renaissance Florence in the 1810s. Twenty years later, Birmingham, Glasgow, Manchester, and Newcastle all had flourishing private societies or academies which supported local art and architecture as well as trade and invention.

Not that many British cities of the period were beautiful or pleasant places. Such was the haste, scale, and rawness of urbanization after 1820 that many artists and moralists came to believe that cities represented all that was worst about the period and the nation, and symbolized cultural degeneracy. Even those who admired the vitality of the early industrial city were repelled by it at the same time; Alexis de Tocqueville described the Manchester of 1835, with its towering factories, its noise and its teeming energy, as a 'foul drain', a 'filthy sewer' from which nevertheless 'pure gold flows. Here humanity attains its most complete development and its most brutish; here civilization works its miracles, and civilized man is turned back almost to a savage.'

Mechanisms for ordering the unstoppable urban influx long remained inadequate. Until the very end of the century there was no conscious science or art of town planning. The layout of city-centres and their streets or of industrial quarters seldom fell to architects. Economy-minded politics in the town halls meant that the replanning of central streets and the slum-clearance schemes which became common after 1870 were not regarded as aesthetic matters and were entrusted in the main to engineers and sanitarians. By Continental standards, Victorian city-centres are incoherent and unplanned, though graced by individually magnificent monuments; where they are successful as a whole, as in Edinburgh, there is an element of topographical luck about it.

Architecture

Yet if architects could do little to alter the scale and configuration of the city, nineteenth-century urbanization made a huge impact on the nature of architecture. The eighteenth-century British town seldom consisted of much more than housing, adapted where necessary to selling and making things, plus a church and inn or two and perhaps a market hall and assembly rooms. The late-Victorian city, by contrast, boasted a plethora of specialized building types: among them, railway stations, town halls, banks, offices, factories, warehouses, shops, hotels, theatres, markets, hospitals, schools, prisons, police stations, fire stations, libraries, and flats. All this was the staple of the local architect, often a respected civic figure, who seldom failed to embellish his buildings with touches of style and ornament. But they were usually undertaken singly, with scant regard to context.

Urban housing

Until the middle of the century British cities were densely built, if not so packed as their Continental counterparts. Coal fires and poor water supply and drainage had long ago turned their centres into noxious places, where prosperous people preferred not to live. Yet so bad were roads and transport that most families dependent upon the urban economy had to live within walking distance of the commercial centre.

The Georgian terrace-house tradition therefore prospered up to the coming of the railways and beyond. In the 1820s Bath, Bristol,

Dublin, and Edinburgh, cities which had flourished in the eighteenth century, were all still raising classical squares, streets, and crescents. The main change was a feeling for broader composition and for the relationship between building, street, and landscape. Architects were now increasingly employed by landowners to design layouts for new quarters of towns and make elevations for the fronts of whole blocks, thus bringing rhythm and movement to suburban street architecture. In Edinburgh, when the New Town was enlarged, the new streets were curved, not gridded, with the objective of attaining 'a happy union of foliage and building'.

The originator of this art of the picturesque suburb within a confined landscape was John Nash. His skilful groupings of stuccoed terrace fronts for Regent's Park, London (1812–26) were quickly taken up both by fashionable development in the capital and by the new resort towns like Cheltenham, Leamington Spa, St Leonards, and, above all, Brighton. Stucco, enriched after 1840 with French or Italianate detailing, continued in vogue for town-house fronts in London, Brighton, and such other south-coast towns as Plymouth until the 1860s. Elsewhere, plainer façades were favoured. Liverpool embarked in the 1830s on a programme of squares and terraces in sober brickwork within a grid of wide streets, modelled on Dublin. At the same time, Newcastle was graced by a set of rising streets and squares laid out by the speculator Richard Grainger, with masonry fronts by John Dobson, one of many capable neoclassical architects working in provincial cities. Glasgow took advantage of its sand-stones to further monumental classicism in a fine series of terraces which culminate in Alexander Thomson's Great Western Terrace (1869), crowning a stretch of high-class ribbon development along Great Western Road.

Though architects dressed up the fronts of terraced houses, they were seldom the prime movers in urban housing. This role remained in the hands of speculative builders, a few of whom, like Thomas Cubitt in London between 1820 and 1850, advanced to become busi-nessmen on the largest scale with high social status (Cubitt offered a complete 'design and build' service which extended to providing the whole of Osborne House on the Isle of Wight for Queen Victoria and Prince Albert). Town-house interiors were fitted out to individual taste by upholsterers or, as time went on, specialist firms of decor-ators. From the 1850s drawing rooms *en suite*, generally in a French taste, occupied the first floor of the largest houses. The up-and-down planning of such houses was stretched to a tiring four or five storeys or, in London, even six; at the rear, gardens gave way to ugly back extensions. After 1880, London succumbed to the opportunities of horizontal living afforded by the hydraulic lift and by the improvements in transport, which made the keeping of private horses and carriages in mews no longer necessary. Demand for such flats was always ahead of supply. By 1890 the building of blocks of large urban terrace houses had collapsed, as professional people opted for detached houses in the suburbs. Yet the terrace type continued at two-storey scale for clerks and artisans in most towns up to the First World War.

Purpose-built housing for the working classes was an invention of the Industrial Revolution. Housing the workforce first became an issue where a fall of clean water had drawn a mill to a site far from existing settlements. Discipline and control were the key to planning and managing such communities. New Lanark (1799–1819), the most famous early mill village, was created and run by its begetter, Robert Owen, with a blend of benevolence and authoritarianism. The Victorian factory villages that followed, notably Saltaire outside Bradford, Bournville outside Birmingham, and Port Sunlight on the Wirral, followed the same pattern of paternalist control. Yet they were to become archetypes for progressive planning. Port Sunlight and Bournville in particular, laid out in the more liberal 1880s and 1890s with updated cottage plans and much open space, transformed self-interest on the part of their founders into civic art; at Bournville, the houses had ample gardens and could even be rented by those who did not work in the factory. Prompted by Ebenezer Howard's *Garden Cities of Tomorrow* (1898), the factory village was the practical model from which the garden city was to spring soon after 1900.

By contrast, Britain's industrial towns mostly expanded by means of shrunken versions of the middle-class terrace house, built for profit and rented out. Their unhealthiness, overcrowding, and meanness earned ringing condemnation from Engels when he investigated Manchester in 1844. By then a sequence of epidemics and government commissions had clinched the connection between mortality rates and bad housing, water supply, and drainage. New building regulations followed and standards slowly improved, in response to Public Health Acts in 1848 and 1875. In the reformed house-type for the

Victorian artisan's family, water would be laid on to the kitchen alone, and there would be a water or earth closet in an outhouse in the yard; there was no fixed bath, and all cooking and water-heating were done from the kitchen range. Where housing came in big concentrations, blocks were fitted into standardized grids of 'byelaw streets'. Roadways were paved in setts; the two-storey brick houses came up to the pavement and often had a common alley behind the yards. In dense cities, Leeds notoriously, back alleys and even yards were dispensed with, so that row houses became 'back-to-backs', enclosed on three sides and with ventilation from the street front alone. In Yorkshire hill towns (Halifax, Hebden Bridge) and the iron-and-coal communities of the south Wales valleys, rows straggled out into the countryside along the contours.

City authorities began to clear slums from the 1840s, but were hampered by their lack of rehousing powers. Instead, private 'philanthropic' companies offering limited dividends began to build purpose-built flats for artisans, constructed like warehouses, with five storeys, concrete floors, flat roofs and tough internal finishes. These initiatives expanded after 1870 following a series of laws aimed at easing clearances, but rents remained high, and affordable only by skilled workers. Housing reformers preferred to rehouse workers in the suburbs, but the cost of transport to and from work was beyond many families' incomes. A new drive for slum-clearance and better housing followed a royal commission in 1884, after which municipalities began to take the lead. In the Boundary Street Estate, Shoreditch (1893–1900), the London County Council developed the flat-plans of the philanthropic companies and gave their blocks a smarter setting and appearance. This scheme was to set the pattern of the twentieth-century urban council estate.

Scotland had its own flatted or tenement tradition. As developed in Glasgow and Edinburgh for artisans and the middle class alike, the tenement remained a dwelling with anything between two and ten rooms off a common stair, which often projected at the back; behind was a common back court or drying green. In later extensions to Glasgow's grid, the tenement blocks occupy the sides of a broad square while the court enjoys open space in the centre. An improvement trust was formed in the 1860s to redevelop slum property, but as in England the municipality only built working-class flats from the 1890s.

Public parks

If the landscaping of the country house was at the cutting edge of garden design in the eighteenth century, the urban park was its successor. It epitomized the mid-nineteenth-century passion for linking health and welfare with didacticism and civic order.

The public park started out as an amenity intended to raise the value and status of suburban estate development, around or even within it. Such were Nash's Regent's Park in London of the 1820s, and the first two parks designed by the gardener, inventor, and entrepreneur, Joseph Paxton: Prince's Park, Liverpool, and Birkenhead Park on either side of the Mersey (1842–47). Only a portion of Regent's Park was at first open to all; other sections were leased as botanic and zoological gardens with limited public access. The zoo's exotic structures and inmates in their parkland setting became a nineteenth-century equivalent to Georgian follies, mixing instruction and entertainment. Dedicated enclosures of this type were to become features of the grander Victorian parks, or sometimes parks in themselves.

The pressure to create parks irrespective of their economic benefits stemmed from the Select Committee on Public Walks. At the time it reported, in 1833, urban death rates were cause for alarm and the value of public space for exercise and good air was gaining acceptance. Piecemeal legislation followed, making it easier for towns to create public parks. Their strongest advocate and publicist was J. C. Loudon, who believed that 'gardens are works of art, rather than of nature'. He developed his ideas in the privately sponsored Derby Arboretum (1839–40). This was a small park with serpentine paths round the periphery, straight ones in the middle, mounds in between to give a sense of size and privacy, benches for relaxation, and trees labelled with names. Such was to be the language of the municipal parks laid out from the 1840s, with Manchester, Preston, and other English northern towns taking a lead.

The Franco-Italian formalism which was a feature of early Victorian country-house gardens found its way into public parks with the landscape created by Paxton to accompany the rebuilding of the Crystal Palace at Sydenham (1854)—a panorama of carpet-bedded terraces, statues, pavilions, and waterworks running downhill to less formal lakes and islands, where models of prehistoric animals and geological strata could be enjoyed. Crystal Palace, with its red-and-yellow bedding, developed the ponderous colour displays of bedded plants that have become synonymous with the idea of the Victorian public park. And indeed the design of urban parks did not evolve much after this, though many filled up with bandstands, conservatories, tea pavilions, playgrounds, and other sources of supervised, 'rational recreation'.

Classicism

Despite challenges to its authority, classicism of one type or another remained the commonest idiom for secular urban architecture in Britain throughout the century. In the years after Waterloo it had ceased to be the universal style, but was riding high in Britain's cities in the guise of neoclassicism. This was an international movement, stimulated by the opening-up of Greece and Egypt to travellers and by the fortunes of revolutionary France, whose ambitions had often been measured against the values and achievements of antiquity. Neoclassicism stressed the origins of architecture, and looked to Greece rather than Rome or the Renaissance. Greek proportions, porticoes, orders, and ornament lent civic buildings a gravity lacking in earlier Palladianism. Interiors were less affected by this Hellenizing fashion, because archaeology offered less information about ancient interiors. Nevertheless, a few interior decorators and connoisseurs experimented with a sensuous Graeco-Egyptian taste.

A boost to Hellenism was given in 1815–16, when the world of art persuaded the government to purchase for the British Museum the sculpture looted from the Parthenon by Lord Elgin. Acquisitions of such antiquities, notably treasures from Egypt, Babylonia, and Assyria, were repeated throughout the century. They boosted Britain's cultural credentials, encouraged tourism, and gave artists authentic originals to learn from. They also made Greek the inevitable choice for Sir Robert Smirke's heavily colonnaded British Museum (1823–46), the grandest of London's neoclassical buildings. But the city where Greek architecture made the most impact was Edinburgh. As a climax to the golden age of Edinburgh's culture, the 'Athens of the North' was graced with a necklace of neoclassical public buildings ranging from W. H. Playfair's Royal Scottish Academy (1822–26) and National Gallery of Scotland (1850–57) to Thomas

Hamilton's Royal High School (1825–29). Edinburgh even has an acropolis of its own upon Calton Hill, where Playfair and C. R. Cockerell started a 'national monument' in temple form (1824–29). This was one of many neoclassical projects—columns, gateways, and arches were the commonest—intended to commemorate the Napoleonic wars. Such memorials could have many purposes. The greatest was the Euston Arch, a gateway in front of Euston Station, London, built in 1835–37 by Philip Hardwick in homage to the momentous destiny of the railways. The general cemeteries built in the 1830s and 1840s to solve the urban burial crisis were also mostly neoclassical in their architecture and in their earliest memorials.

Most architects of the 1820s welcomed the Greek orders into a wider language of 'romantic classicism'—indeed into the ever-broadening family of emotive architectural forms. Among those of an older generation to do so, the greatest were Sir John Soane and John Nash. Soane's architecture mingled a set of personal obsessions involving light, primitivism, and melancholy with a deep comprehension of classicism; all these qualities can be felt in his miraculous house-museum at Lincoln's Inn Fields, London (1792–1824). Nash, his rival, was expert in using the classical orders to picturesque effect. But his temper ran too shallow for the highest level of architecture. His Buckingham Palace (1825–30) for George IV ran into multiple problems and was savaged for its shortcomings. It contrasts lamely with the exotic vulgarity of the Brighton Pavilion, Nash's previous work for the king (then the Prince Regent). Many classicists of the eclectic 1820s took much from Nash and a little from Soane. One such was John Foulston, who endowed the new centre of Devonport with 'an "Egyptian" library, a "Hindoo" Nonconformist chapel, a "primitive Doric" town hall, and a street of houses dressed with an orthodox Roman Corinthian order'.

After 1840, classicism remained the natural choice for city buildings. But in England it lost its ideological edge to Gothic. C. R. Cockerell, an architect of scholarship and refinement, was accused by A. W. N. Pugin of 'paganizing in the universities' when he built the Ashmolean Museum, Oxford and University Library, Cambridge, in a Franco-Greek idiom; and Lord Palmerston had to exert pressure in 1856 to force Sir Gilbert Scott, a well-known Goth, to build the Foreign Office in the classical style. Pure neoclassicism now lost ground to Italian Renaissance styles, more adaptable to modern uses.

Cockerell and Sir Charles Barry ushered in the 'Italianate' idiom, popular for banks, insurance offices, and clubs in mid-Victorian cities. Among the best manipulators of this 'palazzo' style, redolent of Florentine or Venetian mercantile prosperity, were John Gibson, architect of many banks, and Edward Walters of Manchester, where inner-city warehouses after 1850 often sported magnificent façades. Aspiring textile towns in the north of England built rich classical town halls with towers, notably Bolton, Halifax, Leeds, and, smaller but exquisite, Todmorden (by Gibson). Despite frequent defections to other styles, Victorian public and cultural buildings long clung to classicism. Liverpool boasts the grandest of all British classical buildings, St George's Hall, by H. L. Elmes and C. R. Cockerell (1841–56); and behind it runs a backdrop of library, art gallery, and courts, dating from the 1850s to the 1880s and all deploying the orders with force and scholarship. A brassier form of classicism was the mansarded French style popular for the monster hotels of the 1860s. Among these, Cuthbert Brodrick's Grand Hotel, Scarborough, stands out for verve.

Scotland alone retained unwavering loyalty to classicism after 1850, in part because of its distinct religious history, in part because of its tradition of building in dressed stone, which the classical orders of architecture needed to manifest their full power. The foremost of many Scottish architects to persevere with classicism was Alexander ('Greek') Thomson of Glasgow, who created churches, villas, and terraces of great originality from the Greek language of column and lintel long after it had lost its *chic* in England.

Nevertheless, there was a sense of renewal everywhere when, after years of flirting with Gothic and other styles, English civic architecture reverted to the European classical tradition after Victoria's golden jubilee in 1887. Increased consciousness of empire and respect for the clarity of French classicism had much to do with this change. The precursor of what was to be known as 'Edwardian baroque' was John Belcher's Institute of Chartered Accountants, London (1889–93), an essay in the form of a rich North Italian palazzo, laced with sculpture. English classicism was also revived: various civic buildings and government offices in the 1890s brought the wheel full circle back to 'Wrenaissance' and even 'Neo-Georgianism'. As the century closed, the architectural journals abounded in classical competition designs for town halls and law courts. Such was the competition for Cardiff

Town Hall, won in 1897 by H. V. Lanchester and E. A. Rickards with a flamboyant design that was to be the starting point for that city's amply planned new centre at Cathays Park.

The Gothic Revival

The Gothic Revival was the most dynamic movement in British nineteenth-century architecture. Though it had started out in the previous century as an exercise in nostalgia or whimsy, by 1815 it had matured into a flexible and semi-scholarly idiom in much demand for large country houses. Metropolitan and regional specialists in this 'castle style' (like Thomas Hopper, John Nash, and Jeffry Wyatville in London; Francis Johnston and Richard Morrison in Dublin) offered their clients mansions with medievalizing elevations, balanced by plushly upholstered interiors in classical or light Gothic taste. It found special favour in the remote or rugged landscapes of rural Ireland, Scotland, and Wales, as well as for such forbidding building types as gaols.

During the 1820s, the craze for Sir Walter Scott's best-selling novels and for antiquarianism in general relaxed the castle style into something broader and vaguer, summed up by the phrase 'the mansions of the olden times'—a kind of indiscriminate nostalgia for the medieval and Elizabethan periods. This 'Waverley' phase of the Gothic Revival found royal recognition when George IV translated his coronation ceremony into a medieval pageant in 1821, and Wyatville enlarged and romanticized Windsor Castle (1824–40). All this helped to deepen the claims of Gothic to be the one truly authentic national style. Hence the historic decision of 1835 that the fire-ravaged Palace of Westminster should for reasons of context and national sentiment be rebuilt in the Gothic or Elizabethan style.

The revival of Gothic was to reach its apogee in church building, an activity then seen as critical to public order and culture. The mass of remaining medieval churches offered ready inspiration. The 1800 Act of Union had already prompted Parliament to vote sums towards cheap churches for the established Church of Ireland, many in a stunted Gothic style. This set a precedent for larger subsidies voted in 1818–19 for England, where the Anglicans had failed to supply enough seats for potential worshippers in the manufacturing districts and city suburbs. The 'Commissioners' churches' built with this government money in the 1820s tended to be classical still in city-centres, but took to Gothic elsewhere, notably in Yorkshire and Lancashire. Though criticized on many grounds, they were to be the starting point for Victorian church building.

The artistic impetus for improving Gothic church building came above all from A. W. N. Pugin. Pugin had grown up in his father's drawing atelier, which specialized in Gothic detail; this gave him his passion and feeling for medieval precedent. In 1835 he joined the Roman Catholics, six years after they had won official freedom of worship, and in 1836 he published his celebrated *Contrasts*, which by juxtaposing drawings of medieval and modern buildings purported to show the degeneracy of taste and morals. Pugin preached an impossible return to medieval principles in art, religion, and politics, guided by the Catholic Church and Gothic example. But though deeply conservative by instinct, he was an innovator in practice. Up to his early death in 1852 he turned out a cascade of influential tracts, images, churches, and designs for the applied arts. His churches vary in quality; often they suffered from lack of funds and Pugin's prickly relations with the Catholic hierarchy.

Pugin's lead was taken up by the Tory patrons and architects of the Oxford Movement, the High-Church wing of the Church of England, and its church-building counterpart, the 'Ecclesiological Movement'. Since government funding was blocked for further Anglican churches because of protest from Dissenters and Catholics, the aims of the movement had to be forwarded instead by private patronage. Between 1850 and 1870 many forceful churches were built in which motifs from Continental Gothic overlaid the English thirteenth- and fourteenth-century styles that Pugin recommended. 'High-Church' architects identified with the ecclesiologists and planned their churches in the Catholic manner, emphasizing the altar and the mass; 'Low-Church' ones tried to reconcile Gothic axiality with the auditorial and preaching traditions of Protestant worship. All were abetted by an army of craftsmen specializing in church fittings and by the rhetoric of John Ruskin, who in *The Seven Lamps of Architecture* (1849) and *The Stones of Venice* (1851–53) proved a fleeting advocate of the Gothic Revival. The colourfulness and passion of the best High Victorian churches owe much to Ruskin's persuasive prose.

In the same years, countless medieval cathedrals and churches were restored and rearranged—too radically by today's standards, yet with real scholarship. After 1870, English church building became cooler. G. F. Bodley and G. G. Scott Junior drew the High-Church Anglicans towards a more spiritual taste, mingling English and Netherlandish fifteenth-century inspiration. Towards the end of the century, the dogmatism of Gothic dissolved; the finest church of the 1890s, the Catholics' Westminster Cathedral by J. F. Bentley, a Goth by training, espoused an Italo-Byzantine basilican style.

Beyond England, the Gothic Revival had mixed fortunes. Ireland, where Catholic church building proceeded apace after the emancipation of 1829, came under Pugin's spell and soon took to Gothic. Yet, though there are good native buildings in the style (notably by J. J. McCarthy), the country's finest Victorian churches, G. E. Street's Christ Church Cathedral, Dublin and William Burges' Cork Cathedral, were designed by Englishmen bolstering up the ailing Church of Ireland. In Scotland and Wales, the classical temple type remained popular as the best plan form for congregational worship. Most Gothic churches built in these countries had an English aura and lacked the intimacy of the galleried, rectangular kirk or chapel. In the towns, that type began after 1850 to abandon Calvinist simplicity in favour of luxurious classical fronts with towers, claiming kinship with Solomon's Temple.

Gothic as a Victorian secular style was less convincing. Its early triumph was Charles Barry's Palace of Westminster. The largest single building in the world in its day, this *gesamtkunstwerk* involved every known modern art and technique, from quantity surveying, heating and ventilating systems, and iron roof construction to revived fresco painting. The design even managed to incorporate allusions to English medieval parliaments, so stimulating historical interest in parliamentary evolution. Pugin came in to help Barry detail and furnish the interiors. The building's success owes much to the way in which intricate planning and services are disguised by medieval detail. Later public projects like Alfred Waterhouse's Manchester Town Hall and Natural History Museum, London, Sir Gilbert Scott's Glasgow University, Basil Champneys' John Rylands Library, Manchester, and Thomas Deane and Benjamin Woodward's University Museum, Oxford, mixed modern planning and ancient detail in the same spirit. Often, fronts modelled on the old town and market halls of Germany and the Low Countries disguised many small offices behind.

Other Victorian secular buildings clung to Gothic where there was a religious, educational, or charitable connection, as in hospitals, schools, universities, and parsonages. Plenty of Gothic houses, too, went on being built up to the 1870s, the castle style reaching its acme in the excesses of Cardiff Castle, reconstructed by Burges for the millionaire Marquess of Bute. Many a suburban house sported pointed relieving arches, conspicuous over modern, square-topped sashes. But upon most of the new secular building types and many city-centres the Gothic Revival made little impact. By 1900 it had all but shrunk to a specialist style for churches.

The English house

Until 1780 the aristocratic country house had been the focus of British architecture, governed by ideals taken from the classicism of Palladio as codified by his English disciples. That consensus was dying by the time of the French Revolution and dead by 1815. Country houses held a special place in the national consciousness throughout the new century, even after the collapse of agricultural rents from the 1870s meant that they had to be openly subsidized by urban wealth. But they were now built, landscaped, and decorated to suit the taste of their owners, not in a shared idiom. Hence arose the movement which culminated at the end of the century in the internationally noted phenomenon of 'the English house'.

One reason for the popularity of the castle style for country houses in the early nineteenth century was its flexibility of layout. The wings and basements of the old symmetrical houses no longer satisfied the demand for privacy and comfort. One compromise offering a balance of classical order with asymmetrical planning was the Italianate house. This was the idiom of Barry's Trentham Hall (1834–40), which supplied the ideas for Victoria and Albert's Osborne House (1845–48). More popular, however, was the Elizabethan or Scottish baronial manner, offering patriotic sentiment without the small windows of the authentic castle. Between 1835 and 1870, this was the favourite type for country-house building. Though such houses now often look under-furnished and drab, in their day they were efficient machines for the sharply defined patterns of Victorian home life. Family and servants were firmly segregated, while a respect for privacy and separate domains for the sexes became axiomatic. The décor of 'male' and 'female' rooms was distinguished, with dark panelling prevalent in dining and billiard rooms, lighter plasterwork in drawing rooms, boudoirs, and bedrooms. Central heating often appeared after 1835 as a back-up for coal fires; piped water and WCs started to ramify; and stabling became a science. Houses of this era often had formal parterres with coloured and patterned bedding on the garden side of the house, slipping into picturesque prospects beyond the terrace.

After 1870, as agricultural rents fell, the great mansion on its landed estate ceased to be the archetype for English domestic architecture. That mantle fell instead upon the large middle-class house, in its own ample grounds but free from the ties of an estate. Progressive houses combined the now-familiar techniques of specialized domestic planning with motifs from English vernacular buildings such as half-timbering, tile-hanging, inglenooks, and romantically tall chimneys. Lodges and cottages of this type had long been built. But the 'vernacular revival' movement of the 1870s, led by Norman Shaw and W. E. Nesfield, enlarged the cottage style into a vehicle for middle-sized houses. The quaintness of this idiom gave a sense of rootedness, above all to the railway-commuting bourgeoisie of the Home Counties. A more puritanical approach was taken by Philip Webb, in a personal line of development from his Red House, Bexleyheath (1858–60, for William Morris) to Standen (1892–94), the masterpiece of the late-Victorian country house. Regional variants to the vernacular revival style took account of local materials and building traditions. Architects in the English Midlands and north-west, led by John Douglas of Chester, explored the area's timber-building traditions, while Scotland revisited its legacy of harling-faced houses. Only Wales and Ireland were too poor to profit from this railway-dependent boom in 'small country houses'.

The climax of this movement came after 1890, when the English and Scottish middle-class house found a balance of tradition, originality, comfort, and freedom. The key to this was the refinement and simplification of house planning and of local motifs and materials, underpinned by cheap land, building, and craftsmanship and a spread of enthusiasm for artistic houses and gardens, latterly diffused by the magazine *Country Life*. M. H. Baillie Scott, W. R. Lethaby, Edwin Lutyens, C. R. Mackintosh, Ernest Newton, and C. F. A. Voysey were the leading architects of this so-called Arts and Crafts house, while William Robinson and Gertrude Jekyll brought freshness to the layout and planting of flower gardens around it. This equipoise was delicate, however. By 1900, larger country houses had reverted to full-blooded classicism, presaging an imperial pomp which few Edwardian architects could resist.

In English towns, the late-Victorian desire for freedom and individualism found a variant outlet in the so-called 'Queen Anne' style. The name referred to the red-brick and white-windowed architecture of Queen Anne's reign, which was then fitted to modern plans, and energized with shaped gables and ornament from the 'Northern Renaissance'—the old mercantile town houses of Belgium, France, Germany, and Holland. The Queen Anne recipe found a fertile field after 1870 in town houses, schools, seaside buildings, theatres, shops, and offices. It could be spare, as in the London studio houses designed by Norman Shaw, riotous, or just pretty. Sometimes it connoted a liberal and secularizing philosophy; it was popular for the urban board schools built for state elementary education, offering well-lit classrooms and an image of liberty from Gothic gloom and religious control. In its richer, 'Free Renaissance' form it implied unabashed bourgeois individualism, as for instance in Ernest George's run of fantastically gabled town houses in Harrington and Collingham Gardens, Kensington.

By the 1890s Queen Anne had gone commercial and was despised by the avant-garde. A boom late in the decade promoted a rash of extravagant pubs, and of theatres and music halls, a type dominated nationally by Frank Matcham, whose buildings gainsaid *fin-de-siècle* effeteness with a thumping heartiness. A handful of architects made the transition at this time from Queen Anne to something like an urban art nouveau. Among them was C. Harrison Townsend, whose terracotta-clad Bishopsgate Institute, Whitechapel Gallery, and Horniman Museum were aesthetic beacons of reform in the poorer parts of London. The most famous building of this moment is C. R. Mackintosh's Glasgow School of Art, begun in 1897 and balanced between traditionalism, ornamentalism, and a quite personal style. But most of the buildings of the late Victorian urban reformers were Arts and Crafts in taste, that is to say, softer and quieter than either Townsend's or Mackintosh's idiom.

The legacy of engineering

Definite divisions between architect, engineer, surveyor, and builder had yet to be fixed in the early nineteenth century. Apprenticeship or articles were the usual training; the only schools for engineers were military, and full-time education for architects began only in the 1890s. In England, the Institution of Civil Engineers was formed in 1818 and the (Royal) Institute of British Architects in 1834; the Institute of Architects in Scotland followed in 1840. Slowly these bodies clarified professional boundaries. But the titles of the early-Victorian architectural weeklies—the *Civil Engineer and Architect's Journal*, *The Builder*, and *The Building News*—indicate their broad audience.

In the century's heroic new constructions, engineers took the lead. By 1815 a wave of canals, docks, port, and road improvements, waterworks, lighthouses, and bridges were establishing the profession of consulting engineer. John Rennie, for instance, a Scottish millwright by origin and briefly an erector of steam engines for Boulton and Watt, devoted his independent career entirely to civil engineering: among his works were canals, aqueducts, harbour improvements, breakwaters and docks, a road tunnel, a system of stone water pipes, coining machinery, a steam-powered smithy for Woolwich Dockyard, innovative sheds with mobile cranes for the West India Docks, and no less than three bridges across the Thames in London. His sons, George and Sir John Rennie, pursued both the civil and the mechanical sides of the business into the railway age. Thomas Telford, Rennie's contemporary, started out as a mason and architect, then shifted into public engineering. His roads, canals, and bridges in the Highlands, and his London to Holyhead road, opened up remoter areas of the kingdom for economic development. Telford also built the world's first enduring bridge on the suspension principle, across the Menai Straits (1819–26).

The next generation of engineers was caught up by the railway mania. Stations, bridges, and even tunnels played a modest part in the first railways, but grew bolder as the network extended and investment paid off. Isambard Kingdom Brunel, for instance, learnt his trade on two long-drawn-out and troublesome projects, his father's Thames Tunnel, London (1824–43), and the Clifton Suspension Bridge (1830–63). His Great Western Railway was more ambitious in scale than most rivals. Yet his early Temple Meads Station, Bristol

(1839–40), is a tentative building with a medievalizing roof. On the GWR extension into Devon, many of the original structures were also at first lightly built in timber. Not until 1851–54, when the company's London terminus at Paddington was rebuilt, did Brunel team up with the architect Matthew Digby Wyatt to supply the first of the wide-span iron railway sheds with aesthetic ambitions. It was soon sur-passed by others, including Birmingham New Street, York, and St Pancras, London, where the engineer W. H. Barlow spanned the whole station without intermediate supports. St Pancras is one of many termini where the shed is hidden behind a hotel in a different style, here Sir Gilbert Scott's boastful Midland Grand Hotel; the con-trast and concealment, though often criticized as illogical, add to the drama.

Brunel's last contribution to railway building was the Royal Albert Bridge, Saltash, on which his name and the year of his death, 1859, are conspicuous. It belongs to a sequence of bold railway bridges, ranging from Robert Stephenson's High Level Bridge at Newcastle and the same engineer's box-girder Britannia Bridge across the Menai Straits (which greatly advanced the sciences of calculation and testing) to Sir Benjamin Baker and Sir John Fowler's Forth Railway Bridge. In this, the last of the great British railway bridges (1888–90), mild steel superseded wrought iron.

The engineers' contribution to urban infrastructure was profound. In the pre-Victorian period, water was the only service piped underground. Cast-iron pipes had started to supplant wooden ones to cope with higher water pressures by 1815. Gas mains started to ramify from the 1820s, to be joined by electricity conduit in the 1880s, as these services came into operation—at first reaching only pros-perous districts but later whole towns—often under municipal ownership.

Water engineering continued to make strides throughout the cen-tury, though it has attracted less notice than the construction of the railways. In the second half of the century, clean water was brought to cities from increasing distances. Manchester's Longendale scheme, started in 1848, was the first of significance. Glasgow took its water from Loch Katrine 35 miles away after 1859, but such distances were being more than doubled by the time the great masonry-dammed reservoir at Lake Vyrnwy in the hills of Montgomeryshire began in 1891 to supply Liverpool. Nor did canal construction cease with the advent of the railways, the great Manchester Ship Canal (1887–94) transforming Manchester's position as a port.

But perhaps the greatest engineering achievement of the mid-Victorian period was the design and construction of entire urban sewage systems, uniting older brick-lined sewers with new iron ones that fed the waste out to pumping stations. No technology did so much for the slow improvement in health and reputation of British cities. The most famous example was the London network carried out by Joseph Bazalgette for the Metropolitan Board of Works in 1859–65. In underground engineering for transport, London was again in the forefront. The Thames Tunnel of 1828–43, the world's first underwater tunnel of significance, pioneered tunnelling techniques which finally came into their own in the 1890s when electric traction allowed the building of the first deep-level tubes.

Iron made its way unevenly into architecture proper. By the 1820s, cast-iron supports carrying floors in mills or galleries in churches and theatres were common. Concealed iron beams in floors to achieve wider spans and permit heavier loadings, and conservatories with curved ribs of iron and glass panes, were also familiar. The next step was the glasshouses built by Joseph Paxton at Chatsworth in the 1830s and developed in the 1840s by Richard Turner for the botanical gardens at Kew, Dublin, and Belfast. The Kew Palm House (1844–48), constructed by Turner with the architect Decimus Burton, is the most graceful of them. The climax of this line of invention was the Crystal Palace, developed for the Great Exhibition of 1851 by the engineer contractors Fox and Henderson from a concept patented by Paxton. The main innovations of the Crystal Palace were its size, the method and speed of its erection, and the publicity that it attracted. Its spacious interiors and colour scheme were admired, but many people found its repetitiousness boring. When Paxton re-erected the Crystal Palace at Sydenham, South London, in 1855 he took care to amend the design. Yet the structure's fame gave people confidence in iron and glass buildings. It also transferred techniques of prefabrication, fast-track construction, and time management from the railways into ordinary building.

Multi-storey warehouses, mills, or factories, mixing walls of masonry with internal frames of iron, had been invented in the eighteenth century but mushroomed in number and scale after 1815, to the astonishment of foreign visitors. Schinkel drew, and de Tocqueville described, the brutally plain six-storey cotton mills of Manchester, in which maximizing internal space for manufacture or storage was the sole criterion. After 1865 factories were often accompanied by high chimneys, and occasionally boasted ornamental elevations (for example the Templeton Carpet Factory, Glasgow). The rented office buildings, and the larger urban shops and department stores which began to appear after 1870, tended to be constructed in the same way behind more elaborated fronts, while covered markets, arcades, and corn exchanges typically had masonry fronts but open interiors mixing iron, timber, and glass in the roof. Wholly iron-framed permanent buildings of several storeys were erected in small numbers from the 1850s. The first was the Sheerness Boat Store, one of a series of remarkable buildings designed by the Royal Engineers, whose technical competence caused Henry Cole to commission them for museums and other structures at South Kensington, including the Royal Albert Hall. A few commercial buildings in Liverpool and Glasgow were built with iron fronts as well as frames. But most cities forbade the practice, fearing the treacherous behaviour of structural iron in fire. This was the main reason why Britain failed to emulate either the brio of the French department stores of the Third Republic or the tall iron-framed office buildings which started to rise in New York and Chicago after 1880.

Concrete was likewise developed after 1865, at first as a cheap form of construction for cottages, warehouses, and even churches (for example St Barnabas, Oxford). It was considered unsightly, and always covered with either a cement render or a skin of brickwork. Reinforced concrete, which had been investigated by the Brunels and others after 1830, made belated headway in Britain, using a French patent. The first major building to employ the technique was Weavers Mill, Swansea (1897).

Art

Painting

British painting enjoyed a boom in the early nineteenth century, in response to growing middle-class prosperity and leisure. More people were learning to paint, as amateurs especially, but there were more professional painters, too. More people, too, were commissioning and buying art, especially in London, the undisputed centre of the art market. The annual Royal Academy exhibition, the most important 'showcase' for painters, expanded fourfold between 1779 and 1855, while other London venues sprang up to satisfy demand. By the end of the century London was awash with private galleries and dealers, while other cities (Edinburgh and Manchester in particular) had their equivalents.

In 1815 the strengths of British painting lay in portraiture, animal painting, and landscape. Portrait painting was shortly to go into relative decline. In London, Sir Thomas Lawrence, President of the Royal Academy and heir to Reynolds' crown as a society portraitist, died in 1830, his counterpart in Edinburgh, Sir Henry Raeburn, in 1823. Portraiture went on as an instrument of family record and professional commemoration, even resisting the inroads of the portrait photograph. Yet despite a scatter of psychological masterpieces, no painter rivalled Lawrence's capacity for glamour before John Singer Sargent settled in London in the 1880s. The originality of Victorian art was not primarily about the portrait. Nor was it about animal painting. Here, however, there was a change in tone, from the objective, old-style sporting picture, still practised by James Ward and others into the 1850s, towards open sentimentalism. What interested Edwin Landseer, the king of Victorian animal painters, and his many imitators was the expression of kinship between human beings and animals and their shared capacity for emotion.

In the twin careers of John Constable and J. M. W. Turner, English landscape painting of the 1820s was to shine with its brightest lustre. Around and after them came a host of painters who celebrated the romantic love of nature at points along a range stretching from pagan mysticism to worship of botanical and geological detail.

Though different in temperament and technique, Constable and Turner shared some characteristics. Both were more learned than the average painter, and longed to raise British landscape to the status enjoyed by history painting. In the light of their ambitions, the work of most popular landscapists of their time looks anodyne. By the 1820s, both were also in mid-career and in the process of conscious change, in response to the restlessness of society around them. Constable had left his native Suffolk, was painting larger pictures, and enriching his interpretations of nature and weather with hints about the decline of the settled order of things in England, as in his various versions of *Salisbury Cathedral from the Meadows*.

Turner, meanwhile, was creating a style of his own. As with many painters at the time, much of his work came from topographical books which he was commissioned to illustrate. His novelties in technique often flowed from these tasks; he experimented with mezzotint, and worked closely with the engravers who translated his pictures into print. Turner by no means repudiated the inspiration of the past. His finished paintings are in part recapitulations of Claude's work, paying experimental homage to the glories of sunlight and water with new tonalities of colour made available by modern chemistry—notably yellows. Turner's work baffled the public for a period in the 1830s. But it enjoyed a revival in the 1840s through the patronage of a handful of manufacturer collectors and the enthusiasm of Ruskin, who first came to public attention as the self-appointed champion of Turner. Ruskin's *Modern Painters*, in five volumes finally completed in 1860, became the rambling bible of Victorian art criticism, in which truth to nature was presented as the highest value and intricately defined. The book ranges widely across the English landscape school with an unpredictable mixture of insight and prejudice.

As passionate as Constable and as original as Turner were a youthful group of artists called 'the Ancients', who flourished in the late 1820s. They were followers of William Blake (still working till his death in 1827, notably on his woodcuts from Virgil) and of his disciple John Linnell. Like Blake, they were more draughtsmen-engravers than painters, and much of their work was in miniature. They met often at Shoreham in Kent, to study religion and antiquity as well as to make art. Samuel Palmer, the most famous of the Ancients, created hills, trees, and cornfields pregnant with spiritual force. His lesser-known equal, Edward Calvert, created small, sensuous engravings, imbued with wistful longing for a lost Arcadia. Many of the Ancients went on working for years, but only George Richmond the portrait painter improved upon his youthful reputation.

The individuality of the English landscapists of this period owed much to watercolour. Watercolour technique was neat and quick and did not need a large studio. The colours, available in sticks, could be manipulated for sketching and outdoor painting by professionals and amateurs alike. A consciousness of the wider potentialities of water-colour was rising in the early years of the century. Societies of paint-ers in watercolour sprang up in London in 1805 and 1831, offering exhibition space to a medium which the Royal Academy neglected and raising the sights of watercolourists beyond landscape.

In the pre-Victorian period, English watercolour specialists in landscape and topography were exploring broad washes and splashes of strong colour on white paper, so as to convey a generality and transparency impossible with oils. Such were J. S. Cotman, leading figure of the Norwich school of landscape, John Varley, and David Cox. But painters moved with increasing ease between the media. Constable used watercolour liberally for sketching, but exhibited in it only in his last years. The breadth and brightness of Turner's developed style in oil drew upon his devotion to watercolour, while R. P. Bonington's dashing sketches in wash likewise lightened his whole palette. The mid-Victorian love of precision depended upon a watercolour technique in which 'body' was added to the paint to make it more opaque and show finer gradations of detail. Painstaking watercolours of rustic scenery were a feature of late-Victorian art. Yet the medium kept its freshness: even so ponderous a painter as Rossetti refound spontaneity when he turned to wash.

History painting

Since Hogarth and Reynolds, British artists had been calling for a school of history and narrative painting. Nineteenth-century painters managed to establish one, but the achievement proved short-lived. After 1870 the demand for such paintings fell off; and our own age still finds art of this type wanting in immediacy.

History painting was supposed to commemorate, instruct, and ele-vate. To do this convincingly needed a structure of public patronage and exhibition that was missing before the 1830s. Pre-Victorian painters who chose this route took risks; James Barry starved, and Benjamin Haydon, the chief propagandist for history painting, committed suicide for lack of recognition. Benjamin West, more suc-cessful, prospered by means of well-publicized shows in his London studio, fees from engravings, and a sideline in portraiture. The Royal Academy was passive about history painting, while the British

Institution, set up in 1805 to promote the 'national school', proved ineffective. Not until the National Gallery opened its doors in 1824 did public opinion accept that the scope of British painting should be broader and bolder.

Where were painters to look for narrative subject matter? Classical and biblical scenes had limited appeal. Scenes from national history were more acceptable, but the conventions of high art made them hard to depict; uniforms and trousers were felt to look undignified. One answer was to avoid the heights of drama, and by selecting intimate or allusive scenes from history and literature to depict the past in the popular manner of Dutch genre painting. Thus David Wilkie scored a sensational hit with his *Chelsea pensioners reading the Waterloo dispatch* (1822), which showed not the battle itself but the reception of the news outside a suburban inn.

For the next fifty years the Royal Academy's exhibitions abounded in romantic or patriotic scenes from the margins of British history and literature. Shakespeare, Milton, Goldsmith, Sterne, and Scott were favourite authors, while episodes from the lives of Elizabeth I, Lady Jane Grey, Mary Queen of Scots, and Cromwell reinforced Lord Macaulay's view of British history as a line of noble struggle and constitutional progress. Many such paintings found their way into illustrated history books. The antiquarian passion for dress, armour, furniture, and architecture contributed to this movement. Painters hired researchers to ensure accuracy, and deployed props and costumes just as in the theatre.

The stage was indeed a great influence upon British painting. At this period the arts of the theatre, the book, the museum, and the gallery were bound together by ingredients of illusion, entertainment, and popular instruction. Theatrical scene painters like David Roberts and Clarkson Stanfield turned to the gallery and were hailed as major artists. Shipwrecks were a favourite theme among marine painters; and gigantic canvases reconstructing scenes from ancient and modern history were interpreted as educational aides, both when first exhibited and later in engraved and published form. The sensational painter of Biblical disasters, John Martin ('The King of the Vast'), was one of many who enjoyed a wide vogue in reproduction.

Gallery paintings, however, failed to satisfy the call for a more public profile for British art. Since the purchase of the Elgin Marbles, Benjamin Haydon had led a campaign to promote history painting by the public commissioning of works of art. In effect he was asking for patronage to pass from the monarchy to parliamentary democracy— a radical idea, and one that for many years fell on deaf ears. But in 1843 Parliament did agree to adorn its new home, the rebuilt Palace of Westminster, with historical subjects in fresco. The task was shared between many artists and the quality of the pictures, done in an unfamiliar technique, proved uneven. Worse, the medium of fresco turned out to be a disaster. Many paintings had soon to be restored, and few today present more than a shadow of their first appearance. The best include monumental scenes in the heroic style of history painting by Daniel Maclise in the Royal Gallery, of Wellington and Blücher, and of Nelson's death; and a series in a cooler, more linear style by William Dyce.

The experiments in fresco at Westminster were the results of an enquiry by Dyce and Sir Charles Eastlake into the German Nazarene school. The Nazarenes' reverence for the pure line, colour, and spontaneity of early Italian art corresponded to a taste among British connoisseurs of the 1830s and 1840s for the *quattrocento*, and promised a fresher idiom for narrative painting. So, despite the setbacks at Westminster, historical and religious cycles influenced by Italian frescoists were spasmodically tackled in Victorian buildings. Sometimes there were fresh failures: at the Oxford Union, when a group of Pre-Raphaelites frescoed the upper walls in 1857 with Arthurian scenes, decay set in immediately. Happier were the vignettes of Northumbria, past and present, painted under Ruskin's influence round the hall at Wallington House, Northumberland, by William Bell Scott (1856–61). But the late masterpiece of Victorian fresco painting was Ford Madox Brown's mannered cycle in Manchester Town Hall (1879–92), showing 12 events in the growth of the city and its industries. Later didactic murals on town-hall staircases and library walls tended to be executed on canvas and then stuck up, rather than laboriously painted *in situ*.

The Pre-Raphaelite Brotherhood, founded in 1848, owed its style to the researches of Dyce and Eastlake and its subjects to Victorian medievalism in poetry and religion. Its members wanted to reinvigorate painting with the colourfulness, naturalism, and 'truthfulness' of the early Italian painters, as the Nazarenes had done. At first they had a certain amount in common, in particular an angular originality aimed to shock, apparent in *Christ in the House of his*

Parents by J. E. Millais (1849–50). Soon enough, Millais and the other main talents of the 'PRB', Dante Gabriel Rossetti and William Holman Hunt, diverged: Millais into a medley of narrative, portrait, and landscape painting, Rossetti into obsessively depicting one type of female beauty, and Hunt into experiments with religious subjects. But Pre-Raphaelitism survived and spread with the support of Ruskin, who turned its naturalism to his own critical ends, and through the merging of its colourfulness and passion for detail, into the broad current of mid-Victorian painting. Many older artists such as Dyce, Ford Madox Brown, and another Hunt, William Henry Hunt, a painter of amazing verisimilitude, stood on the verge of Pre-Raphaelitism without identifying with it. In the next generation the term came to be applied to the younger medievalizing friends of Rossetti, notably the painter Edward Burne-Jones and the poet-designer William Morris.

The precision and 'truthfulness' of mid-Victorian art in the face of nature may seem a strange preoccupation, given the rise of photography at just this time. In fact, art photography was at first regarded as an adjunct to painting; some of its early practitioners, such as Hill and Adamson in Edinburgh, were indeed painters by origin. From another perspective, naturalism in painting and architectural ornament were part of a half-scientific, half-religious spirit of pedagogic classification which united such different Victorians as Ruskin and Darwin, turned many artists into passionate gardeners and zoologists, and made cases of geological and botanical specimens an apt accompaniment to Pre-Raphaelite paintings in drawing rooms. For the mid-Victorians there was no boundary between art, science, religion, and education; 'art for art's sake' had yet to arrive.

Painters of modern life

During the 1850s painters overcame their aversion to depicting modern life on the grand scale. Hitherto, contemporary scenes beyond the scope of portraiture, landscape, or caricature had fallen to two types of artist: topographers and genre painters. The topographers were often book illustrators by trade, and depicted urban life with an accepting eye. The genre painters tended to be narrators and moralists, drawn towards homely rural or suburban scenes. Perhaps the first modern voice in British genre painting was William Mulready, whose pictures of street life in a scruffy London suburb go beyond Dutch humour to hint at violence and dereliction. Victorian imitators of Mulready and his Scottish contemporary, David Wilkie, mostly softened and sentimentalized their vision. A common theme in genre painting, as in landscape, was the passing of pre-industrial village life. Cranbrook in Kent during the 1850s attracted a colony of summering or weekending artists, committed to recording rustic lore and incident. It was to be a predecessor of harsher venues like the fishing village of Newlyn in Cornwall, where a later community of painters gathered in the 1880s.

The first artists to paint large panoramas of Victorian life were W. P. Frith and Ford Madox Brown. Both also painted historical romances, but today Frith is remembered only for his popular sequence of crowd pictures, *Ramsgate Sands* (1854), *The Derby Day* (1858), and *The Railway Station* (1862). Brown's *Work* (1852–65) is more enigmatic and moralistic, but like Frith's work owes to Hogarth its relish for the vitality of the crowd. Such paintings court the viewer's curiosity, but make no appeal to feelings of pity, fear, or outrage. After 1870 came a change, as magazines like *The Graphic* began to use illustrations to confront the public with the facts of poverty and homelessness; from this time also date the first photographic studies of urban misery in London and Glasgow. Realist painters like Luke Fildes, Frank Holl, and Hubert von Herkomer often worked up their magazine drawings into Academy paintings; the most sensational example was Fildes' *Applicants for Admission to a Casual Ward* (1874). To the extremes of this approach belong the claustrophobic plates of deprivation and despair drawn for Blanchard Jerrold's *London: A Pilgrimage* (1872) by the Alsatian émigré Gustave Doré. They contrast with the merely ludicrous or picturesque images of poor Londoners presented by the early illustrators of Dickens.

Many Victorian painters objected to so brutal a depiction of life's perils, feeling that the moral pill should be present in painting, but sugared. The Pre-Raphaelites sometimes toyed with allegory, as in Holman Hunt's *The Hireling Shepherd*, on the state of the Anglican Church, or Rossetti's *Found*, a veiled commentary on prostitution. Some artists felt that they should address the working classes by illustrating social issues relevant to them, but inspire rather than shock or depress. Thus G. F. Watts's picture *When Poverty Comes In, Love Flies Out of the Window*, donated in 1889 to the Whitechapel

Gallery, made its point allegorically, using the label (often a lengthy appendage in Victorian painting) to hammer home its message. But it was far commoner to depict a domestic scene from which audiences could infer what might follow from a loss of self-control—violence, intemperance, extravagance, ruin, or infidelity. The genre goes back to Hogarth, and sometimes his precedent was explicitly invoked, as in Augustus Egg's triptych *Past and Present* (1858).

Late-Victorian painting

Art in France had never been so obsessed with moral standards; and it was to French subject matter and techniques—long an influence, but latterly revered—that British painters without a political or social axe to grind turned with relief in the last third of the century. The pioneer was an American, James Whistler, who settled in London in 1863 after a spell in Paris. Whistler's aesthetic revolution was influenced by the poet critics Gautier and Baudelaire, and akin to his friend Oscar Wilde's views on literature. While far from abjuring modern subject matter, he denied that the subject was the point of the painting. Whistler termed his urban vignettes 'nocturnes', and his portraits 'arrangements'. Under the spell of Japanese art, he flattened the picture plane and picked his viewpoint almost casually, 'painting across form', as his disciple Walter Sickert was to call it. Adopting this technique, Sickert himself was to create a memorable series of 'low life' images of London music halls and circuses between 1886 and 1895. Sickert deliberately represses sympathy with his subjects, to the point that their pathos presents itself in intensified form. Whistler's indifference to his subject matter, by contrast, seems genuine. It was no doubt among the reasons why Ruskin accused him in print of 'wilful imposture'. A libel trial ensued in 1878, which Whistler won. He received only nominal damages, but from that date the decline of moral subject matter, and of Ruskin's standing among painters, became precipitous.

A second side to aestheticism in painting was the recovery of classicism, but now in sensual or symbolic guise. Here the prime mover was the president of the Royal Academy, Frederic Leighton, but its ablest exponents were Albert Moore, Sir Lawrence Alma-Tadema, and Burne-Jones. Inspiration came from France (from Ingres in particular), from Michelangelo and Venetian art, and from the more personal interpretation of life in the ancient world and Renaissance presented by writers like Walter Pater. Influential, too, were 'orientalist painters' like J. F. Lewis, one of several painters who specialized in titillating scenes of the harem and slave market.

One concern of these artists was to revalidate the nude. Nudity and sensuality had never been absent from nineteenth-century art. The greatest British painter of the female nude, William Etty, was active and admired up to his death in 1849. Victoria and Albert even gave each other nude paintings as presents in the early years of their marriage. Still, toleration of the nude had always been tenuous, especially during the mid-Victorian climax of religious rhetoric. Everything depended on presentation; for example, the soap king W. H. Lever justified his ownership of Ettys and Alma-Tademas in terms of the purity and cleanliness of the nude figure. Even the late Victorians had to portray nakedness according to the classical canons of painting, as ideal or historical. But the aesthetic stress on technique and on the picture as a self-sufficient object helped to legitimize Moore's narcoleptic sequences of draped and undraped goddesses, or Alma-Tadema's glimpses of bathing, gossiping, and flirting, set against exquisitely rendered Roman marblework.

Burne-Jones was the most celebrated of the aesthetic artists, with a reputation in France and the United States as well as Britain. By the 1880s he had shed much of his medievalism in favour of a style based on Botticelli and Michelangelo, and was concentrating on other-worldly scenes of folk-tale and myth (for example the Briar Rose series at Buscot Park, Berkshire, 1874–90). These pictures float on the tide of late-Victorian escapism in art, yet also bear a burden of sorrow that few of the plethoric paintings and illustrations of nymphs and fairies produced at the time manage to catch. In another side to his personality, Burne-Jones was a practical man, who to the end of his career collaborated creatively with the enterprises of his friend William Morris in the fields of stained glass and book illustration. English line illustration enjoyed a short golden age in the 1890s, in tandem with the typographical revolution led by Morris' Kelmscott Press. The decadent plates drawn for *The Yellow Book* (1894) by the short-lived Aubrey Beardsley and the stirring images contributed by Walter Crane to the socialist tracts of the time are both indebted to Burne-Jones's drawings for the Kelmscott Press, as if in homage to his contradictory qualities.

By the end of the century British painting had lost its self-sufficiency. Progressive landscapists and artists of rural life looked candidly to France for inspiration. Among the leaders of this movement were Stanhope Forbes and George Clausen in England and James Guthrie in Scotland. They were especially attracted to *plein-air* painting, and their hero was the French realist Bastien Lepage. Impressionism was familiar but less important, the one true early 'English impressionist' being Wilson Steer. These artists distanced themselves from the exhibiting policies and teaching methods of the national academies, and some settled permanently in the countryside. Yet the great cities were still the only reliable marketplaces for their art. In London their preferred venues for exhibition were first the Grosvenor Gallery (1877) and then the New Gallery (1888), while a focus for debate was the New English Art Club (1886). Like the Royal Academy, the Royal Scottish Academy in Edinburgh lost kudos in the 1880s to the Glasgow Institute, where a group of French-influenced artists, later labelled the 'Glasgow Boys', exhibited. By 1900 the academies had ceased to be the national focus for the fine arts—a position they were never to recover.

Patronage and museums

By Victoria's accession the bourgeoisie had become more important than the aristocracy in the business of picture collecting. Merchants and manufacturers were dominant, for instance, among the later patrons of Etty and Turner. In due course this affected subject matter, but the change in fashion was not a simple one. Some middle-class collectors wanted to ape aristocratic taste; others employed dealers and art advisers to choose their paintings for them with investment in mind, while others had strong preferences or altruistic aims. Such was the Leeds cloth merchant and manufacturer John Sheepshanks, who in 1857 gave his collections (mainly of British genre and landscape) to the South Kensington (now Victoria and Albert) Museum, as a representative display of national art available to a wide public.

By then there were just sufficient public galleries and museums to make sense of such a bequest. Earlier, most museums had been private and sensational, mixing art with science, 'curiosities', waxworks, and sheer fraud for the sake of profit. Madame Tussaud's, permanently installed in London from 1830, still survives from this tradition.

The greatest showman of the Regency age was William Bullock, a naturalist and collector who began his career in Liverpool. Among the items shown at Bullock's exotic Egyptian Hall in London were Napoleon's carriage (which went on tour and was allegedly seen by 800 000 people), Géricault's *Raft of the Medusa* (1819), and the spoil from Belzoni's archaeological excavations in Egypt.

A favourite art attraction of the first half of the century was the panorama, in which vast illusionistic paintings were exhibited on a circular backdrop and viewed from a high platform. The most famous of the panoramas, the Colosseum in Regent's Park, London, opened in 1826 with an accurate copy of the views from the top of St Paul's Cathedral. Its rival was the diorama, a French invention; this showed scenes modulated by illusionistic tricks to a seated and darkened audience in a form that foreshadowed the cinema (brought to Britain by the brothers Lumière in the 1890s). Panoramas, dioramas, and 'cosmoramas' (chic versions of the peep-show) relied on a changing menu of exotic and topical scenes: battles and volcanic eruptions were favourites. Even so censorious a critic as Ruskin saw them as useful in an age hungry for popular information. They were superseded as literacy and illustrated journalism improved.

The modern idea of a government-supported museum or gallery with a building of its own and ready access for the public begins with the rebuilt British Museum (1824–43) and new National Gallery (1834–37) in London. At first they were still reckoned to be primarily for connoisseurs and artists and had awkward opening hours. Wider provision and access had to await the 1850s—a crucial decade for museums. An Act of 1850 allowed municipalities to support museums and libraries. One of the first towns to do so was Warrington where, typically, the museum started out with a local and trades collection, adding works of art a little later. The same decade saw the foundation of the South Kensington Museum, endowed with an exemplary collection for craftsmen to learn from, and soon lit by gaslight in order to encourage working people to visit the collections in the evening.

In 1857 Manchester held its Art-Treasures Exhibition. This famous event drew together pictures of all dates and types on loan and was enjoyed by over a million visitors of all classes. From the success of the Art-Treasures Exhibition stemmed the grandiose series of late-Victorian and Edwardian museums and galleries built by manufacturers and municipalities all over the north of England (for example the Harris Museum, Preston, and the Bury Art Gallery). Many of these institutions reflected the taste of donors and had no precise educational programme. Rather different were the Whitechapel and the South London Art Galleries of the 1890s, where the sponsors encouraged prominent artists to give, or even create, uplifting or otherwise apposite artworks for these drab quarters of the metropolis. These galleries relied on the idea that the public ought to see original pictures rather than just the reproductions by now copiously available in books or accessible through one of the 'art unions' that promoted the sale of artistic prints. Yet as 'authentic' art became more accessible, it was becoming less and less clear whom it was for at all.

Sculpture

British sculpture moved from strength through decline back to a certain strength again during the course of the nineteenth century. As the natural art of commemoration, sculpture took heart from romanticism, which fostered the remembrance of piety, power, talent, loyalty, or valour. The Napoleonic wars brought the cult of the hero into vogue. Public statues not only to kings but to commanders and statesmen arose in streets, squares, and public gardens, soon to be followed by judges, explorers, inventors, and even (as in the Scott Monument of 1840–46 in Edinburgh) literary figures. Nelson was celebrated with statue-topped columns in London and Dublin and countless lesser memorials, while Wellington during his lifetime received two colossal accolades: Westmacott's manly iron figure of Achilles in Hyde Park, London, and an obelisk in Phoenix Park, Dublin.

The commonest field for sculpture was always the church or grave-yard monument. At the top of the scale, Parliament voted money for memorials to a few of the officers who died in the Napoleonic and Crimean conflicts; far more were erected by private subscription. St Paul's Cathedral became the nation's equivalent to the French Panthéon, and other major churches, too, filled up with relief groups laden with fulsome epitaphs. Most pre-Victorian monuments in churches paid scant regard to their context. They were modelled on the antique, usually in pure white Carrara marble. John Flaxman and Francis Chantrey were the leading exponents, Flaxman excelling in grace and line, Chantrey in a plasticity and emotion evident in his 'Sleeping Children' monument in Lichfield Cathedral (1817).

The climax of heroic commemoration was the towering monument in St Paul's Cathedral to Wellington (begun in 1857, not finished till 1912). Its creator, Alfred Stevens, pioneered a richer, more energetic style in emulation of Michelangelo. But by then a reaction had taken place. An Act of 1853 having practically prohibited new burials inside English churches, funerary sculpture migrated into the new, impersonal cemeteries, where it never achieved consistency or development. At the same time, church reformers frowned upon the secularism and vanity of monuments. Instead they urged donors to give commemorative fittings or stained glass, the revival of which by specialist firms so much enriched the Gothic Revival. The able mason carvers of capitals, fonts, pulpits, and reredoses in mid-Victorian churches and town halls were subservient craftsmen more than designers, and so seldom rose to great heights. In major churches sculptural monuments did continue, sometimes in the form of recumbent, medievalizing tombs; many cathedrals boast a well-crafted series of such memorials to Victorian bishops. More original are the smaller reliefs and painstakingly lettered epitaphs of the Arts and Crafts Movement, which often mix bronze, marble, gesso, and gold.

Victorian sculpture was at a low ebb by the 1870s. It had missed out on the energy of the Gothic Revival, and under the influence of the Danish neoclassicist Bertel Thorvaldsen had too often shrunk to 'the white marble portrait bust, the impassive Grecian goddess, and the enervated funerary angel'. Attempts at collaboration between architects and sculptors had consistently misfired. Nash's programme for adorning Buckingham Palace and the Marble Arch with neoclassical reliefs was disastrously curtailed in 1830. The external statues for the Palace of Westminster were lacklustre compared to the fittings and ornament, where the architects had greater control. Likewise, on the costly Albert Memorial (1863–72), designed and coordinated by Sir Gilbert Scott, the metalwork and mosaics had impressed far more than the free-standing sculptural groups; only the frieze won much admiration.

Reform came after 1880 in the shape of the so-called 'New Sculpture'. This was a London-based movement, headed by such artists as Harry Bates, Alfred Drury, Onslow Ford, Alfred Gilbert, George

Frampton, and Hamo Thornycroft. It relied upon better teaching and modelling techniques learnt from France; upon the pioneering work of Alfred Stevens and the Italian sculptors who had been his inspiration; upon the late Victorian fondness for psychology, sensuality, and symbolism; and upon an increased public respect for collaboration in the arts. The Institute of Chartered Accountants, London (1891–93), with its dense frieze by Thornycroft and high-relief figures by Bates, was a turning point. Thereafter architects began regularly to offer sculptors integrated space on their buildings. Frampton was an artist who responded especially well to the challenge of architecture, and Glasgow Art Gallery (1897–1900) and Lloyds Registry of Shipping, London (1898–1901), show his relief work at its delicate best.

Bates, Frampton, and others also created some numinous gallery pieces, imbued with the taste for mystery and symbolism rampant in the 1890s. But the great individualist of the New Sculpture was Alfred Gilbert, a perfectionist who struggled constantly with inner torment. In three bronze memorials, the popular Eros at Piccadilly Circus, London (1886–93), the Queen Victoria monument, Winchester Castle (1887), and the Duke of Clarence's tomb, Windsor Castle (1892–99), Gilbert produced unsurpassed masterpieces of symbolist sculpture.

The applied arts

By the 1820s British industrialists in the textile and metal trades were aware of national deficiencies in the emergent field of 'art manufacture'. The growing use of machinery, they complained, was already separating design from production in these trades, leading to the decline of craft and the importing of pattern designs and designers from abroad. While France and several of the German states were subsidizing art and design schools, the British government spent little money on teaching art techniques. The Royal Academy's schools in London, the Trustee School in Edinburgh, and the schools of the Dublin Society all supported fledgling painters and sculptors, however feebly; but for the applied arts, apart from military mapping, there was nothing.

The upshot was a Select Committee on Arts and Manufactures, set up by the reforming Whig–Liberal Government in 1835. It led to the founding in 1837 of a Normal School of Design in London, intended as the centre of a national network of schools training designers for local trade and industry. The early years of the venture were fraught with quarrels over design teaching. These disputes reflected the chasm between manufacturers who worked repetitiously from moulds and patterns, and the skilled manual trades; production-minded teachers favoured standard exercises and patterns, while the purer artists called for originality and for drawing from nature or the human figure. The School of Design's early star pupil was Christopher Dresser, who followed the pattern-minded approach later to be laid down by his teacher Owen Jones in *The Grammar of Ornament* (1856). An expert in botany, Dresser devised strict functional principles for art design, whereby plant forms were systematically abstracted and geometrized. He was much in demand after 1870 for the design of high-class ceramics, glass, and metalwork and was in effect Britain's first independent industrial designer.

In 1852 Henry Cole, the organizing genius of the Great Exhibition, persuaded Prince Albert and the government to second some of the exhibition's profits to create what soon became the Department of Science and Art, as a coordinating agency for the reformed and enlarged schools of design. Cole presided over the South Kensington (now Victoria and Albert) Museum, founded as a repository of the applied arts to which designers could refer for ideas and techniques; and over a National Art Training School, which took over from the Normal School as the model for the network of regional design schools.

The rigidity and abstraction of the 'South Kensington' system attracted criticism: its methodology turned out uninspired art teachers, and it avoided involvement in technical crafts processes, for fear of seeming to subsidize particular trades. But the network of schools was gradually fulfilled. In Ireland, for instance, schools of design were set up in Belfast, Cork, and Dublin in 1850, after the famine; the Belfast one failed, only to be refounded in 1865 at the behest of local linen and printing trades. Birmingham and Sheffield's schools naturally specialized in design for metalworking, while the Lambeth school at first taught modelling for the local ceramics and stone-carving industries, but developed into a source of training for the London art sculpture movement. In due course the South Kensington system loosened up and played its part in the burgeoning of municipal and other art schools in the 1890s.

A contrary side of Victorian reformism in the applied arts is reflected by the emergence of the Arts and Crafts Movement. The origins of this movement go back to Pugin and Ruskin. In the 1840s, Pugin made great efforts to make 'truthful' designs for his Gothic ornament and fittings, reflecting the varying nature of the materials for which they were conceived, and to build up a network of skilled craftsmen to execute them. This was the origin of the partnerships between architects and craftsmen which were to be so creative a feature of mid-Victorian Gothic buildings. Ruskin then raised the stakes further; he argued, in reaction to the South Kensington system, that ornament was the most important aspect of architecture, but that it had no value unless it was executed by hand, and unless the craftsman had liberty and took joy in his labour.

It was William Morris who did most to carry these principles through to the next generation. In the first instance, the crafts firm which Morris founded in 1861 was chiefly involved in the genre of church decoration championed by Pugin. But it soon developed its secular side and revolutionized Victorian pattern designing of domestic wallpaper and fabrics. Handwork and an entire understanding by the designer of every stage in the manufacturing process were always the ideal if not always the reality in Morris' productions. At the same time, the Ruskinian ethic of dignified and creative work for all as the key to human welfare became the basis of the ardent socialism he professed during the 1880s.

By the end of that decade the Arts and Crafts Movement was an explicit and widespread network. It took two main forms. One was a plethora of small workshops, guilds, and cooperatives producing hand-finished goods for sale—mainly art, metalwork, jewellery, furniture, and fabrics for the bourgeois home and person. The other was a growth of crafts activity among middle-class women, whether amateur or professional. Embroidery and dressmaking were the commonest pursuits, but some women made stained glass, others painted, while others became interior designers, the most famous today being Margaret Macdonald, wife of C. R. Mackintosh.

The Arts and Crafts philosophy stood for a reaction against standardized products, and against the shortcomings of Victorian urbanism and industrialism. Yet, though the movement (in England especially) looked back to earlier and simpler patterns of life and idealized the countryside, it relied upon urban skills and methods of training. One of its regional strongholds was Birmingham; and this chapter concludes with a sketch of the history of design in that city, as a token of the achievements and the contradictions that characterized the applied arts in Britain at the end of the century.

Craft production had been a speciality in Birmingham since the early days of the Industrial Revolution. Matthew Boulton, James Watt's partner in the manufacture of steam engines, also made silver, Sheffield plate, and ormolu, while another of his associates, Francis Eginton, was a pioneer in the revival of stained glass. Pugin depended upon John Hardman of Birmingham for the precision of his metal-work and the rich colouring of his glass.

Precisely because the link between artisan skills and industrial production was taken for granted, Ruskin's insistence upon the value of handwork in art received a warm welcome there during the 1870s. Among the elite of manufacturing families who had transformed Birmingham into 'The Best Governed City in the World' were several who collected Pre-Raphaelite paintings and took as gospel the link-ages between art, craftwork, personal morality, and social reform preached by Ruskin and Morris. William Kenrick, for instance, mayor of Birmingham in 1877, was also an amateur artist and 'wrote poems about pale knights in dim cloisters'.

In 1883 Birmingham became the first British city to municipalize its art school. Its new building was designed by a disciple of Ruskin's, J. H. Chamberlain, who also built the distinctively Gothic local board schools and supplied Kenrick with a richly furnished suburban house to show off his art. The Birmingham art world became a focus of creative tension between artisans training for the metal trades and the middle-class young men and women of the School of Art, intent on acquiring the less competitive skills of drawing, fresco, book illustra-tion, and embroidery. The Birmingham Guild of Handicraft, estab-lished in 1890, took as its motto 'By Hammer and Hand' and as its aim 'to supply handmade articles superior in beauty of design and soundness of workmanship to those made by machinery; and to make only such as shall give pleasure both to the craftsman and to the buyer of them.' Such was the noble but innocent ethic of British design at the turn of the century, as Germany strove to catch up and surpass the United Kingdom in all aspects of manufacture. It would not survive the Great War.

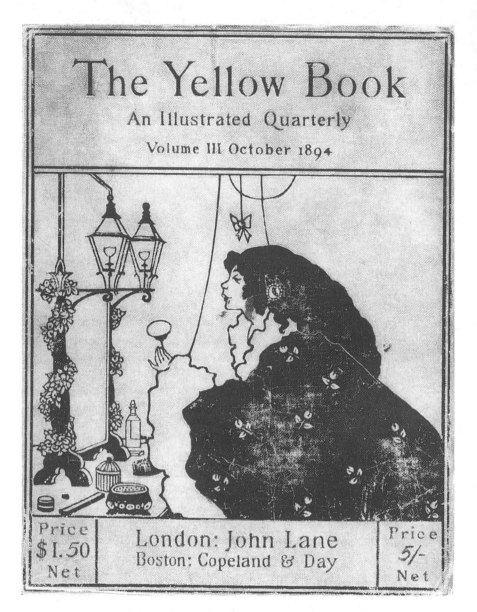

Plate 10 Design by Aubrey Beardsley for the October 1894 issue of *The Yellow Book*. In the same year Beardsley produced his illustrations for Wilde's *Salome* and Malory's *Morte d'Arthur*, and gave contemporary 'decadence' its enduring visual identity – though in practice his decisive, strong, linear style was an agent of invigoration and renewal rather than a symptom of over-ripeness and decay.

Conclusion: *fin-de-siècle*[1]

Colin Matthew

'Yes, there was to be . . . a new Hedonism that was to re-create life, and to save it from that harsh, uncomely Puritanism that is having, in our own day, its curious revival . . . Its aim, indeed, was to be experience itself . . .' Oscar Wilde in *The Picture of Dorian Gray* (1890) correctly identified the Janus face of the 1890s. And the trials of Oscar Wilde in 1895 reflected much that was typical of *fin-de-siècle* London: in addition to the ambiguous figure of Wilde himself, they involved an eccentric aristocrat and his family, the aesthetic movement and its ethos, the stage, the rough trade of hotels and clubs, and, in an indirect and largely undocumentable way, several members of the government, including perhaps Lord Rosebery, the prime minister. They brought face-to-face, on the one hand, anti-homosexual legislation (at the time almost casual in its enactment through Henry Labouchere's amendment to the Criminal Law Amendment Bill (1885)) and the 'Social Purity' campaigners of the *fin-de-siècle* years, and, on the other, the sense of liberation through the aesthetic movement from the Victorian emphasis on the priorities of work and duty.

The Wilde affair was matched on the imperial side by the Jameson Raid in December 1895, an attempt by Cecil Rhodes—perhaps in cahoots with the Colonial Office and possibly with the connivance of Joseph Chamberlain, the colonial secretary—to overthrow the government of the Transvaal. The raid, which failed, was followed by a

[1] '(1890): Pertaining to, or characteristic of, the end of the (nineteenth) century; characteristically advanced, modern, or decadent' (*Oxford English Dictionary*).

lengthy and inconclusive inquiry by a select committee of the Commons, at which Rhodes acted with unconcealed contempt and arrogance. The raid and Rhodes showed an imperialism almost out of control, with the priorities of money and company profit openly flaunted and the imperial virtues of order, responsibility, and trusteeship set aside. Their proximity through the telegraph and the press gave South African affairs an immediacy in the United Kingdom which the Opium Wars of the mid-century, which they in part resembled, had lacked.

These two almost simultaneous scandals—Wilde and Rhodes—matching each other in convoluted complexity, and in avid press coverage, seemed in retrospect characteristic of a decade anxious to show its difference from the rest of the century. In the sense that sexual and imperial scandals occurred in every decade of the century, it is easy to dilute the significance of the 1890s, and Wilde and Rhodes were typical of extremes rather than of the decade generally considered. Yet the latter years of the century did reflect significant change across a wide range of public and private life. The aesthetic movement of the 1870s (brilliantly satirized in Gilbert and Sullivan's *Patience* (1881)) became almost respectable by the 1890s. The *fin-de-siècle* years saw a considerable change in art, architecture, and design, the Celtic revival and French impressionism both contributing to a lightness and simplicity of design and depiction, exemplified in the work of Charles Rennie Mackintosh in Scotland and William Nicholson and Aubrey Beardsley in England.

There was a striking change in personal appearance. Women's fashions, especially in London, became brighter and lighter. Men of property began to wear suits and bowler hats instead of morning coats and top hats, and urban working men increasingly wore flat caps as a mark of distinctiveness of identity (though modernity in dress was not thoroughgoing: agricultural labourers still wore smocks in parts of Oxfordshire at the end of the century). Many men became clean-shaven—a marked change from the heavy beards of the mid-century, which, in their turn, had been a striking innovation, for beards had not been worn with wigs, the omnipresent hairpiece of the eighteenth century. As the wig ceased to be fashionable at the beginning of our period (though a few wore it in London as late as the 1840s), so the beard, which to an extent replaced the wig as a means of male adornment, and which became especially fashionable from the 1850s, declined as the century advanced. Nine of the members of Glad-stone's first cabinet (1868) sported beards; in his fourth cabinet (1892), only three.

Changes in clothing and personal presentation reflected a self-conscious sense of modernity. Leonard Woolf, who went up to Cambridge with Lytton Strachey in 1899, recalled himself and his contemporaries as 'sceptics in search of truth and ethical truth': the expectation was of change not of certainty, and the emphasis in high-er education had changed from being taught truths to pursuing self-discovery and experience.

The young generation of the 1890s were surrounded by the tech-nical developments which were, in the next century, to accelerate still further the velocity of 'intelligence and communication', and many other things besides: bicycles and automobiles, electrical devices, the cinema, telephones, and radio (in 1899 Marconi successfully transmit-ted a message from France to Chelmsford in Essex). As yet these changes were embryonic — in 1904 there were only about 8000 private cars, 5000 motor buses and taxis, and 4000 goods vehicles on British roads and Leonard Woolf records the astonishment he caused in Shetland when he cycled the length of the main island in 1896. The rapid expansion of these *fin-de-siècle* innovations was to come in the Edwardian years. Indeed, in important respects, it was 1900–14 that was, for the mass of the population, the *fin-de-siècle* period. Innov-ations were the most obvious proof of Alfred Marshall's observation that 'we are moving at a rapid pace that grows quicker every year'. The large *fin-de-siècle* literature of futurology and science fiction, epitomized by H. G. Wells's *The Time Machine* (1895) and *The War of the Worlds* (1898), emphasized this escalation of technical change while often questioning humanity's ability to control it, with war the possible consequence.

The mid-Victorian state, so energetically promoted by the Liberals and given considerable acceptance in practice by the Tories, came under strong criticism from a wide spectrum of political commenta-tors, and old party allegiances sometimes began to be awkward and intrusive. Moreover, rising wealth began to encourage a new view of poverty: instead of being seen as omnipresent and insoluble, poverty began to be understood as a measurable, containable, and con-sequently soluble problem. This optimism was by no means confined to Socialists. In his *Principles of Economics* (1890), written before social surveys revealed the extent of chronic poverty, Alfred Marshall observed: 'Now at last we are setting ourselves seriously to inquire whether it is necessary that there should be any so-called "lower classes" at all.' The sort of mid-century view typified by Samuel Smiles, that 'civilization itself is but a question of personal improvement', was replaced by a more sophisticated analysis of society. A consensus began to emerge that public expenditure must rise and that the mid-Victorian tax corset, so carefully designed and tightened by Gladstone and the Treasury, needed relaxation, though there was fundamental disagreement as to whether this should be on the direct (income tax) or indirect (tariff) side.

The 1892–95 liberal governments paid for increased social reform and imperial expenditure by imposing for the first time an effective death duty: a stimulus and a precedent for the increases in direct taxation so important in the 1900s. Unionists responded by increased enthusiasm for indirect taxes, some of them intended to encourage imperial integration through an Imperial *Zollverein* (and German models of supposedly greater efficiency were an important influence on British thought at this time). Three strands of thought— sometimes described as 'Social Imperialism'—conditioned Unionists' thinking, which was becoming tinged with a sense of decline even at the moment when they urged Britain to yet greater acts of imperial exertion. They believed that young industries—chemicals, electricals, automobiles—needed protection from foreign competitors, especially those in Germany and the USA; they wished to promote imperial union through an integrated imperial economy; and they wished to pay for increased domestic expenditure by indirect rather than direct taxes. But, despite the large Unionist majorities in both Houses, they took no action until the South African War's soaring expenditure provided the financial context for the introduction of several temporary duties.

On the left of British politics—the terms 'left' and 'right', like 'unemployment', came into common use in the 1880s and themselves indicated an important change—the Liberals began to look beyond Gladstone and constitutional reform to a 'new Liberalism' which would be more pro-active especially in the area of social reform. This reflected a change of view among 'advanced' Liberals (as they were known) about the nature of Liberalism and a recognition that the Liberal Party itself faced a real danger of being outflanked 'on the left' by the various labour groups founded in the 1890s, particularly the Independent Labour Party (1893) and the Labour Representation Committee (1900). These groups were not as yet strong, but they were strong enough to alarm Liberals who saw the maintenance of a non-class-based party as central to their objective of political and social progress in a system of representative government.

The extent of these changes in attitude should not be exaggerated. The Liberal leadership could not persuade local Liberal associations to adopt working-class candidates. Many Liberals *and* Unionists opposed the idea that government spending should generally rise (though often ready to promote spending on their own particular causes); some Unionists strongly opposed protection, and a few Liberals were willing to contemplate it. Lord Salisbury's governments did almost nothing to arrest the 'decline' which some of their Unionist supporters sensed and the introduction of 'Prussian' methods to arrest 'decline' could not have been further from the languid ethos of the 'Hotel Cecil'.

British politics in the 1890s seemed ripe for major restructuring, but the high boundary fence of Home Rule kept the Unionists and the Lib-Lab parties confined to their respective camps. 'New Liberals', as the Liberal innovators sometimes called themselves, felt that their progress within their party was slow, and imperialists despaired of getting their message taken seriously. A complex network of inter-party political relationships developed, epitomized by the Rainbow Circle (a discussion group on the 'left'), the Fabians (a Socialist pressure group with links to both the Liberal and Unionist parties as well as to the new Labour groups), and the various imperial organizations, such as the Imperial Federation League, which attracted a cross-party membership.

These networks sometimes produced surprising results. The Fabian booklet edited by George Bernard Shaw, *Fabianism and the Empire* (1900), was an energetic defence of imperialism as the coming means of progress, and related to the enthusiasm for the eugenics movement found in progressive as well as imperial circles. Benjamin Kidd's books, especially *Social Evolution* (1894), are representative of this approach, often called Social Darwinism. The idea that evolution should apply to moral as much as to material life was an important corrective to Marxism for many in the emerging Socialist movement, notably the young Ramsay MacDonald. It led some to see the Liberal

Party as having evolved to the end of its useful life, with a Labour/ evolutionary Socialist movement picking up the torch of progress. This view relates to Thomas Arnold's Broad-church notion of the 1830s that a nation had a life cycle similar to that of a person; consequently, many at the end of the century sought a rebirth for the United Kingdom in a wider imperial context.

The end of the century found the empire overstretched and under-defended, but until the South African War began in October 1899 the extent of this was not generally apparent. Indeed, the Colonial Office rather casually allowed war to be provoked in southern Africa by the imperial 'men on the spot' in the autumn of 1899, and the government was uncertain whether to meet German naval expansion in the 1890s by an alliance with Germany or by a larger British fleet to defend against Germany. British perplexity was the result of self-deception. World responsibilities had been allowed to increase, and, outside the Far East and Latin America, virtually no possible imperial gain had been foresworn. 'Pegging out claims for posterity'—Lord Rosebery's phrase—had gained the British many prospectors' plots, some of them as large as Europe itself. But the British had failed to notice that most mining claims are valueless, that claims have to be defended and exploited if they are to be maintained, and that the chartered company—the legal device for imperial expansion so beloved of late nineteenth-century governments—made the British government ultimately responsible for the capitalists to whose activities a chartered company gave legal sanction and cover.

The advantage of these imperial gains, especially in the last third of the century, had been uncertain and unquantified. The acquisitions had been accompanied by an attempt to develop an imperial ethos, which followed rather than caused the acquisitions. This reached its most vocal point in the 'khaki election' of 1900, fought at short notice during the South African War at a moment when that war (mistakenly) seemed a breezy walk-over. But the ethos of *fin-de-siècle* imperialism was for the most part cautious rather than bombastic. For some, it became a de-Christianized religious ethic of the state, exemplified in Rudyard Kipling's verses, 'Land of our birth, we pledge to thee/Our love and toil in the years to be ... Oh Motherland, we pledge to thee,/Head, heart and hand through the years to be' (quickly much used as a school hymn). For others, it provided the context for a move away from party government, either towards some grand coalition of the centre or, more boldly but even less probably, towards the suspension of representative government.

The nineteenth century had been Britain's moment as the world power, exercising a hegemony not seen again until the USA's dominance in the latter years of the next century. Free trade, a Liberal society, representative government, the idea of improvement and of economic, political, intellectual, and moral progress—all of these were powerful contributions and challenging priorities to put before the rest of the world. But by the end of the century, despite the enthusiasms and parades of the queen's jubilees in 1887 and 1897, it was starting to become apparent that the British moment was passing, and had even, perhaps, already passed:

> There's a whisper down the field where the year has shot her yield,
> And the ricks stand grey to the sun,
> Singing:- 'Over then, come over, for the bee has quit the clover,
> And your English summer's done.'
>> Rudyard Kipling, 'The Long Trail' (written 1891)

Further Reading

Introduction

Briggs, Asa, *The Age of Improvement*, new edn. 1979.

Dyson, H. J., and Wolff, Michael, *The Victorian City: Images and Realities*, 2 vols, 1976.

Gatrell, V. A. G., Lenman, Bruce, and Parker, Geoffrey, *Crime and the Law. The Social History of Crime in Western Europe since 1500*, 1980.

Girouard, Mark, *The Return to Camelot: Chivalry and the English Gentleman*, 1981.

Harris, José, *Private Lives, Public Spirit: A Social History of Britain 1870–1914*, 1993.

Hilton, Boyd, *The Age of Atonement: The Influence of Evangelicalism on Social and Economic Thought, 1785–1865*, 1988.

Hobsbawm, Eric, *Industry and Empire*, 1990 edn.

Hoppen, K. Theodore, *Ireland since 1800: Conflict and Conformity*, 2nd edn, 1986.

Hoppen, K. Theodore, *The Mid-Victorian Generation, 1846–1886*, 1998.

Jones, Aled, *Powers of the Press: Newspapers, Power and the Public in Nineteenth-century England*, 1996.

Lambourne, Lionel, *Victorian Painting*, 1999.

Mingay, G. E., *The Victorian Countryside*, 2 vols, 1981.

Morgan, Kenneth O., *Wales in British Politics, 1868–1922*, 1991 edn.

Prest, John, *Liberty and Locality: Parliament, Permissive Legislation and Ratepayers' Democracies in the Nineteenth Century*, 1990.

Smout, T. C., *A Century of the Scottish People 1830–1950*, 1986.

Thompson, E. P., *The Making of the English Working Class*, 1963.

Thompson, F. M. L., *English Landed Society in the Nineteenth Century*, 1963.

Thompson, F. M. L. (ed.), *The Cambridge Social History of Britain 1750–1950*, 3 vols, 1990.

Waller, P. J., *Town, City and Nation: England 1850–1914*, 1983.

Young, G. M., *Victorian England. Portrait of an Age*, 1953.

Chapter 1

Alborn, T. I., *Conceiving Companies: Joint-stock Politics in Victorian England*, 1998.

Broadberry, S., *The Productivity Race*, 1997.

Daunton, M. J., *Progress and Poverty: An Economic and Society History of Britain, 1700–1850*, 1995.

Floud, R., and McCloskey, D. (eds), *The Economic History of Britain since 1700*, 2nd edn, 1994.

Hennock, F. P., *Fit and Proper Persons: Ideal and Reality in Nineteenth-Century Urban Government*, 1973.

Hilton, B., *Corn, Cash and Commerce: The Economic Policies of the Tory Governments, 1815–30*, 1977.

Johnson, P., *Saving and Spending: The Working-Class Economy in Britain, 1870–1939*, 1985.

Lazonick, W., *Comparative Advantage on the Shop Floor*, 1990.

Pollard, S., *Britain's Prime and Britain's Decline: The British Economy 1870–1914*, 1989.

Stedman Jones, G., *Outcast London: A Study in the Relationship between Classes in Victorian Society*, 1971.

Szreter, S., *Fertility, Class and Gender in Britain 1860–1940*, 1996.

Thompson, F. M. L., *English Landed Society in the Nineteenth Century*, 1963.

Chapter 2

Bateson, C., *The Convict Ships*, 1969.

Blewett, Neal, 'The franchise in the United Kingdom, 1885–1918', *Past and Present*, 1972.

Cannon, John, *Parliamentary Reform, 1640–1832*, 1972.

Cornford, James, 'The transformation of conservatism in the late 19th century', *Victorian Studies*, 1963.

Crowther, Anne, *The Workhouse System 1834–1929*, 1981.

Dewey, Clive, 'Celtic agrarian legislation and the Celtic revival: historicist implications of Gladstone's Irish and Scottish Land Acts 1870–1886', *Past and Present*, 1974.

Hoppen, K. T., *Elections, Politics and Society in Ireland 1832–1885*, 1984.

McKibbin, Ross, 'Why was there no Marxism in Great Britain?', *English Historical Review*, 1984.

Matthew, H. C. G., *Gladstone 1809–1898*, 1997.

O'Gorman, Frank, *Voters, Patrons and Parties: the Unreformed Electoral System of Hanoverian England 1734–1832*, 1989.

Ostrogorski, M., *Democracy and the Organization of Political Parties*, Vol. 1, 1902.

Parry, J. P., *The Rise and Fall of Liberal Government in Victorian Britain*, 1993.

Smith, Paul, *Disraeli*, 1996.

Vincent, John, *The Formation of the British Liberal Party, 1857–1968*, 2nd edn, 1976.

Wright, M., *Treasury Control of the Civil Service, 1854–1874*, 1969.

Chapter 3

Bayly, C. A., *Imperial Meridian: The British Empire and the World, 1780–1830*, 1989.

Bayly, C. A., *The Raj: India and the British, 1600–1947*, 1990.

Eddy, John, and Schreuder, Deryck (eds), *The Rise of Colonial Nationalism: Australia, New Zealand, Canada, and South Africa First Assert their Nationalities, 1880–1914*, 1988.

Fieldhouse, D. K., *Economics and Empire, 1830–1914*, 1973.

Gillard, David, *The Struggle for Asia 1828–1914: A Study in British and Russian Imperialism*, 1977.

Hyam, Ronald, *Britain's Imperial Century 1815–1914: A Study of Empire and Expansion*, 2nd edn, 1993.

Koebner, R., and Schmidt, H. D., *Imperialism: The Story and Significance of a Political Word, 1840–1960*, 1964.

Marshall, P. J. (ed.), *The Cambridge Illustrated History of the British Empire*, 1996.

Owen, Roger, and Sutcliffe, Bob (eds), *Studies in the Theory of Imperialism*, 1972.

Porter, Andrew (ed.), *The Oxford History of the British Empire: Vol. 3 The Nineteenth Century*, 1999.

Porter, A. N. (ed.), *Atlas of British Overseas Expansion*, 1991, 1994.

Porter, Bernard, *The Lion's Share: A Short History of British Imperialism, 1850–1990*, 3rd edn, 1995.

Robinson, Ronald, and Gallagher, John, *Africa and the Victorians: The Official Mind of Imperialism*, 1961; 2nd edn, 1981.

Ward, John Manning, *Colonial Self-Government: The British Experience, 1759–1856*, 1976.

Warwick, Peter (ed.), *The South African War: The Anglo-Boer War 1899–1902*, 1980.

Chapter 4

Bland, L., *Banishing the Beast. English Feminism and Sexual Morality, 1885–1914*, 1995.

Breitenbach, E., and Gordon, E., *The World is Ill Divided: Women's Work in Scotland in the Nineteenth and Early-Twentieth Centuries*, 1990.

Clark, A., *The Struggle for the Breeches: Gender and the Making of the British Working Class*, 1995.

Colley, L. *Britons. Forging the Nation, 1707–1837*, 1992.

Cullen, M., and Luddy, M., *Women, Power and Consciousness in 19th-Century Ireland: Eight Biographical Studies*, 1995.

Davidoff, L., and Hall, C., *Family Fortunes. Men and Women of the English Middle Class, 1780–1850*, 1987.

Gillis, J. R., *For Better For Worse: British Marriages, 1600 to the Present*, 1985.

Hammerton, A. J., *Cruelty and Companionship: Conflict in Nineteenth-Century Married Life*, 1992.

Holton, S. S., *Suffrage Days: Stories from the Women's Suffrage Movement*, 1996.

John, A. V., *Our Mothers' Land: Chapters in Welsh Women's History, 1830–1939*, 1991.

Midgley, C., *Women Against Slavery. The British Campaigns, 1780–1870*, 1992.

Porter, R., and Hall, L., *The Facts of Life: The Creation of Sexual Knowledge in Britain, 1650–1950*, 1995.

Purvis, J. (ed.), *Women's History. Britain, 1850–1945*, 1995.

Ross, E., *Love and Toil: Motherhood in Outcast London, 1870–1918*, 1993.

Sharpe, P. (ed.), *Women's Work. The English Experience, 1650–1914*, 1998.

Summers, A., 'Public functions, private premises. Female professional identity and the domestic service paradigm in Britain, c. 1850–1930'. In *Borderlands. Genders and Identities in War and Peace, 1870–1930* (ed. B. Melman), 1998.

Tosh, J., 'The making of masculinities: the middle classes in late nineteenth-century Britain'. In *The Men's Share? Masculinities, Male Support and Women's Suffrage in Britain, 1890–1920* (ed. A. V. John and C. Eustance), 1997.

Walkowitz, J., *City of Dreadful Delight. Narratives of Sexual Danger in Late-Victorian London*, 1992.

Chapter 5

Ash, M., *The Strange Death of Scottish History*, 1980.

Bowler, P., *The Invention of Progress: The Victorians and the Past*, 1989.

Brown, C., *A Social History of Religion in Scotland since 1730*, 1987.

Desmond, A., and Moore, J., *Darwin*, 1991.

Foster, R., *Paddy and Mr Punch: Connections in Irish and English History*, 1993.

Gill, R., *The Myth of the Empty Church*, 1993.

Humphreys, E., *The Taliesin Tradition: A Quest for the Welsh Identity*, 1983.

Levine, P., *The Amateur and the Professional: Antiquarians, Historians and Archaeologists in Victorian England, 1838–1886*, 1986.

Lightman, B. (ed.), *Victorian Science in Context*, 1997.

Lynch, M., 'Scottish culture in its historical perspective' in *Scotland: A Concise Cultural History*, 1993.

McLeod, H., *Religion and the People of Western Europe, 1789–1970*, 1981.

McLeod, H., *Religion and Society in England 1850–1914*, 1996.

Parsons, G. (ed.), *Religion in Victorian Britain*, 4 vols, 1988.

Shattock, J., and Woolf, M., *The Victorian Periodical Press: Samplings and Soundings*, 1982.

Stocking, G. W., *Victorian Anthropology*, 1987.

Turner, F. M. *Contesting Cultural Authority: Essays in Victorian Intellectual Life*, 1993.

Watts, M., *The Dissenters*, Vol. 2, 1978–95.

Chapter 6

Altick, Richard, *The English Common Reader*, 1957, revised edn, 1998.

Armstrong, Isobel, *Victorian Poetry: Poetry, Poetics and Politics*, 1993.

Beer, Gillian, *Darwin's Plots: Evolutionary Narrative in Darwin, George Eliot and Nineteenth Century Fiction*, 1983.

Booth, Michael R., *Victorian Spectacular Theatre 1850–1910*, 1981.

Brantlinger, Patrick, *Rule of Darkness: British Literature and Imperialism 1830–1914*, 1988.

Ehrlich, Cyril, *The Music Profession in Britain Since the Eighteenth Century: A Social History*, 1985.

Fallis, Richard, *The Irish Renaissance*, 1977.

Gallagher, Catherine, *The Social Reformation of English Fiction 1832–1867*, 1985.

Gilmour, Robin, *The Victorian Period: The Intellectual and Cultural Context of English Literature 1830–1900*, 1993.

Levine, George, *The Realistic Imagination: English Fiction from Frankenstein to Lady Chatterley*, 1981.

Pearsall, Ronald, *Victorian Popular Music*, 1973.

Poovey, Mary, *Uneven Developments: The Ideological Work of Gender in Mid-Victorian England*, 1989.

Rowell, George, *The Victorian Theatre: 1792–1914*, revised edn, 1978.

Showalter, Elaine, *A Literature of their Own: British Women Novelists from Brontë to Eliot*, 1977.

Temperley, Nicholas (ed.), *The Athlone History of Music in Britain*. Vol. 5: *The Romantic Age 1800–1914*, 1981.

Tucker, Herbert F. (ed.), *A Companion to Victorian Literature and Culture*, 1999.

Walker, Marshall, *Scottish Literature since 1707*, 1996.

Wheeler, Michael, *Death and the Future Life in Victorian Literature and Theology*, 1990.

Chapter 7

Altick, Richard D., *Paintings from Books*, 1985.

Beattie, Susan, *The New Sculpture*, 1983.

Bell, Quentin, *The Schools of Design*, 1963.

Conway, Hazel, *People's Parks*, 1991.

Davey, Peter, *Arts and Crafts Architecture*, 1980.

Dixon, Roger, and Muthesius, Stefan, *Victorian Architecture*, 1978.

Girouard, Mark, *Sweetness and Light*, 1977.

Girouard, Mark, *The Victorian Country House*, 1979.

Macleod, Dianne Satchko, *Art and the Victorian Middle Class*, 1996.

Maas, Jeremy, *Victorian Painters*, 1969.

Muthesius, Stefan, *The English Terrace House*, 1982.

Nadel, Ira Bruce, and Schwarzbach, F. S. (eds), *Victorian Artists and the City*, 1980.

Penny, Nicholas, *Church Monuments in Romantic England*, 1977.

Reynolds, Graham, *English Watercolours*, 1988.

Smith, Alison, *The Victorian Nude*, 1996.

Strong, Roy, *And When Did You Last See Your Father?*, 1978.

Summerson, John, *Architecture in Britain 1530–1830*, 1970.

Treuherz, Julian, *Victorian Painting*, 1993.

Waterfield, Giles, (ed.), *Palaces of Art*, 1991.

Lambourne, Lionel, *Victorian Painting*, 1999.

Chronology

1821   resumption of convertibility

Elizabeth Fry founds the British Ladies' Society for Promoting the Reformation of Female Prisoners

De Quincey, *Confessions of an English Opium Eater*

death of Keats

1822   patent on power loom; Liverpool introduces 'Liberal Tories' to cabinet

W. H. Playfair's Royal Scottish Academy

David Wilkie's painting, *Chelsea Pensioners*

1823   Demerara slave rebellion

Anti-Slavery Society founded

Royal Society of Literature founded

Meteorological Society founded

death of Shelley

work begins on Robert Smirke's British Museum

death of Sir Henry Raeburn

1824   repeal of Combination Laws against trade unions; common standard of weights and measures

Heyrick, *Immediate not Gradual Abolition: or, an Inquiry into the Shortest, Safest, and Most Effectual Means of Getting rid of West-Indian Slavery*

death of Byron

J. Wyatville's restoration of Windsor Castle

1824–   first Burma War
26

1825   first patent on automatic spinning machine

opening of Stockton–Darlington railway

financial mania

penalties on anyone using threats to enforce union membership or strikes

Female Anti-Slavery Society for Birmingham formed

Thompson, *Appeal of one Half of the Human Race, Women, Against the Pretensions of the other Half, Men . . .*

Coleridge, *Aids to Reflection*

Hazlitt, *Spirit of the Age*

John Nash begins work on Buckingham Palace

1826   financial panic; ban on issue of banknotes under £5 in England; joint-stock banks permitted outside a radius of 65 miles from London
Society for the Diffusion of Useful Knowledge founded
University College London founded
Zoological Society founded
Disraeli, *Vivian Gray*

1827   Liverpool resigns, Canning prime minister, then Goderich
death of Blake

1828   Wellington prime minister
Test and Corporation Acts repealed
Meredith born
D. G. Rossetti born

1829   metropolitan police introduced by Peel
Catholic Emancipation Act
Jerrold, *Black-eyed Susan*

1830   completion of automatic spinning machine
Swing riots
Liverpool–Manchester railway
William IV king
Whigs win general election
Lyell, *Principles of Geology*
Geographical Society founded
Coleridge, *On the Constitution of the Church and State*
Comte, *Cours de Philosophie Positive* (–1842)
Tennyson, *Poems Chiefly Lyrical*
death of Sir Thomas Lawrence

1830–32   First Reform Bill

1831   arrival of cholera (epidemic 1832)
Truck act prohibits payment of wages in goods
Jamaican slave rebellion
non-sectarian school system introduced in Ireland
British Society for the Advancement of Science begins its annual meetings

1832   defeat of miners' strike in north-east of England
Reform Act passed, restricts the vote to male persons
Charles Dodgson (Lewis Carroll) born
death of Scott

1833   joint-stock banks permitted in London
end of East India Company monopoly on tea
state support for education
Althorp's Factory Act begins effective restriction of working hours of children and women in factories
Act of Emancipation ends slavery in British colonies
Keble's *Assize Sermon* starts the Oxford Movement
Penny Magazine begins
Carlyle, *Sartor Resartus*
Newman, *Tracts for the Times*

1834   transportation of Tolpuddle Martyrs
Grand National Consolidated Trade Union formed
Poor Law Amendment Act
London tailors strike against employment of women
Bulwer Lytton, *Last days of Pompeii*
death of Coleridge
National Gallery, London

1835   Municipal Corporations Act
Melbourne prime minister
Dickens, *Sketches by Boz* (1st series)
Hardwick's Euston Arch, London
Select Committee on Arts and Manufactures

1836   Marriage Act
Botanical Society founded
Dickens, *Sketches by Boz* (2nd series)
Dickens, *Pickwick Papers*
A. W. N. Pugin, *Contrasts*

1836–
37   railway mania starts

1837   Victoria becomes Queen

rebellions in Upper and Lower Canada
Carlyle, *French Revolution*
Dickens, *Oliver Twist*
Macready becomes manager of Covent Garden
National School of Design, London

1838   formation of Anti-Corn Law Association in Manchester
New Poor Law for Ireland
Sarah Stickney Ellis, *The Women of England; their Social Duties and Domestic Habits*

1839   formation of Anti-Corn Law League in London
first Chartist petition
first Custody Act
Carlyle, *Chartism*
I. Brunel, Temple Meads Station, Bristol

1839– J. C. Loudin's Derby Arboretum
40

1839– First Opium War; First Afghan War
42

1839– Rebecca riots in Wales
43

1840   penny post
marriage of Victoria to Albert
New Zealand annexed under Treaty of Waitangi
World Anti-Slavery Convention meets in London
William Whewell, *Philosophy of the Inductive Sciences*
Agnes and Elizabeth Strickland, *The Lives of the Queens of England* (–1848)
Hardy born

1840– Barry's Palace of Westminster built
60

1841   census begins to record women's occupations
Landseer's painting, *Windsor Castle in Modern Times*
Punch begins

Chemical Society founded
Pharmaceutical Society founded
Carlyle, *Heroes and Hero Worship*
Macready becomes manager at Drury Lane

1842   reintroduction of income tax
Coal Mines Act on employment of women and children
opening of Pentonville prison
second Chartist petition
Treaty of Nanking ends Opium War
Hong Kong acquired
Whitelands College founded
Sarah Stickney Ellis, *The Daughters of England*
Illustrated London News begins
Tennyson, *Poems*
Robert Browning, *Dramatic Lyrics*
Macaulay, *Lays of Ancient Rome*

1842–   O'Connell's 'monster meetings' advocating repeal of the Act of
44   Union

1843   annexation of Sind
Ellis, *The Mothers of England* and *The Wives of England*
Secession from the Church of Scotland to form the Free Church
John Stuart Mill, *A System of Logic*
Thomas Carlyle, *Past and Present*
Ethnological Society founded
Ruskin, *Modern Painters*
Theatre Regulation Act
Wordsworth becomes Poet Laureate

1843–   O'Connell prosecuted
44

1844   Rochdale pioneers
Bank Charter Act
miners' strike defeated
Factory Act introduces further controls on employment of
women and children

Railway Act; further railway mania
anonymous publication of the *Vestiges of Natural History of Creation* (by Robert Chambers)
Disraeli, *Coningsby*
Elizabeth Barrett, *Poems*
Phelps becomes manager of Sadler's Wells
Decimus Burton's Kew Palm House

1845   controls of Scottish banks
Maynooth affair
Irish famine begins
Peel resigns, Russell unable to form government; Peel returns
John Henry Newman enters the Roman Catholic Church
Disraeli, *Sybil*
Prince Albert's Osborne House

1846   repeal of Corn Laws
Tories split
Russell prime minister
Brontës, *Poems*

1847   ten-hour day for women and children in factories
Tennyson, *The Princess*
von Helmholtz, *Uber die Erhaltung der Kraft* (On the conservation of force)
formation of the United Presbyterian Church in Scotland
Emily Brontë, *Wuthering Heights*
Charlotte Brontë, *Jane Eyre*
Anne Brontë, *Agnes Grey*

1848   outbreak of cholera
Chartist demonstration
Public Health Act
Marx and Engels, *The Communist Manifesto*
Queen's College, Harley Street founded
Macaulay, *History of England*
John Stuart Mill, *Principles of Political Economy*
Thackeray, *Vanity Fair*
death of Emily Brontë

Gaskell, *Mary Barton*
founding of Pre-Raphaelite Brotherhood
revolutions in Europe

1849   repeal of Navigation Laws
annexation of Punjab
Bedford College, London, founded
Thackeray, *Pendennis*
Ruskin, *Seven Lamps of Architecture*
Charlotte Brontë, *Shirley*
Millais' painting *Christ in the House of his Parents*

1850   Don Pacifico affair
North London Collegiate School for Girls founded
Brougham's Act
Public Libraries Act
Agnes and Elizabeth Strickland, *The Lives of the Queens of Scotland* (–1858)
death of Wordsworth
Wordsworth, *The Prelude*
Tennyson becomes Poet Laureate; *In Memorium* published
Charles Kingsley, *Alton Locke*

1851   Great Exhibition, Paxton's Crystal Palace, Hyde Park
formation of Amalgamated Society of Engineers
Ecclesiastical Titles Act
the census begins to record marital status
Owens College, Manchester established
Spencer's *Social Statics*
Ruskin, *The Stones of Venice*

1852   Russell resigns; Derby's first minority Tory government
Aberdeen prime minister of coalition government
Second Burma War
Stowe, *Uncle Tom's Cabin*, published in Britain
Dickens, *Bleak House*
Thackeray, *Henry Esmond*
Department of Science and Art, South Kensington
Brown's painting, *Work*

1853 Gladstone's first budget
Aggravated Assaults Act
National Association for Vindication of Scottish Rights
William Thomson, 'On a universal tendency in nature to the dissipation of mechanical energy', *Philosophical Magazine*
The Positive Philosophy of Auguste Comte translated and condensed by Harriet Martineau
Matthew Arnold, *Poems*
Charlotte Brontë, *Villette*
Gaskell, *Ruth*
Yonge, *The Heir of Redclyffe*

1854 Crimean War starts
Northcote–Trevelyan report on civil service
London Working Men's College founded
publication of Mann's Report on the Religious Census of 1851
Dickens, *Hard Times*
Crystal Palace moved to Sydenham

1854–56 Nightingale works in military hospital in the Crimea

1855 introduction of limited liability
Friendly Societies Act
Aberdeen resigns; Palmerston prime minister
married women's property committee formed
Robert Browning, *Men and Women*
Gaskell, *North and South*
Charles Kingsley, *Westward Ho!*

1856 Peace of Paris ends Crimean War
Froude, *History of England from the Fall of Wolsey to the Defeat of the Spanish Armada*, 12 volumes (–1870)
Elizabeth Barrett Browning, *Aurora Leigh*
birth of Wilde and Shaw
Sir Gilbert Scott's Foreign Office

1856–60 Arrow War with China

1857   Indian Mutiny
       East India Company replaced by Crown government
       National Association for the Promotion of Social Science formed
       Divorce Act
       discovery of Neanderthal man, near Düsseldorf
       Dickens, *Little Dorrit*
       Trollope, *Barchester Towers*
       National Portrait Gallery

1857– Alfred Stevens' monument to Wellington, St Paul's Cathedral
1912

1858   formation of General Medical Council
       Palmerston defeated; Derby's second minority Tory government
       Government of India Act
       Dorothy Beale becomes principal of Cheltenham Ladies' College
       English Woman's Journal founded
       removal of Jewish disabilities
       Clough, *Amours de Voyage*
       Eliot, *Scenes of Clerical Life*
       W. P. Frith's painting, *Derby Day*

1859   legislation of peaceful picketing
       Derby resigns, Palmerston's second government
       Langham Place reading room and offices opened
       Darwin, *On the Origin of Species*
       H. L. Mansel, *Limits of Religious Thought*
       Mill, *On Liberty*
       Smiles, *Self-Help*
       Tennyson, *Idylls of the King*
       Wagner, *Tristan and Isolde*

1859– lecture tour of Sarah Parker Remond
61

1860   Cobden free trade treaty with France
       Gladstone's budget
       Essays and Reviews
       Collins, *The Woman in White*

Eliot, *The Mill on the Floss*
Ruskin, *Modern Painters*, completed

1861 annexation of Lagos
Dickens, *Great Expectations*
death of Elizabeth Barrett Browning
death of Clough
Morris's craft firm founded

1862 Ruskin, *Unto this Last*
Mill, *Utilitarianism*
Meredith, *Modern Love*

1863 Cambridge Local Examinations opened to girls
Anthropological Society founded
Charles Kingsley, *The Water Babies*
Eliot, *Romola*
Gaskell, *Sylvia's Lovers*
Whistler settles in London

1864 Contagious Diseases Act (extended 1866, 1869)
metropolitan railway (partially underground) opens in London
Samuel Crowther, bishop of the Niger, first African consecrated
at Lambeth
Alexandra College, Dublin founded
Dickens, *Our Mutual Friend*
Newman, *Apologia Pro Vita Sua*

1864– Schools' Inquiry Commission
67

1865 death of Palmerston; Russell takes over Liberal government
Morant Bay rebellion in Jamaica
Ruskin, *Sesame and Lilies*
Elizabeth Garrett qualifies as a doctor by licence of the Society of
Apothecaries
Maxwell, *Dynamical Theory of the Electromagnetic Field*
death of Gaskell
Arnold, *Essays in criticism* (1st series)
Carroll, *Alice's Adventures in Wonderland*

birth of Kipling and Yeats
William Burges' restoration of Cardiff Castle

1866   exchequer and audit reform
Russell/Gladstone Reform Bill defeated; Derby's third minority government
petition for women's suffrage signed by 1459 women
Glasgow Police Act
Matthew Arnold's lectures on 'The study of Celtic Ireland'
Eliot, *Felix Holt*
Gaskell, *Wives and Daughters*
Swinburne, *Poems and Ballads*

1867   Queensbury rules for boxing
British North American Act establishes Canadian federation
rejection of women's suffrage amendment to second Reform Act
first permanent women's suffrage societies founded in London, Manchester, and Edinburgh
Sullivan, *The Story of Ireland*
Robertson, *Caste*

1867–   Reform Acts for urban voters
68

1868   Torrens Act gives power to local authorities to enforce repair or demolition of individual houses
formation of Trades Union Conference
Disraeli succeeds Derby as prime minister
telegraph network nationalized
last public execution
end of transportation of criminals
Gladstone's first government
Abyssinian crisis
Cardwell's army reform reduces colonial garrisons
suffrage societies in Birmingham and Bristol
Robert Browning, *The Ring and the Book*
Collins, *The Moonstone*

1869   Charity Organization founded
Church of Ireland disestablished

Suez Canal opened

J. S. Mill, *Essay on the Subjection of Women* (written with Harriet Taylor Mill)

Endowed Schools' Act

Girton College founded at Hitchin; moved to Cambridge 1873

women ratepayers gain vote in municipal elections

Josephine Butler founds Ladies' National Association for the Abolition of State Regulation of Vice

Arnold, *Culture and Anarchy* (first published in *The Cornhill Magazine*, January–August, 1868)

Nature begins

Thomson's classical buildings in Glasgow

1870   Tramways Act

Elementary Education Act and school boards for England

Irish Land Act

Married Women's Property Act gives wives 'separate property' in their earnings

Franco-Prussian War

Women's Suffrage Journal founded

Devonshire Royal Commission on Scientific Instruction and the Advancement of Science

Rossetti, *Poems*

death of Dickens

1871   bank holidays introduced

university tests abolished

Trade Union Act

purchase of army commissions abolished

Football Association and Rugby Football Union founded

English FA Cup competition starts

Darwin, *The Descent of Man*

Eliot, *Middlemarch*

Carroll, *Through the Looking-Glass*

Hardy, *Desperate Remedies*

1872   controls on adulteration of food and drink

agricultural labourers' strike

secret ballot introduced

Scottish Elementary Education Act

Licensing Act

Cape Colony obtains responsible government

Girls' Public Day School Company (later Trust) founded
Butler, *Erewhon*
Hardy, *Under the Greenwood Tree*

1873 Judicature Act
government defeated on Irish universities but Disraeli declines office
Home Rule League (later Association)
Custody of Infants Act
Gull identifies anorexia nervosa
Pater, *Studies in the History of the Renaissance*
death of Mill and publication of his *Autobiography*

1874 Tories win general election
Disraeli's second government
St Leonard's, St Andrews, founded
Hardy, *Far From the Madding Crowd*

1875 Cross Act gives power to local authorities to clear slums
Artisans' Dwelling Act
Public Health Act
Trade Union Act
reform of trade union law in Employers and Workmen's Act
Emma Patterson, first woman admitted to the Trades Union Congress
first woman Poor Law Guardian elected
Trollope, *The Way We Live Now*

1875– eastern crisis involving Ottoman Empire and Russia
78

1876 Merchant Shipping Act
Elementary Education Act
Royal Titles Act makes Victoria empress of India
Disraeli becomes Lord Beaconsfield
Mother's Union founded
Sophia Jex qualifies as a doctor under the 1876 Enabling Act
Freeman, *History of the Norman Conquest of England*
James, *Roderick Hudson*
Eliot, *Daniel Deronda*

1877   tennis at Wimbledon
       trial of Charles Bradlaugh and Annie Besant for republishing *The
       Fruits of Philosophy*

1878   Factory Act
       London University admits women to degrees and University
       College London becomes coeducational
       Salvation Army founded
       Matrimonial Causes Act gives magistrates' courts summary
       jurisdiction to make separation orders in cases of cruelty
       Hardy, *The Return of the Native*
       H.M. Stanley, *Through the Dark Continent*
       Ruskin–Whistler law suit

1879   Agricultural depression
       Zulu War
       Irish National Land League
       women admitted to profession of pharmacy
       Meredith, *The Egoist*
       James, *Daisy Miller*
       Ibsen, *A Doll's House*

1879– Second Afghan War
81

1879– Carnarvon Commission on defence of British trade and colonies
82

1880   Tories defeated; Gladstone's second government
       Burials Act
       elementary education compulsory in England and Wales
       foundation of Mason's College, Birmingham
       women in Isle of Man enfranchised in House of Keys elections
       Y Frythones founded
       Yonge, *The Clever Woman of the Family*
       death of Eliot
       'New Sculpture' movement

1880– First South African War
81

1881   Irish Land Act
       Parnell imprisoned
       death of Disraeli
       death of Carlyle
       Ibsen, *Ghosts*
       James, *The Portrait of a Lady*

1881– Ladies' Land League
82

1882   Parnell released
       Phoenix Park murders
       Crimes and Arrears Acts
       Married Women's Property Act
       British occupation of Egypt
       state grant for cookery teaching to elementary schoolgirls
       Society for Psychical Research founded

1883   Corrupt Practices Act
       Primrose League founded
       Mahdist rising in Sudan
       Women's Cooperative Guild founded
       Contagious Diseases Acts suspended
       Schreiner, *Story of an African Farm*
       Birmingham's municipal art school

1884   Third Reform Act
       Social Democratic Federation and Fabian Society founded
       Imperial Federation League founded
       Moore, *A Mummer's Wife*
       Oxford English Dictionary begins publication

1885   Redistribution Act
       Gladstone's government resigns
       Penjdeh crisis on India's north-west frontier
       death of Gordon in Sudan
       Women's Liberal Federation founded
       Salisbury's first (minority) government
       Ashbourne Irish Land Purchase Act
       secretary of state for Scotland

Pall Mall Gazette publishes 'The maiden tributes of modern Babylon'
Criminal Law Amendment Act
Tories lose election in November
third Burma War
National Vigilance Association founded
Roedean School founded
Rider Haggard, *King Solomon's Mines*
Pater, *Marius the Epicurus*
Meredith, *Diana of the Crossways*
Gilbert and Sullivan, *The Mikado*
birth of D. H. Lawrence and Ezra Pound
Dictionary of National Biography begins publication

1886   unrest in London
third Gladstone government
first Irish Home Rule Bill defeated in Commons
Liberals split and lose election
second Salisbury government, supported by Liberal Unionists
Royal Niger Company receives government charter
Guardianship of Infants Act
Contagious Diseases Acts repealed
White Cross Army founded
Allbutt, *The Wife's Handbook*
James, *The Bostonians*
Stevenson, *Dr Jekyll and Mr Hyde*
Alfred Gilbert's 'Eros', London

1887   Irish Crimes Act
Parnell fraudulently vilified by *The Times* (Piggott forgeries)
queen's golden jubilee
Conan Doyle, 'A study in scarlet'
Hardy, *The Woodlanders*
Manchester Ship Canal

1888   Jack the Ripper murders in London's East End
Women's Liberal Unionist Association founded
Kipling, *Plain Tales from the Hills*
Mrs Humphry Ward, *Robert Elsmere*

death of Arnold
invention of Kodak box camera
Sir John Fowler's Forth Railway Bridge

1888– County Councils for England, Wales, and Scotland
89

1889 formation of National Union of Gasworkers and General
Labourers and Miners Federation of Great Britain
London dockers' strike
Navy Defence Act
Nineteenth Century publishes women's 'Appeal against female
suffrage'
P. Geddes and J. A. Thomson, *The Evolution of Sex*
National Society for Prevention of Cruelty to Children founded
Stevenson, *The Master of Ballantrae*
Yeats, *The Wanderings of Oisin*
Gilbert and Sullivan, *The Gondoliers*
deaths of Robert Browning, Hopkins, and Collins

1890 Housing of the Working Classes Act
Marshall, *Principles of Economics*
Wilde, *The Picture of Dorian Gray*
Ibsen, *Hedda Gabler*
Mark Rutherford (William Hale White), *Miriam's Schooling*
Birmingham Guild of Handicraft

1891 Parnell cited in O'Shea divorce suit
Hardy, *Tess of the D'Urbervilles*
Kipling, *The Light that Failed*
Gissing, *New Grub Street*
Morris, *News from Nowhere*

1892 Tories lose election; fourth Gladstone government
Wilde, *Lady Windermere's Fan*
Kipling, *Barrack-Room Ballads*
Conan Doyle, *The Adventures of Sherlock Holmes*
death of Tennyson

1892– Scottish universities admit women to degrees
95

1893　Independent Labour Party founded
second Irish Home Rule Bill, passes Commons, rejected by Lords
first two women factory inspectors appointed
Thomas Huxley, *Evolution and Ethics*
Egerton, *Keynotes*
Gissing, *The Odd Woman*
Grand, *The Heavenly Twins*
Wilde, *A Woman of No Importance*
Pinero, *The Second Mrs Tanqueray*

1894　Gladstone resigns; Rosebery's Liberal government
Local Government Act
Harcourt death duties
Kipling, *Jungle Book*
Shaw, *Arms and the Man*
Mona Caird, *The Daughters of Danaus*
Moore, *Esther Waters*
first issue of *The Yellow Book*
death of Stevenson

1895　trials of Oscar Wilde
Liberals lose election; third Salisbury government in coalition
with Liberal Unionists
Joseph Chamberlain appointed secretary of state for the colonies
in Salisbury's government
Wycombe Abbey School founded
Wells, *The Time Machine*
Conrad, *Almayer's Folly*
Hardy, *Jude the Obscure*
Wilde, *The Importance of being Earnest*

1896　*Daily Mail* begins publication
agricultural rating reform
Jameson Raid
Carpenter, *Love's Coming of Age*
Housman, *A Shropshire Lad*
women in Ireland eligible for election to Boards of Guardians
Leighton ennobled

1896–　British reconquest of the Sudan
98

1897   queen's diamond jubilee
        second colonial conference in London
        National Union of Women's Suffrage Societies founded
        Commons passes second reading of Women's Suffrage Bill by 228
        votes to 157
        Havelock Ellis, *Sexual Inversion*
        Mary Kingsley, *Travels in West Africa*
        Wells, *The Invisible Man*
        Conrad, *The Nigger of Narcissus*
        Bram Stoker, *Dracula*
        C. R. Macintosh, Glasgow School of Art
        Country Life founded

1898   County Councils for Ireland
        death of Gladstone
        Hong Kong enlarged by lease of 'New Territories' on Chinese
        mainland
        Spanish–American War
        Anglo-German agreement
        Fashoda crisis
        women in Ireland eligible for election to district councils
        Alice Zimmern, *The Renaissance of Girl's Education in England*
        Vagrancy Act increases penalties for male homosexual soliciting
        James, *The Turn of the Screw*
        Wilde, *The Ballad of Reading Gaol*

1899   Second South African War (to 1902)
        International Congress of Women meets in London
        Ward, *Naturalism and Agnosticism*
        Elgar, *Enigma Variations*

1900   Labour Representation Committee founded
        conquest of Orange Free State and Transvaal
        Boxer Rising in China
        amalgamation of the United Presbyterian Church and the Free
        Church in Scotland
        granting of Royal Charter to transform Mason's College into the
        University of Birmingham
        Conrad, *Lord Jim*
        deaths of Ruskin and Wilde

1900– nearly 30 000 Lancashire women millworkers petition for suffrage
01

1901 death of Queen Victoria (22 January); Edward VII king
Commonwealth of Australia
B. Seebohm Rowntree, *Poverty, a Study of Town Life*
women's commission of inquiry into conditions in South African concentration camps
British Psychological Society founded
Kipling, *Kim*

1902 Peace of Vereeniging ends South African War
William James, *Varieties of Religious Experience*

1903 Owens College becomes Manchester University

Maps

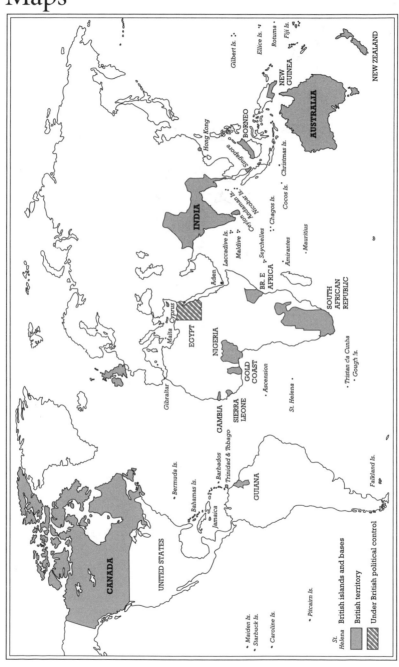

Map 1 The British Empire by the 1890s

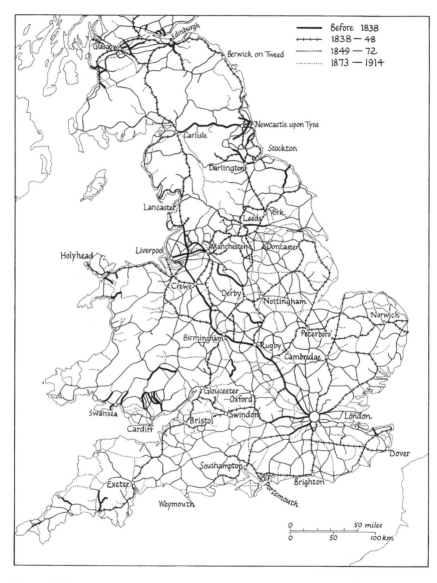

Map 2 Railway construction, 1825–1914

Index